Hope for the Children

Hope for the Children

A Personal History
of Parents Anonymous
by Patte Wheat
with Leonard L. Lieber

Library of Congress Catalog Card Number: 78-65520
ISBN: 0-03-049401-X
Printed in the United States of America

Cover design: Esther Malabel
Text design: Holly Ramsey

5 4 3 2 1

Winston Press, Inc.
430 Oak Grove
Minneapolis, MN 55403

Other Books by the Author

By Patte Wheat
Three for a Wedding
By Sanction of the Victim

By Dale Hale and Patte Wheat
You're Getting Closer

This book is dedicated to our children—Kerry, Colleen, Kelly, and Michael—and to all the other children who have been granted growth.

And to Jeffrey Lansdown and all the other children who
"... shall grow not old as we, that are left, grow old;
Age shall not weary them nor the years condemn;
At the going down of the sun and in the morning,
We will remember them."

—Anonymous
War Memorial
Edinburgh Castle

Special Acknowledgments from Leonard

The body of the following text is not constructed to allow mention of all the special people who have been important to us during the past ten years. For this reason, I would like to thank some of them here.

Peter Guzvitch is a psychiatrist in Long Beach, California. I learned from him some very creatively unique ways to work with groups when we did volunteer work together at the Long Beach Free Clinic from 1969-1970. His teachings were invaluable.

Joyce Will was my supervisor at two job locations from 1968-1971 and 1972-1973. It was she who gave me much support and encouragement to help initiate the P.A. concept. Without her backing, our beginning struggles would have been far more difficult.

Carol Johnston, founder of Parental Stress Services in Alameda County, California, has been a very special friend during our organization's ten years of existence. She has been a "human oasis" to rely on when the going has been rough.

Rex Levering has been a national board member of P.A. and its personnel committee chairperson since 1975. His expertise in management issues and his coolness in times of stress have helped ease us through some very tough times.

Kee MacFarlane became our H.E.W. project officer in 1976. She has worked terribly hard on our behalf and exemplifies what we all like to see in government service—dedication, honesty, and perseverance.

To all of our P.A. colleagues in the United States and beyond, we extend our deep thanks for their hard work and sacrifices. Without them there would be nothing to write about.

From Patte

My heartfelt thanks to all the P.A. parents who have willingly and honestly shared their pain with me over the past ten years in the hope that this book would help save others from similar pain.

And to Alice Loper, P.A. secretary, typist, and friend, thanks for consistently bringing order out of chaos with unflagging cheer and great good humor.

... And from the two of us

Special thanks go to Chris Herbruck, our friend and colleague in Ohio, whose gracious assistance led to the production of this book.

And special thanks to Dee, Pamela, and all the other good people at Winston Press for their great support in its production.

Contents

1
Beginnings

"At first, many years ago, I thought maybe abusers were somebody else that lived over there, or somewhere else. Gradually, I found out they're not somewhere else. They're in the same city, the same town. Sometimes they're down the street. Sometimes they're people who are working along with you in the same hospital where you work. And you find out that all your early ideas about who the abusers were were complete nonsense. They're people just like we are. And we are all people who happen to live in ways that we were brought up to live, and the child abusers are no different from the rest of us, except through the accidents of very early life experience and happenings that have led them to behave in somewhat different ways than the rest of us behave...."*

Brandt Steele, M.D
Professor, Department of Psychiatry
University of Colorado Medical Center
Denver, Colorado

* An excerpt from his presentation "Who are the Child Abusers?" at Parents Anonymous National Child Abuse Conference, Long Beach, California, February, 1975

Patte's story

On December 7, 1978, at 7:30 A.M. California time, I happened to answer a crisis call that came in from Florida on the Parents Anonymous National Hotline. The woman on the other end sounded bright, friendly, and open. She told me in a matter-of-fact way that the day before, when her three year old had come in with a load of sand in his pants and trailed it all over the house, she'd spanked him so hard that she'd left little bruises on his bottom.

"I don't know if this constitutes child abuse or not," she admitted, "but my husband and I are a little afraid to send him to nursery school today. What if somebody had to change his pants and saw the bruises? Would they report us as child abusers?"

Her voice caught; I could hear that she was upset with herself, but she went on in the same forthright manner: "I'm getting too angry at him too often, and I'd better look for some help, some alternatives. This child is very special to me. I love him very much, and it's just unthinkable to me that my parenting has deteriorated to spanking him that hard, even if he *was* driving me up the wall."

I gave her the phone number of the sponsor of a Parents Anonymous chapter in her area and suggested that she might also benefit from a parenting class like Parent Effectiveness Training (P.E.T.),[1] which helps parents to establish better communication with their kids. I had taken the class, and I had learned a lot from it. Then I went on to reassure her that we had all been where she

4

was—unsure of ourselves, worried about how we were dealing with our children, a little scared.

Twenty years ago, I had spanked my own three-year-old boy with a hairbrush, hard enough to leave ridgemarks on his bottom. I don't remember what he did to trigger my anger, but in my mind I can still see those little bruises. I do remember having felt lousy as I looked at them, trying to convince myself that he deserved it, knowing, even then, that he hadn't earned that kind of response. He'd simply been the victim of one of my occasional outbursts of temper under stress.

How wonderful it would have been if I could have called somebody, *anybody*, and talked normally and naturally about what I'd done. If only I could have aired *my* feelings and openly sought ways to help myself so that I could have understood episodes like those and defused them before they erupted. But twenty years ago was 1958, and millions of "good," conscientious parents like me were sweeping their outbursts under the rug, swallowing hard, and trying to erase abusive incidents, pretending they hadn't happened. Back then, there wasn't anybody to call; there wasn't anybody who'd listen.

My professional involvement with child abuse began four years before Parents Anonymous was founded. My children were eleven, nine, and four years old at the time. In the spring of that year, the crime section of *Time* magazine carried an account of a pretty teenage girl whose parents had left her for the summer with a woman they barely knew. When her parents returned from their travels, the girl was dead, apparently scapegoated and disciplined to death over a period of three

5

months by the woman and her children. The story was treated as a grisly, isolated incident of brutality, a crime perpetrated by monsters who weren't part of the human race as we prefer to think of it. There was no mention of child abuse.

As I reread the details, I couldn't help wondering: Why didn't the girl run away when things became unbearable? She apparently had opportunities to reach out and seek help, but she didn't take advantage of them. Did she want to die? If so, why? Did she perhaps feel that she *deserved* to die? Maybe that was it. Maybe she thought of herself as being so worthless that she deserved whatever punishment she got. But why did she feel worthless? Maybe she was convinced that her parents didn't care much about her or they wouldn't have left her there.

I saved that article; I couldn't get the girl and her circumstances off my mind. In the months that followed, other news articles about child murders came to my attention, and I found myself filing those away, too: a woman and her common-law husband charged with the neglect and beating of their ten-month-old son; a six year old found chained in a box, his mother and nine others charged with felony child abuse. Ten years ago, "battered-child syndrome" and "child abuse" were phrases used by only a handful of medical experts and lawyers. In the clippings I was collecting, each story was treated as an isolated phenomenon and forgotten until the next freak occurrence.

I soon had a file folder packed full of stories about such "isolated" events. In the meantime, I was curious about how many of these events *weren't* reaching the news. As I researched the subject over the next five years, I learned that I

6

had discovered the tip of an iceberg, the mere surface of a huge subculture comprised not of monsters but of human beings who had been conditioned from birth to hate themselves, who perpetuated their self-hate through their own children, forming a continuous chain of generation-to-generation brutalization.

In late 1967, some cautious statistics began to emerge: A California assemblyman estimated that 50,000 children in that state alone were neglected to the point where specialized assistance in their homes was badly needed. The American Medical Association concluded that parental abuse ranked alongside automobile accidents as a major cause of childhood deaths. A study cited in their report showed that most abusive parents came from homes where they had been ignored or harmed—homes like the ones they were providing for their own children.

Then the news magazines occasionally began to print sickening photographs of battered children, together with very brief descriptions of the pioneering work with abusive parents being done at the University of Colorado Medical Center in Denver. After diligent searching, I found that the results of the Denver studies had first been published in *The Battered Child*, a textbook that came out in 1968 and was edited by Doctors C. Henry Kempe and Ray E. Helfer.[2] They and their colleagues at the National Center for the Treatment of Child Abuse and Neglect in Denver had worked with several hundred abusing families during the 1960s, and their findings showed that while parents with abuse problems might be very different from one another, almost all of them had themselves been abused as children, either physically or emotionally. The book explored in depth what was known about child abuse at that time and included a state-by-state summary of related legislation. It also included a history of child abuse that would lead anyone who read it to conclude that society in general has not been overly concerned about the problem. Infanticide, abuse, deprivation, and sexual molestation of children have been going on for centuries in conjunction with the attitudes that children are the property of their parents and that harsh punishment is necessary to maintain discipline.

In the past ten years, more and more people have become interested in the subject of child abuse, and as a result, more literature has become available. In 1968, though, aside from a few articles in medical journals, *The Battered Child* was about all there was in the way of reference. It sold for $12.50, was difficult to find in libraries and bookstores, and didn't come out in paperback until 1974. For this reason, the general public never heard of it, and many persons working in the field were not even aware of it.

The more I studied the dynamics of child abuse, the more obsessed I became with the murdered teenage girl whose case had first led me to research. I wanted to know more about what her life had been like. I began to recall encounters with "significant others" in my own life who had made me feel worthless as a child, like my grandmother, who had come to live with us after my mother and father were divorced. I was only six at the time, but I remember her standing over me, drunk, with her hands on her hips, looking huge and all-powerful as she told me that I was either shit mean or stupid. I remember feeling that

I *had* to be one or the other of those things, even though I didn't *want* to be. She defined me with those words, defined what I was, and I had no weapons until I learned to laugh at her. In the meantime, she controlled my world, and I lived daily with the depressing knowledge that I did not please her, I *could* not please her.

Looking back at my own life made me think about what must have happened to the murdered girl. She had obviously gotten the message from her parents that she didn't have much personal worth, that she deserved whatever punishment she got; and then she was handed over to another emotionally crippled, self-hating adult. I started looking for answers, sensing that when I found out more about her, I would find out more about myself and a lot of other people as well—people who had spent their growing-up years in the shadow of their caretakers' disapproval.

I decided to write a book about the girl and call it *By Sanction of the Victim*; the first draft was completed in late 1970, and it was then that I first heard about a self-help, crisis-intervention group called Mothers Anonymous. It consisted of parents who met on a weekly basis to help each other stop their abusive behavior toward their children. I was given permission to sit in on their meetings as part of the research I was doing on my book. Mothers Anonymous—its name was changed to Parents Anonymous the following year—was nine months old at that time and had only one chapter, in Redondo Beach, California. (At this writing, there are over 1,000 chapters nationwide and many overseas.) My interest in the fledgling organization grew with each meeting I attended, and my role of researching writer quickly blurred into that of

9

friend, sometime volunteer, and unofficial historian who photocopied printed materials and taped public presentations and meetings. And when Parents Anonymous was funded by the Office of Child Development, Department of Health, Education, and Welfare in 1974, I became their staff writer and the editor of their publication, *Frontiers*.

The ten years I have spent with P.A. people have spelled personal growth for me. My involvement with them has enabled me to take a more honest look at the quality of my own parenting and my own life and has helped me to recognize the interpersonal abuse—and the self-abuse—that has taken place over the years in my own family. I have learned how self-esteem can be built and how it can be destroyed. I have painfully faced the fact that the occasional feelings of uncontrollable anger I had toward my own children were not that different from the feelings of those parents whose anger resulted in excessive abuse or murder. As educator Eda LeShan has said,

We seem to behave most angrily and irrationally toward our children when they remind us, at a deep, unconscious level, of the helpless, anxious, terrified feelings we had during our own childhood and don't want to remember. Our rage is our defense against those feelings; we feel once again threatened and not in control. There is not one of us who has left childhood behind forever. Inside each of us is a helpless two-year-old.[3]

My work with Parents Anonymous has freed me and members of my family from a painful silence. When he was twenty-seven, my half-brother, a victim of generations of paternal abandonment, told me about the relentless emotional abuse he had suffered at the hands of a woman who had posed as his benevolent caretaker for years. He had swallowed that abuse and accepted it as his due. My father, who seldom shows any kind of emotion, stood with tears in his eyes at the age of sixty-five and told me how much he wanted to get in the car with my uncle, his brother, and hunt for *their* father, who abandoned them when they were children. "We were living in Illinois," he said. "I remember watching him go down the road with just one suitcase. I watched him until I couldn't see him anymore." There is an old unfounded rumor that he was last seen in Arizona many years ago and is probably dead by now. All we have left of the man who was a complete stranger to his son, his grandchildren, and his great-grandchildren is a faded snapshot of him on board a ship taken sixty years ago.

My twenty-four-year-old son and I can both laugh now when he describes how helpless and terrified he felt as a child when I became enraged at his dawdling and tried to stuff a cheese sandwich down his throat. And my daughters and I can talk about the hair-pulling and our family heritage of hair-pulling as a means of discipline. We can discuss the laughter and the love as well. We can look at one another with compassion as we reveal what things were like for us then and what they're like now. I have learned that when I can remember to stay in touch with the child in me, I can get closer to my own children.

More importantly, I have learned that child abusers aren't people who live "over there" or "somewhere else." When we become willing to let go and look honestly at our own lives, we find that child abuse is a personal issue with every one of us. A child can be killed just as easily by inches over a lifetime as in a moment of uncontrolled rage. If we choose to examine ourselves, we can see that all of us have been emotionally crippled all our lives by varying kinds and degrees of child abuse.

Like many of the people who have been associated with Parents Anonymous over the years, I have journeyed through my own personal awakening to look hard at my own life and make the decision to grow. I have come to realize that the best gift I can give my children—and myself—is my own emotional maturity. And finally, I've learned that while growing toward that goal is messy and painful, refusing to grow toward it is even more so.

November 1969

An excerpt from a November 14 *Los Angeles Times* story:

Bakersfield

Little J—— was found clutching a fence beside Interstate 5, about 25 miles south of here Oct. 25. She told the highway patrolman who found her that her father and her mother had let her out of the car and told her to wait by the fence. She had been there about 12 hours.

Officers said she apparently had been trained to say her name was Smith and that she lived in Bakersfield.

Subsequent investigation revealed the Fouquets had another missing child, Jeffrey Lansdown.

January 1970

An excerpt from a January 15 follow-up story:

"Daddy," a battered, half-dead 5-year-old told his stepfather on Sept. 16, 1966, "I don't want to live anymore."

"Then, why don't you just die?" asked the stepfather.

"All right," said the frail youngster, "I will."

And the next day, Jeffrey Lansdown did.... Mrs. Fouquet said her husband first became enraged at the little boy because he knocked a shoe out of a window and later spilled a can of paint.

* * *

Jeffrey Lansdown obediently joined tens of thousands of his brothers and sisters, and his death voiced the unasked question, "If I die, will you love me?"

By 1970, there were 60,000 reported cases of child abuse per year in the U.S. But the relative handful of experts who were studying the problem conceded that because of erratic reporting, this figure was probably well below the actual number. During that same year, Dr. James Apthorp,[4] the Pediatric Trauma Coordinator at Los Angeles Children's Hospital, wrote in *Family Weekly* magazine:

Child abuse is one of our most serious social problems today. It is also one of the most difficult to correct. The real tragedy is the battered child whose injuries, delving far beyond the visible scars, last a lifetime. Physical injury heals in time. Emotional scars seldom do.

To help such children, we must first help the parents. We must increase our knowledge on how to treat the troubled parents, then provide adequate help for them.[5]

This echoed the research findings being published by the team of doctors at the Denver Center.

I stared at the newspaper picture of Betty Lansdown Fouquet. She looked like a stupid, unfeeling creature beyond salvaging. Expendable human refuse. Why had she stood by and allowed one of her children to be murdered, another abandoned? And the article stated that she was pregnant with another child. Was this one of the "troubled parents" the doctors wrote about? In 1970, child abusers were still people who, in the eyes of the general public, made the headlines and then disappeared. They still lived "over there," "somewhere else."

I looked once more at the woman's photograph before stuffing the article into my bulging file. Her expression wasn't exactly blank; it was more like the glazed, unseeing look of an animal that has been caught in a trap for a long time and is waiting to die. I was sure I would never know what, if anything, went on in her head—but I was wrong. In another year, I would come face to face with the woman behind the headlines.

November 1970

One evening, a friend who knew about the research I was doing for *By Sanction of the Victim* called to tell me about a self-help group of abusive parents who called themselves Mothers Anonymous. She'd learned about them from a brief segment of a local T.V. newscast. I called the station and was directed to Dr. Edward Lenoski, then a trauma consultant at the University of Southern California's Pediatric Pavilion. He told me that the founder of Mothers Anonymous was a woman named Jolly K., a child abuser who had begun the self-help group nine months earlier in desperation because she couldn't find help anywhere else. He gave me her phone number and reassured me that she wouldn't mind my calling her or attending the meetings, as long as I was sympathetic to the group's cause and made it clear that I meant them no harm. The meetings were held every Monday night at St. Paul's Methodist Church in Redondo Beach; the mothers were known by their first names only.

I hesitated for a long time before calling Jolly K. Book research was one thing, but now I was actually going to talk with a real child abuser—one of "them."

*　*　*

The voice that answered the telephone was strong and friendly and had an optimistic quality to it that helped me relax. Jolly K. was an easy talker, seemingly honest and very open. I explained that I was revising a novel I'd written about child abuse and wanted to do some further research. Could I sit in on some Mothers Anonymous meetings?

"You're welcome to come," she said, "but the women in the group are a little edgy. If you take notes they might want to see what you're writing."

I could hear a child talking in the background. Although she became increasingly demanding, Jolly was very patient with her.

"A year ago I would have belted her," she commented. "I was certain that if I didn't get help then, I'd end up killing her."

How many children did she have?

"Two—Faith and Roz."

Had she abused only one of them?

"Yes, the younger one, Faith, the eight year old. I came near strangling her to death one day because she'd stolen money at school. I heard Roz, my older daughter, screaming at me to stop. That's what brought me to my senses before it was too late."

From what I had learned about child abuse, her actions seemed to fit a prescribed pattern. "They" usually abuse only one child. I asked Jolly how she herself had been treated when she was young.

She answered that she didn't recall being beaten, or whipped, or physically battered or abused. She had simply been in and out of over thirty-eight foster homes and state schools from the time she was born until she was seventeen. Her mother had been a nomadic circus performer who was emotionally unequipped to nurture a child. Her father had been a merchant seaman who was seldom around. Whenever Jolly misbehaved, she suffered a routine punishment: her mother pronounced her incorrigible and turned her over to the juvenile authorities, who put her into a state school or a foster home.

Jolly was so easy to talk to that I soon found myself telling her we were *all* guilty of child abuse. There wasn't a person on our block—myself

16

included—who hadn't hit a child a little too hard because of anger or frustration or frayed nerves.

"Yes," she agreed, "it's a matter of degree and control. We all have pretty much the same thoughts and feelings, if we admit them, and verbal abuse is just as bad as physical abuse. In my opinion, psychological abuse is often worse. I know what it did to Faith—and I know what it did to me."

We talked for a long time. When I hung up the phone, I thought for a while about people I knew who didn't hit their kids, who instead ground them down with words and attitudes that said, "You're stupid; you don't measure up"—people who routinely trampled on their children's feelings. These children didn't have any visible marks on them; they just grew up feeling unvalued as human beings. They fell into the vast category of the emotionally abused.

Then I thought about myself, my three children, and my husband. But I didn't want to think *too* hard about those things. It would be another few years before I could muster the courage to deal with the emotional dishonesty that lay under the surface of our happy family facade and to comprehend the extent of my emotional neglect of myself and my children.

December 1970

It was an unusually cold, windy night when I drove into the parking lot at St. Paul's Methodist Church. There was a light on in the annex, and a short man with bushy red hair was standing just outside the door. He asked me if I was looking for the Mothers Anonymous meeting.

"Yes," I answered. "I'm Patte Wheat. I spoke with Jolly earlier."

"I'm Leonard Lieber," he said.

So this was the therapist I'd heard about who had challenged and nagged Jolly into starting her own group when she couldn't find the help she needed anywhere else. He hardly looked like anybody's idea of a rescuing knight.

We walked together into a room that was bright with fluorescent lighting. In a semicircle on straight chairs and two sagging couches sat approximately eleven women eyeing me. Jolly didn't come forward to introduce herself but instead spoke from the end of one of the couches and asked me to tell the women who I was and why I was there. The group appeared to accept me at face value and got on with their discussion. Jolly's hair was blonde and severely short then. I don't know what I had been expecting, but it wasn't somebody that fierce looking or that tall—Junoesque, with glasses, eyes the color of light melted chocolate, and a glittering, teasing smile. There was a tigress air about her. Her demeanor at that time belied the warmth I'd felt over the phone. She was very much in charge here, and nothing was going to get out of hand. This big, leggy woman was wearing a frilly yellow little-girl dress, which somehow made her appear even more formidable.

She was verbal and volatile—a chameleon. She moved back and forth easily between what I thought of then as "our" world and "their" world. When she'd spoken with me on the telephone, she'd sounded like an unusually communicative, articulate young woman who was perfectly capable

18

of handling her life in a healthy fashion. Now, as I listened to her talk to the group, I was surprised to hear her lapse freely into street language. Was she using gutter phrases for shock value, I wondered, or because she wanted to encourage the group to respond to her gut-level words with their own gut-level feelings? She had an instinctive skill for helping the women to express their real feelings, getting them back on the track if they rambled or halting them if they seemed too upset for their own good.

A woman across the room looked as though she was having a silent argument with herself. We all turned to her as she spoke up suddenly. "What *should* my reaction be when another kid beats up my kid? I know I didn't handle it right. I told him, 'Kick the shit out of him, or I'll kick the shit out of *you.*'"

"How do you feel about your husband, Bea?" somebody asked.

"He's a *goddamn coward*, and when he's pushed in a corner, he goes to kill. I don't want my boy to handle anger like that. I don't want him to wait that long, letting it build up."

"But fighting shakes me up emotionally," a woman named Karen interrupted. She was grossly overweight, frankly vulnerable, articulate. She expressed herself like somebody who reads a lot. She wasn't resorting to the repeated catch phrases that tend to kill communication. Karen was groping for words, ideas.

Later, Jolly told me that Karen had been in Mothers Anonymous for three months and had a baby girl a year old. She had verbally abused her child regularly but had physically abused her only once when she had hit her and bruised her face

19

during a feeding. Not long after that incident, Karen had seen an ad in a local newspaper inviting "mothers who lose their cool with their kids" to call Jolly K. She had gathered her courage and called. At Jolly's suggestion, Karen brought the baby with her to the next meeting, and with Karen's permission, Jolly had shown the baby to the rest of the group as a dramatic example of what can happen when verbal abuse goes unchecked and is allowed to erupt into a physical attack.

"It isn't chicken," Jolly told Bea, "to walk away from a fight. If a child doesn't want to fight, the mother should uphold him in that decision." This sounded strange coming from Jolly, who looked as if she had never in her life walked away from a fight.

Then Leonard added, "Physical confrontation between children *is* sometimes necessary, but only as a last resort." This observation seemed to satisfy the group, and they went on to a new topic.

I watched and listened during this meeting as an increasingly familiar pattern emerged. Although the women stated and restated their problem in varying ways, they were all suffering from the same chronic and cumulative hostility. They all voiced a low threshold of stress tolerance and an inability to cope with constant feelings of personal inadequacy. At these M.A. gatherings, they were beginning to learn how to handle their anger *before* it exploded into destructive behavior. Jolly consistently monitored their outpourings, trying to keep the discussion centered on the real reason why they were all there: the relationships that were destroying them, their children, and their families.

20

Later during the meeting, Jolly announced, "I have a Christmas present for the group." She'd just gotten her eight-year-old daughter, Faith, back from the Hathaway Home for emotionally disturbed children. "I had to fake affection at first," she admitted. "I saw her sitting there, waiting for me, and I knew she wanted me to put my arms around her, and I couldn't. But I made myself do it, and when I did, it felt great. I liked it! Maybe if you *force* yourself to change your behavior, you can start feeling like you know you really want to feel. Maybe you can *make* it become real."

The discussion came around to the fear of full and open communication, the fear of being vulnerable, the fear of losing another person's love if you dare to expose your deepest feelings to him or her. Then Karen said that she had another Christmas present for the group: For the first time since she'd had her baby, she was beginning to enjoy her. Even her husband had noticed the change.

Enjoy. How many people in "our" world, I wondered, really enjoy their children? Not my neighbors, who jerked their kids around by their arms in the market and put up a smiling front when their minds were really on the next bridge game. Not my friend, who role-played even for her husband and then stepped into the shower every night after her two children were in bed and sobbed unheard against the wall. And what about me? How many times had I let go and enjoyed my children when they were small instead of looking upon them with dread, boredom, or a sour sense of duty?

I remembered a piece of advice that had been passed along to me by some wealthy and successful friends of ours. Their son was suicidal at eighteen, and he had already gone through some $50,000 worth of psychiatric care.

"If we've learned anything from the pain we've been through," they said, "it can be summed up in one word: *enjoy*. Learn to *enjoy* your kids."

I stood up and looked around as the meeting came to a close. Jolly passed a shoebox for voluntary contributions, and we all wished one another a Merry Christmas. As I looked at the crumpled dollars and the ravaged faces, I knew that I had encountered more honesty in that shabby little room than I would ever see in the community where I lived. And I knew with dreary certainty that my smug little neighborhood was typical of so many others across the U.S. where "child abuse didn't exist."

I had turned a corner and stepped into another world that night, and while I knew I couldn't go back, I was damn nervous about going forward.

* * *

Jolly began to call often to tell me of the group members' triumphs, setbacks, and crises. She was going through a crucial time with her own daughter Faith and she needed moral support. There'd been a blow-up one night when Faith had stuffed toothpaste into the cat's mouth—one of the signs of Faith's emotional illness had been her extreme cruelty to animals. Jolly had panicked at what seemed to be a relapse, screamed at Faith that she was crazy, and sent her off to bed. She had managed to catch herself before any physical abuse began. When she'd tried to call Leonard, he hadn't been available, so she'd called an advisor at the

22

Hathaway Home. After calming down, she'd gone to Faith's room, awakened her, and apologized—something she'd never done before. Jolly was able to take what she'd learned from that incident and share it with the other members: "If you do slip and lose your temper, let the kids know it's *your* problem, not theirs, and tell them you're sorry."

When I asked her why she hadn't called one of the other members of Mothers Anonymous during her crisis rather than an advisor whom she'd met only once or twice, she answered, "The girls don't expect me to have problems. I'm supposed to be this tower of strength. I'm pretty healthy now, and that's a great feeling, but I've been healthy for only a year."

Healthy for a year. How old was she? "I'm thirty-one now, and for thirty years, whenever I did anything good, I'd immediately destroy it. I can't do anything about those first thirty years—they're wasted—but I can do something about the next thirty."

I told her that she could call me when she was close to the edge, if she wanted to—and if somebody more expert wasn't available.

"I will," she said. "I like you."

"I like you, too," I confessed, surprised. Her friendship was a gift and a responsibility that I hadn't really counted on or wanted. I had expected to stay apart and objective, to analyze and comprehend; I hadn't expected to really like her. She never called me when she was in crisis, though. I think she needed always to show me her best side, the child side that wanted desperately to be mama's good girl.

Around the same time, Jolly was busy trying

to put together all the knowledge that she and a few other core members had gleaned about child abuse. She wanted to print up some guidelines for new members and a pamphlet describing Mothers Anonymous. Jolly came over to my house one day carrying a battered black briefcase. Just about everything that had been put on paper about M.A. was jammed into that briefcase, I found out, including official files, newspaper articles, and letters.

I lent her the Helfer-Kempe book, *The Battered Child*, and offered to share my own files with her. Over bologna sandwiches and coffee, she told me that their M.A. group had broken child abuse down into six categories: physical abuse, physical neglect, sexual abuse, verbal abuse, emotional abuse, and emotional neglect.[6] They were in the process of defining these, and two members who had been attending meetings regularly for several months were putting together *Guidelines for Achievement* and *Guidelines of Allegiance*.[7] (These were eventually incorporated into the booklet *I Am a P.A. Parent*.)

We spent the day learning from each other, and after she left late that afternoon, I realized I didn't even know her real name. I hesitated to ask her about it until I knew her better. Anonymity was guaranteed to all members of the group, and I had no idea how she might feel about the question. Several weeks later, when I finally did ask her, she told me that Jolly was a nickname she'd picked up during her marriage to a fellow named Green. "Some of our friends called me the Jolly Green Giant and it stuck," she said. "Actually, I was named after a movie star."

Jolly K.'s story

She was a winter baby, born Maureen Maude Barton in late November of 1940. Her father had named her after Maureen O'Hara. One of her earliest memories is of being taken by her mother to a stranger's apartment in San Francisco. The woman gushed over her while her mother was there, but it wasn't long before things changed.

"I remember the woman put me down for a nap, and when I woke up, she was standing there with a note in her hand, saying, 'Well, your mother's left you, and you're not stayin' with me.' I kept telling her, 'No, Mama's going to come back and take me to a movie.'

"Then I was taken to a big gray building, and just like in the movies, I found myself sitting on the police sergeant's desk eating ice cream while the officers talked and joked and asked each other what they were supposed to do with a four year old. After that, I was put into a room by myself. It was night, and I could hear rain, and there was the smell of damp wool clothing drying on an open radiator. I was only four, but what I remember most of all was that there were crying babies in there who were a lot younger than I was.

"They told me I was bad and that's why all this had happened. I don't remember my mother coming back.

"When I was five or six, I was taken to the Children's Farm Home in Corvallis, Oregon, and I stayed there until I was nine. I was mostly happy there, except for the times when I was spanked with a razor strap. I got the belt end once; I still have the scar. My mother visited me, and I always had plenty of money for comic books and things; I had plenty of clothes. My mother still tells me that I had twenty dresses during the war.

"But when I got out, my mother had sold my dolls. We got into fights, my mother and I, over radio programs. And I was always bawled out for slamming screen doors. Then this very nice, kindly, white-haired lady came up to the house one day, and I was told that I was leaving again, this time with the lady. I didn't want to go, but somehow the lady made it all sound very nice. My mother told her I was incorrigible, that I wouldn't stop running in and out of the house slamming the screen door. For years I thought I was taken away because I slammed doors. To this day I have a phobia about anyone slamming doors. It drives me up the wall to hear a door slam."

Jolly spent her tenth birthday in Portland Juvenile Hall, where she got her first tattoo, smoked her first cigarette, and had her first introduction to institutional lesbianism. From there she went to a Catholic home for girls in Melhurst, Oregon. "My father came to see me there and said I was going to go home. My parents lived in Long Beach, California, then. I didn't want to leave, but he put me on a bus for Long Beach. I remember looking out the bus window and thinking the jackrabbits were baby kangaroos. Everybody on the bus laughed, they thought that was cute.

"I don't remember my homecoming at all. My mother put me in a foster home in Long Beach, and I hated the place. I was taken out of there and put in another one. I ran away and was raped by a forty-nine-year-old Mexican farm worker. My mother put me in juvenile hall again—she said I was incorrigible and it was all my fault I got raped. The court didn't see it that way. They convicted the guy. She told *them* I was incorrigible; she called me a fuckin' little slut. She'd called me that since I was seven; it was a favorite phrase.

"Next I was transferred from Long Beach Juvenile Hall to Los Angeles Juvenile Hall. I spent my eleventh birthday in Los Angeles Juvenile Hall. I was placed in the Good Shepherd Home after the rape. I was there for about ten months. Then after that it was in and out. I'd be someplace for a week or two, then somehow back to juvenile hall, then home for a few days, then back in another place. I was in Los Angeles Juvenile Hall eleven times, Bakersfield Juvenile Hall twice, Las Vegas Juvenile Hall once, Santa Ana Juvenile Hall twice."

The California Youth Authority released her when she was eighteen. She moved in with a girlfriend, relied on the generosity of men, and eventually became pregnant. She spent the last months of her first pregnancy in The Big Sister's Home in Los Angeles. She and the baby then went to live with another girlfriend.

Not long after the baby was born, Jolly was assailed by a morbid fear that she would hurt her: "All I could think about was, 'I'm so big and awkward, and she's so tiny.' " The baby was placed in a foster home until she was eighteen months old.

In 1961, Jolly gave birth to a boy. She named him Sean and kept him home for two months, and then made arrangements for a private adoption. "I gave him away because he was a boy; I felt completely incapable of even trying to raise a boy. But I was determined that he should have a good home. I picked out the kind of parents for him that I would have picked out for myself. I was in New Mexico at the time, and that's where he lives.

I know where he is. He has a wonderful, nurturing home, and I don't interfere. I haven't seen him since he was ten months old."

Then came another man, a short marriage, and a legitimate pregnancy. Jolly named the baby Faith, after her mother. She placed her in a foster home when she was eight days old and brought her back on her second birthday. Verbal abuse progressed rapidly to physical abuse. In Jolly's mind, Faith was legitimate and therefore decent and good. Jolly felt herself to be so rotten that anything good or legitimate she did had to be destroyed.

"So whenever Faith misbehaved, it came into my head that I would have to straighten her out like I had been straightened out when I was a child. She was nothing but another me anyway, a damn little brat who shouldn't have been born acting like me. Of course, she wasn't like me or anyone else—she was a completely unique individual. But parents like me see our kids as our lives' whipping posts. They're going to suffer for everything we've suffered for. And the more they're like us, the more they're going to suffer."

Jolly soon remarried, this time to a gentle Japanese who was loyal and sympathetic. But the pattern of scapegoating Faith was too deeply ingrained by this time, and she couldn't let up. For three years, Jolly made the rounds of nine different agencies, seeking psychiatric help. The only solutions they ever suggested were adoption or foster care.

"One day Faith walked into the house and I had packed her things again; I had her ready to go to another foster home. By that time, I knew she was safer in foster care, away from me. I was

28

starting to lose touch with reality. I was thinking that Faith was the bad me, that if she died she would take all the badness in me with her. I knew I had to get her out of my sight."

In her final quest for help, Jolly told a social worker in a child guidance clinic that she was losing control and that she'd almost killed Faith on several occasions. When the woman informed her that there was a six months' waiting list for treatment, Jolly went to pieces and began pounding on the desk.

"I need help *now!*" she shouted. "My daughter will be dead in six months, and you'll be more responsible than me because you're rational and I'm not!"

The next day she was put in touch with Leonard Lieber, a man who was to become one of the most important people in her life.

Leonard's story

Parents Anonymous was born Mothers Anonymous in February of 1970. It had its real beginnings thirty years earlier, however, when a little red-headed Jewish kid named Leonard Lieber played solitary games at his grandparents' house on Hobart Street in Michigan City, Indiana.

"During World War II, my parents both worked at the family supermarket, and I was left in the care of my very loving paternal grandmother, Frieda, who gave me a solid sense of my inner self. When she died in 1950, there were as many strangers at her funeral as friends and relatives. Nobody knew until then that this very special lady had, for many years, saved the change from her family budget and used it for cab fare to sneak across our little town and read newspapers and books to blind people who had little contact with the outside world."

Leonard felt very secure in his grandparents' home. It wasn't until he was thirty-eight years old that he learned about the devastating effects the war had had on his own family. While he was growing up in Indiana, a number of his relatives were being massacred by the Nazis in a small town in southern Poland. People who may have looked like him, may even have had his name and been his age, were lined up in front of an open pit and machine-gunned to death.

When Leonard was three and a half, his sister Ellen Jo was born. She was severely retarded and physically handicapped.

"From the beginning, it seemed as though I sensed more of a closeness with her than my folks did, and I willingly became her surrogate parent. There was a rapport between us, and I lived with the gut-wrenching awareness of what a delight she would have been had she been whole. I loved her; she was mine; but my association with this little person who appeared so strange to my peers effectively sealed me off from most normal interactions with playmates. I remember getting into yelling matches and sometimes physical fights with them when they made fun of her. And there was the inevitable anti-Semitism and taunts of 'damn Jew' that resulted in my fierce retaliation even though I was small for my age. I felt different—I *was* different."

Leonard's family had little support from the professional community in dealing with Ellen Jo's problem. They went from one place to another, hoping for a miracle that never happened. Finally, Ellen Jo was placed in a custodial home in the east. This was the first of a series of homes around the country that the Liebers would try in their search for the right one.

"When I was nine, I accompanied my mother to a treatment center in Florida where Ellen Jo was at that time. It was a home for seriously retarded and cerebral-palsied children and young adults. In this world of the absurd, there were people in bodies that were totally broken; yet their brains in many cases were well developed, their thought processes highly lucid. They were prisoners in bodies that just didn't function. I remember a young Cuban boy—his name was Jesus—sitting in a wheelchair, unable to control his body while he carried on a brilliant conversation.

"In looking back, I think that these vivid pictures of the hideously bizarre circumstances human beings could find themselves in helped me later on to put the child-abuse situations I encountered into a broader perspective."

When Leonard was eleven, his father left the family store and opened a restaurant, which soon failed. By that time, the family included a younger sister, Debbie. On Leonard's twelfth birthday, they moved to California, where Ellen Jo was placed, first in a foster home, then in a state hospital. It was yet another separation from her that Leonard could barely handle.

The stresses—the frustration, sorrow, and confusion—of those dozen years had taken their toll on everyone. Leonard found himself living with a lot of questions, and no one had the answers. Finally, impatient with his large, impersonal public school, he briefly dropped out of high school at sixteen and left home at seventeen. He drove 2,000 miles back to Indiana and finished high school there while living with an uncle. This was followed by a six-month stint in the army and a period of rootlessness—spending a year at the Pasadena Playhouse, taking part-time jobs, moving back home, then leaving again.

"Finally, I got interested in social work. I kept recalling a picture I'd seen in high school of a friendly young adult counseling a teenager—a very warm, brotherly sort of thing that, in my emotional isolation, held great appeal. I finished my B.A. in three years, still a loner, but gravitating more and more toward people with handicaps. During this whole time while I was struggling to make sense of things, I nevertheless felt a strength within myself. I realize now that this came from my father's quiet and constant faith in me, his faith that I would do 'the right thing,' whatever that might be."

Leonard married a woman he met in college. They eventually had a son, Michael; but the marriage ended in 1972 and Leonard became a single parent. By that time, he had been a social worker for eight years.

"My first job as a welfare worker in 1962 brought me into contact with people so far below the poverty level that they were dreaming of food while eating water. I would do a cursory screening and determine what kind of aid they should be referred to. I remember one proud old woman who was attempting to live on $35 a month social security. She was starving, yet she cried at the shame of having to ask for help. I was learning a lot about human misery that I'd thought I was aware of but had never come close to knowing.

"After graduate school in 1965, I went into child welfare and protective services. That's where I got immersed in the issue of child abuse and neglect. I was one of the first protective service workers in Los Angeles County in 1966. Half the time I didn't know what I was doing, and the other half I managed to do something positive simply because of intuition. None of us had been trained to work in child abuse, and the agency didn't know much more than we did.

"I became social-worker supervisor at the county center for the most neglected and battered children (MacLaren Hall) just a few months after my son was born. I saw very, very young children getting over some of the physical wounds of their abuse, and it became damned difficult for me to handle the idea that people could do such things to their kids. My feelings toward abusing parents were very mixed; I wasn't sure what role to adopt in dealing with them and their kids. We would take kids out of their homes without knowing how to prepare them for their return and without knowing how to help the parents understand what they had to do to get their kids back again."

In late 1968, Leonard left the social services agency for a new career at California State Mental Hygiene as a psychiatric social worker serving former mental-hospital patients. Around Christmas of 1969, an ex-colleague, Florence McCaffrey, asked him to evaluate a young woman for possible entry into the state mental hospital. The woman had confessed at a South Bay child-guidance clinic to serious child-abuse problems and had become hysterical when told that she would have to go on a six-month waiting list. Her outburst had prompted a call to protective services and a request for immediate intervention on behalf of her children. Not long afterward, Leonard met Jolly K. for the first time.

He began to see Jolly twice a week in therapy and her daughter Faith once a week. The therapy with Jolly didn't progress well.

"She was playing a lot of games and throwing roadblocks into the therapeutic process. Finally, she told me point-blank that I was failing; I hadn't stopped her from abusing her daughter. I admitted that I was fresh out of ideas and would welcome anything she might come up with."

Jolly was quiet for a few minutes before answering, "If I could sit down with somebody who had problems like mine, maybe we could sort things out together and come up with a better way."

"If you started something like that, what would you call it?" Leonard asked.

"How about Mothers Anonymous?"

Leonard remembers his initial response to Jolly's suggestion: "I felt a tingle and a gut excitement that I have since come to know as the feeling I get when something big is going to break. It was a hell of a good, sensible idea, and there was no reason why it couldn't work."

A week later, when Jolly and Leonard met again, he asked her, "Well, have you done it?"

"Done what?" Jolly answered, bewildered.

"Started Mothers Anonymous," Leonard replied.

"No," she admitted.

Leonard kept after her, realizing that she would have difficulty accepting the idea that she could do something positive. A typical characteristic of a child abuser is a low self-image, and Jolly had been convinced all her life that nothing she attempted could ever turn out well. Finally, Leonard pulled a bright, gutsy woman named Bea out of his caseload. She had confessed to being verbally abusive.

"The three of us had our first meeting at my office. Several decisions were made at that time. First, Jolly and Bea decided that they had to control their behavior, even before they searched for causes. Second, we exchanged telephone numbers so that we could all be available to one another, day and night. And finally, we agreed that we would meet weekly in members' homes and that under no circumstances would members of our group ever be charged any dues or fees.

"Somehow, each succeeding week, we added a few more people. There were referrals from the caseloads of other social workers. One or two members told their acquaintances and relatives about the group, and some of them began to show up, too. Jolly was able to secure the meeting room at St. Paul's Methodist Church. Then she ran an ad in the paper, which began, 'For Mothers Who Lose Their Cool With Their Kids....' "

Parents Anonymous may have had quiet beginnings, but it was not destined to remain inconspicuous for long. The group began to get help from others who saw what the group was doing and wanted to get involved. Then, during late summer of 1970, Fred Anderson of KABC-TV in Los Angeles filmed a Mothers Anonymous group meeting. The segment was shown on the local evening news and picked up by an ABC affiliate several hundred miles east. The word was out.

January 1971

The M.A. meeting was barely under way when Jolly's husband, Jim, arrived to tell her that an emergency call had come in at their home. A woman had beaten her child unconscious, panicked, and called the Mothers Anonymous phone number for help. Jolly asked me to go home with her and wait until the woman called back.

Her house was a clutter of antiques, cats, a sewing table strewn with material, and a large aquarium. The phone sat on the kitchen table. We drank instant coffee and waited. Her two girls, Faith and Roz, came out of their bedroom wearing long flannel nightgowns and looking as if they'd just stepped off the cover of a family magazine.

"Did you come back to help the lady who called?" Roz asked her mother.

"Yes, if I can," Jolly told her. She was chewing on the side of her thumb, and I noticed for the first time that all of her nails were bitten to the quick.

Faith hugged her mother, then asked me if I knew which of the cats was her favorite. I guessed wrong. When I told her that my younger daughter, Kelly, was her age, she looked pleased.

If I had expected to see a woebegone, shifty-eyed, abused child, I had come to the wrong place. Faith looked into my face with friendly affection. When she put her hand on my arm, though, an insistent, intensely pleading quality came through in her touch.

36

We were startled when the phone rang. The voice on the other end was faint and jerky, and there were pauses when we thought the woman had hung up. Her child was still unconscious. Jolly finally convinced the woman that she should take him to a hospital—Morningside was the nearest one. The woman promised to call an ambulance.

"We'll meet you there in half an hour," Jolly said. "Or do you want us to come to your house and help you?"

No, she didn't.

The emergency room at Morningside was crowded with tired-looking people. It was cold outside, but the waiting room was airless. We checked with the attendant just inside the door and explained why we were there. No battered children had been admitted; it was 9:30 P.M.

We spoke with the attendant every fifteen minutes and wandered back and forth between the parking lot and the waiting room until 11:00 P.M. Once we met two policemen in the parking lot who were heading for their car. We explained our mission and told them that we had come to the hospital in order to help the mother. They stared at us suspiciously.

"Sorry, I haven't seen anybody like that tonight," the older one said.

"Yeah, well," the younger one added, "when you do see that woman, maybe you can help her off the nearest bridge. That'd be the best thing for her."

As they got into their car, Jolly called, "That won't help her or her kid either." They didn't hear, or pretended they didn't hear.

The woman never showed up.

37

* * *

In mid-January, we learned that Mothers Anonymous had been given a place on the program at
the Child Welfare League's Regional Conference
scheduled for February 8-10 in San Francisco. We
all felt that this was a turning point. The group
had been in existence for nearly a year, and there
had been some media recognition, but somehow an
invitation to participate in a conference seemed
like the onset of legitimacy. In the meantime, the
M.A.'s treasury had run dry, as it was destined to
do many more times before we began receiving
government funding. But then a $50 donation
came through from the Altrusa Club of Redondo
Beach. The money seemed like another good omen.

In the weeks before the conference, I photocopied newspaper articles that had been written
about M.A. and any other pertinent materials that
we could think of to take with us. I had been
invited to go along so that I could tape Jolly's and
Leonard's presentations; it was time for M.A. to
begin keeping accurate records of its progress.

One afternoon, when I was sitting in Jolly's
kitchen, another emergency call came through. The
woman had been referred by Dr. Gary Faber, who
later became a P.A. board member. Jolly was
barefooted and dressed in jeans and a sweatshirt.
She grabbed her briefcase, and we drove over to
the woman's house. A painfully thin, pretty
woman in a red pantsuit greeted us at the door.
She was very depressed and nervous as she
explained that while she hadn't really done anything yet, she was afraid of what she might do if
she didn't talk to somebody. We spent over an

hour with her, and she showed up at the M.A. meeting two weeks later.

Even today, after nine years, the picture of Jolly hurrying up that driveway, barefooted and swinging her black briefcase, is still very vivid in my mind.

February 1971

The night before we were scheduled to fly up to San Francisco, I went to Jolly's house to help her make some last-minute decisions about what to wear and what to pack. She was in a state of nerves, partly because her mother was in the hospital following a suicide attempt. Jolly's mother protested her going to the conference and had taken an overdose when Jolly had refused to cancel her presentation. This had resulted in a slight cardiac arrest. Since her mother wasn't in serious condition, Jolly was determined to leave as planned the next morning.

"Make sure you have shoes," I kidded her. "They won't let you into the Sheraton Palace barefooted, even *with* a briefcase and credentials."

* * *

The next day, February 8, Leonard was scheduled to speak on "Child Abuse and Treatment of the Abusers" in the Royal Suite, room 264, of the Sheraton Palace Hotel. Jolly wasn't mentioned on the program, and Mothers Anonymous was billed as a "rap session"—not one of the important workshops or general meetings. We were all a little frustrated when we saw the room we'd been given.

Child abuse had built to epidemic proportions; yet the only people at the conference who were going to discuss a functional approach to it were Jolly and Leonard, and room 264 held about thirty people.

Leonard waited for a while before introducing himself. Finally, he stepped to the front of the room.

"I'm Leonard Lieber, a psychiatric social worker for the State Department of Social Welfare Community Services Division in Redondo Beach, California, which services an area of one million people

"I'd like to share some gut feelings about child abuse and talk about what has been done, see where we're going, what we should have been doing, and what we can be doing in the future. Social workers have been reluctant to get involved *beyond the child* with child abuse and neglect. The scope of the problem has centered around the child, and there's been a reluctance to deal directly with the benighted parent who's been accused, convicted of upsetting a child's physical and emotional equilibrium. One of the last things in our society that people are willing to deal with on an accepting level is child abuse. We are unaccepting of the issue of child abuse—emotional, verbal, and physical child abuse—*because all of us have experienced the feeling of wanting to abuse our own children or someone else's children.* And I think having to face somebody who has already gotten to that point produces more guilt in us than we can possibly tolerate.

"I was kidding around today over the fact that I've got my three year old up here with me, and I started contemplating holding him out of the

40

fourth-floor window by his heels because he was really getting to be too much. And although I could laugh about it, I know there are people who couldn't control their feelings, and their feelings would lead to actions, and they *would* hold their children out over a fourth-floor ledge. There's a very thin line between feelings and action, and maybe the difference between those of us who do abuse and those of us who don't abuse is that some of us learn how to have better control than others.

"I think basically we're all abusers of other people—of children, adults, and ourselves—to one degree or another, based upon the stresses that we experience.

"It's very difficult to line up services for yourself if you present yourself as someone who's done something severe to a child. People give you the cold shoulder. About a year ago, someone came into my office, distraught. She'd confessed her problem to several other agencies and received promises, but no real help. She had an idea about establishing a treatment program—a self-help program for child abusers. I challenged, pushed, and cajoled her into working on it. At that point, the office with which I was involved gave her full backing and endorsement, and Mothers Anonymous, as she coined it, began."

Leonard had explained to the roomful of social workers what Mothers Anonymous was. Then he introduced Jolly as "a very unique young woman, who has done a fantastic job of promoting and improving her self-esteem, the self-esteem of another thirty women, and that of one other person, this daddy right here."

Jolly was stunning in her blue velour suit and salt-and-pepper wig. Her makeup covered the thin

41

razor-blade scars on her face left over from a suicide attempt five years earlier. This would be only the third time she'd spoken in public.

"Of the 60,000 reported cases of child abuse per year," Jolly began, "over 700 die as the result of abuse. Ninety-five percent of us survivors who become parents also become child abusers. We produce a chain. As the children grow up to be parents, they abuse *their* children. In a couple of studies, one made at Brandeis University and another at the University of Colorado, there have been cases where abuse has gone back as far as eighteen generations in one family.

"Our group is composed of child abusers, myself included.

"My daughter was abused. Luckily, she wasn't killed. She would get in my way, and I'd give her a blow, kick, slap, or whatever. I wasn't particular about where I hit her. If it was on the head, then it was her tough luck for getting in the way. She was lucky that she never fell against something sharp when I hit her, lucky that she didn't sustain brain damage.

"She was abused in another way, too, one of the worst and most prevalent ways: verbally. From the time she could walk, she was called everything lousy you could think of. I can imagine what kind of self-image she got out of it. I guess any one of you can imagine what would happen to your child if he grew up from the age of two on hearing what a little dummy he was. He'd *become* a dummy. Children are programmed by their parents as to what to think of themselves.

"In our group, we go after these things— physical abuse, verbal abuse, and, of course, neglect.

"Children who are abused usually remind their parents of themselves. In a way, it's as if parents were abusing themselves through their children. It's as if they were getting back at themselves. My child didn't look like me, but she was just as stubborn, just as willful, and got into just as much trouble as I did at her age. I remember how I was punished when I was a child, and I punished her in the same ways."

The room was surprisingly quiet, even though it was filled beyond capacity. There were people standing in the doorway, and the traffic in the hallway had come to a stop. The idea of saving the parents so they in turn could save their children was a novel one, and it seemed to be a solid hit in this roomful of social workers. We knew, though, that our struggle for recognition and acceptance by professionals had only just begun.

* * *

It was late when Jolly and Leonard and I returned to the hotel suite we were sharing with Leonard's parents and three-year-old son, Michael. We were worn out and exhilarated. After we had all had a drink to celebrate, I went into the room I was sharing with Jolly and fell into bed.

Something had awakened Michael, and I could hear Leonard through the wall of our adjoining rooms as he talked softly to him. I listened to them and to the pipes rattling in the night, and I thought about how Jolly had been abandoned in this same city at the age of four. She had lain awake, too, smelling damp wool and steam heat, hearing the creaks in the old Juvenile

Hall building, but there had been no one to tell her that everything was going to be all right.

* * *

February ninth was the day the big earthquake hit Los Angeles. We stood on a windy street corner in San Francisco, reading the newspaper headlines. When we called home, we found out that everybody was all right, but Jolly decided to change her reservation and leave early. I asked her why.

"My mother will be scared, " she said, "and it could bring on another attack."

I didn't ask her how she could care, at this point, whether her mother lived or died, but she seemed to sense what I was thinking.

"I just don't want to think of her being scared and alone," she explained.

Just like you were scared and alone when she left you, I thought. The child had become parent to the parent. This was a phenomenon we would see many times over the years with P.A. parents who managed to grow through their pain while their parents wouldn't or couldn't. There is also another aspect in this: Many abused children grow up still clinging to the hope that their parents will change and love them like they've always wanted to be loved. And, with exposure to P.A., some of them do.

* * *

Mothers Anonymous was growing, slowly but surely. Not surprisingly, it found its way into prison.

The California Institute for Women at Frontera (C.I.W.) is the largest women's prison in the

44

world, located in a cow pasture fifty miles south-
east of Los Angeles. Two weeks after the Child
Welfare Conference, Tobi M., a member of M.A.
who had recently been released from C.I.W. (she
had not been in for child abuse), wrote a letter to
then Superintendent Iverne Carter requesting a
hearing for the M.A. program:

Dear Mrs. Carter:

*... First of all, I think you may already have
heard that since I left the institution behind, I've gone
on and somehow or another been halfway successful in
getting my life straightened away.*

*I married a terrific fella and ten months later had
a baby impulse as usual. She is now a very active nine
month old. Now despite how much I can say about our
girl being my whole life, I cannot cope with her too well.
Blaming a defenseless child is much easier than looking
at my own ineptness. I started an old pattern of taking
my frustrations out on an innocent party ... my own
child. But even though I've never really lost control of
my "physical blood-thirsty" feelings toward her, I have
torn my little girl to shreds emotionally. There isn't a
downgrading word I've left unsaid. I yell at her—or, I
did, at a moment's notice, and not because she is bad.
She is much better than you would expect, if you
remember me. What I am saying is, verbally I am guilty
as all hell of child abuse.*

*I really felt horrible because I couldn't seem to stop
the destruction. So I started looking for help, and I've
found it. I was referred by Harbor General Hospital to
contact a group in Redondo Beach known as Mothers
Anonymous. I felt I had to get myself straightened away
before my little girl was emotionally torn apart for a
lifetime.*

I talked with the group founder, who explained to

*me what was happening and gave me enough strength to
follow through with my need for help. I started
attending this self-help group, and it is helping. I still
lose my cool occasionally, but I know when it's time to
stop now, before the damage has occurred. I am learning
more about myself and my inner thoughts, feelings, and
impulses than I ever have. I know it can work.*

*I can still see the gals on campus in my mind.
Some of their names are failing me, but the faces are
still hanging on. I remember convicted mothers ... some
of whom were not as fortunate as most of us in M.A.
The only difference between the child abuser in prison
and the child abuser out here in society is that the
insiders were brought to the attention of the authorities.
A lot of our M.A. group could have been in prison by
now if they hadn't been fortunate enough to get help for
themselves.*

*Every month there are gals leaving C.I.W. scared
to death of what is yet to be faced, but they are willing
to take a stab at making good. Our group founder and I
have discussed prison life and the return to society in
great depth. We have really thought about those women
coming out soon and wondered how many of them are
mothers with children to go home to.*

*We feel that our group could be of great value to a
number of mothers who will eventually go back into
society, and we are anticipating a possibility that we
might start a pilot program within C.I.W.*

*If this program makes sense to you, please let me
hear from you so that we can arrange to talk with you
further and answer the questions you no doubt have.
Mrs. Carter, you and your staff reached out to help me
(as hellish as I was). In return, I would like a chance to
reach out to other inmates, in cooperation with you and*

your staff. I know we can succeed if you will give our pleas your utmost consideration.

Very hopefully yours,
Tobi M——

The following answer came by return mail:

Dear Mrs. M—— :

This is February 23, and your letter arrived today. I am so pleased with it that I am replying immediately, even though I cannot give you assurance that tomorrow we will start a Mothers Anonymous group. Your honesty and openness about what has happened is the thing that pleased me more than anything else.

The group sounds to me like an excellent idea. I would like to kick it around a little with some of our counseling staff since they know who might be open enough and honest enough to come into such a group. We would need to know how often you would be able to come to the institution, whether there would be someone else coming with you and, if so, who, and a little bit more about how the group meetings might be carried out here.

I will be back in touch with you again as soon as I have had a chance to give this a little more thought. However, I did not want to let the day go by without letting you know your letter had come and interests me.

Sincerely,
Iverne R. Carter, Superintendent

Mrs. Carter acted immediately, and by the following week, Jolly and Tobi had an appointment to present the program to her at C.I.W. I was granted permission to accompany them and tape the meeting.

We drove the sixty miles to the prison. The freeway from Los Angeles to the California Institute for Women goes through a mountain pass that's beautiful in the spring: everything is green and leaping with life. The horizon is limitless, with snow-capped mountains in the distance. Turning off onto a country road into the lowlands, we smelled cows and fertilizer.

Finally, we saw the sign on flagstone: CALIFORNIA INSTITUTE FOR WOMEN. It didn't look like a prison, with its low buildings, new brick, and drifts of pansies in neat flowerbeds.

The staff called it the "campus"; the inmates called it the "joint." The lobby was furnished in steel tubes and vinyl upholstery; there were vending machines, prisoners' handcrafts for sale in glass cases, a switchboard girl, a uniformed attendant. When we signed in, the attendant double-checked to see that we and the tape recorder were authorized and then stamped our hands purple so we could get out again. We walked through a security arch, then to a door, where we waited for an official click to signal its opening, and at last down a hall to Mrs. Carter's large, sunny, carpeted office.

Superintendent Carter came off as something of a *grande dame*, but she was also down-to-earth and keenly perceptive. She listened closely as Jolly told her story and described what she thought M.A. could do for convicted child abusers. When Jolly had finished, Mrs. Carter stared at her without blinking for a few seconds before nodding her head briskly. The program was given eight weeks' probation. Two weeks later, we held the first group meeting at the prison. Jolly and Leonard soon started going there once a week.

Nancy, a twenty two year old who was in for five years to life as an accessory to killing her child, attended from the beginning and was instrumental in getting the group started. She had told Mrs. Carter, "I wouldn't be in prison and my child would still be alive if there'd been anything like M.A. to help me when I needed it."

Mrs. Carter retired shortly thereafter, and Virginia Carlson who took over as the new superintendent was also enthusiastic and supportive. Two prison nurses, Alice Best and Alba Gray, offered to become the in-house sponsors for the group and to make themselves available to the members on a regular basis in case any of them experienced emotional difficulties between meetings. They also did a lot to help educate the rest of the prison staff about M.A. and child abuse and helped to smooth out some of the institutional complications that Jolly and Leonard occasionally ran into.

I knew that the infamous Betty Lansdown Fouquet was in C.I.W. at the time, and I couldn't help asking if she would be attending the M.A. meetings. She was the woman who had fascinated me over a year ago when the newspapers had carried stories about her standing by while one of her children was killed and the other was later abandoned.

"The word has come through that Betty Lansdown's going to attend," Jolly told me. "She doesn't use Fouquet's name anymore."

I observed Betty Lansdown during her first M.A. meeting. She was well groomed and aloof, thinner, not the way I remembered her from the

49

newspaper photograph, but still scared looking. She was wearing a sequined white sweater, and her hair was pulled back in a ponytail. Throughout the meeting, she sat staring woodenly and saying nothing.

The back of her neck looked especially vulnerable. Little tendrils of hair escaped from the ponytail and trailed down, going their own way, lost but determined.

Betty would be in the group for a long time before she would be able to open up and tell her story.

Betty Lansdown's story

Betty Lansdown grew up in Buffalo, N.Y. She doesn't recall having any sense of her own identity until she was nine years old. She never felt any love from her family, and they barely made it financially. Although both her parents worked, her father spent most of his money at a local bar.

"I was sexually abused by my father when I was five. My mother found out and confronted him, and that ended the marriage.

"I knew I was really to blame, or that's what I thought. I withdrew, became a loner, hated myself. When I was nine, a playmate gave me an identity: she called me a stupid, ugly, blundering idiot. I knew then who I was. I had repeated second grade; I went on to fail fourth grade, seventh grade, and then seventh-grade summer school. I quit the summer I was sixteen; I was still in the seventh grade.

"When I tried to get a job in a department store, they gave me an addition problem, but I couldn't do it, so I didn't get a job there or anywhere else I tried."

She was seventeen when she married a man eight years older than herself. They had known each other for a month. They moved to California, and a year later Betty had her first child. At that time, her husband told her, "When I married you I didn't really love you. But I do now because you've given me a son." Betty became a baby machine and had four children, one after another. "What I really wanted was for someone to love me for myself. But if nobody wanted me, I could have kids—they'd want me."

Her husband couldn't hold a job, and the family moved forty-seven times in three years. Finally, the kids were starving, the utilities had been turned off, and they were living on charity from a neighborhood church. Betty painted her landlord's house to earn enough money to take her back to New York. Even though she was sure that her family didn't love her, she hoped that they would care about her kids. That wasn't the case; nobody wanted to be bothered with "Betty's brood." So she went on welfare and lived in a shack.

"Then I met Ronnie. He was nice to the kids and nice to me. He offered to pay for my divorce and adopt my children. It was the best offer I'd had. What I didn't know was that before I met him he'd beaten his first wife and left her for dead.

"We packed up the kids and moved to Cleveland. For three weeks, everything was okay. Then he began to beat me almost daily. I thought his reason for beating me was because I didn't want to become pregnant again. So I let myself get pregnant. He stopped beating me and started beating my children. Jeff was only four then.

"Nothing I did seemed to help. We had no friends; we moved in and out of apartments in the middle of the night. My family made no attempt to find us.

"When my youngest daughter was six months old, Ronnie would hit her with his fist. Or she'd be sitting in the playchair, and he'd kick it over and she'd tumble out. He knew that without the kids I had nothing to live for. That was his hold on me. I knew he'd find us and kill us if I took them and left."

In 1965, they decided to move to California. On the way out, Ronnie made up his mind that Betty's youngest child didn't belong in their family. He wanted to leave her in the desert to die. Betty managed to talk him out of it, and they finally left the baby with her brother, who had also moved to California. When her brother wanted to know where he could reach them, Ronnie gave him the address of a vacant lot.

"My brother said to leave the baby and her clothes with him and told me to get out. I wanted to tell him that there was something terribly wrong, that I needed help, but I couldn't; I felt he didn't really care about me anyway.

"In September of 1966, Ronnie took my five-year-old son's life. He stood in the middle of Jeff's stomach. I tried to push him off, but he threw me to the floor. Jeff died in minutes. I felt like some kind of monster, like there should have been *something* I could have done to stop it. Fear was a big part of what took place. Not only did I fear the man I was with, I feared my own inadequacies as a human being. Most of the time, I didn't even feel human."

No one knew about Jeff's death; his body was disposed of in the desert. To keep from becoming suicidal, Betty had to block out all her feelings about her son's death. She felt that she had to stay alive in order to protect the rest of her children. But Ronnie continued to abuse them; for over two years they lived in constant fear. By this time, Betty's contact with the outside world had been completely and effectively cut off by his threats to kill her and the children if she so much as made a telephone call. He had her convinced that he had ways of knowing every move she made.

One day, Ronnie decided that he didn't like five-year-old Jannie because she cried too much. He claimed that she was "ugly" and "stupid" and began to talk about shooting her. Betty got him to agree to abandon Jannie instead and talked him into leaving the child in a gas station or on a back porch. He said that he'd drive Jannie to San Francisco because it was far enough from Los Angeles that no one would be able to trace her back to them.

"A couple of days before he planned to abandon her, he took one bullet out of the house, and the next day he took the gun. I knew that if he took my daughter out of the house alone, she would never reach San Francisco alive. Finally, he agreed to let me and the other children go with him. We decided to go only as far as Bakersfield and then leave my daughter at a relatively safe place. We drove into Mettler, and I saw a house that gave me good feelings. I felt that loving and kind people lived there and that they would love

53

my daughter. By this time, I wasn't capable of giving my children love.

"Ronnie wouldn't let her out at that house. I prayed that he wouldn't kill her. We finally put her out on the freeway. Three days later, the police found her. She told them about her life, and we were arrested."

* * *

Betty Lansdown's trial for child abandonment began in December of 1970. It was then the most infamous and widely publicized child-abuse case in California.

While I was busy cutting out newspaper articles for my file, a woman named Louise was getting directly involved in Betty Lansdown's life.

"The first time I recall seeing her," Louise remembers, "my kids were out of school, and we were downtown Christmas shopping. They wanted to do something special, so I decided to take them into the courthouse since we were parked near there anyway. I thought they should see how the law was carried out at a trial.

"So we wandered in. The prosecuting attorney had just chosen the last juror and was making his remarks. I sat there, thoroughly disgusted with the whole thing, and I thought, 'If there's any answer to this, I want to hear it.' At first I was on the side of the prosecuting attorney. My first impression was, 'Boy, they ought to hang this lady. Good thing I'm not on the jury or I'd have her out of here and in prison in nothing flat.' I was sure there couldn't be a decent answer for what she had let happen to her children.

"I took my kids, and we went back on the

second day. That's when I discovered that there *was* a very sufficient answer: Betty's own life.

"I came back on the third day, and the fourth, and the fifth. Why? Well, she looked like she needed someone to talk to. The first time our eyes met in the courtroom and I really *saw* her, I asked this lady sheriff if I could hold her hand when they took her away. She said, 'No, you can't touch her.' When I asked why not, she answered, 'You just can't.' So I said, 'Well, you tell her to consider her hand held.'

"So she went up and told Betty. And Betty turned around and looked at me. Our eyes locked—and I just knew that I had a friend. There's a way you know something like that; I can't describe it, but there's a way you know it in your heart. It wasn't necessarily that *I* was *her* friend, but that *she* was *mine*. And she's been a good friend to me."

On the fifth day of the trial, Louise suddenly held up a large sign in the courtroom with the words NOT GUILTY printed on it.

"I couldn't believe that the jury would find her guilty, but they did. She was guilty of child abandonment. They sentenced her to one to ten years."

For his crime, Ronald Fouquet was sentenced to die in the gas chamber. Later, in the wake of restrictions on the use of capital punishment, his sentence was reduced to life in prison. He is currently incarcerated in the California State Prison system.

* * *

Even as an adult, Betty was convinced that she was

55

still the "stupid, ugly, blundering idiot" a playmate had labeled her so many years ago.

"I continued through the years to build on
that identity. I almost destroyed my life and a lot
of other people's lives because I felt I had to
project everything I'd learned about myself. And I
did a darned good job of it. I did so well that I
finally took myself to prison.

"When I reached prison, I found an identity
that was even worse. I knew there had to be
something else, something better, somewhere—at
least I hoped so. Somehow, I didn't give up that
hope. I realized I needed help, that I couldn't
better myself by myself. So I asked to go to the
psychiatric unit at C.I.W., and they wanted to
know why.

"I answered, 'Because I need help, and I don't
know what to do about myself.' Then they said,
'Betty, if you're together enough to ask for help,
you don't need it.'

"That was bullshit—I needed it very much. So
I slammed doors; I tore my bed up; I threw some
glasses around, and they sent me to PTU [Psychiat-
ric Treatment Unit]. But I didn't get any help over
there—the psychiatrist was always busy. I think he
took an eight-hour-a-day coffee break because none
of the other girls ever got any help from him
either. We all wondered, 'What's the guy here for?
Where's our help coming from?' When you read in
the paper that some girl is being sent to prison for
psychiatric help, that's bullshit. There isn't any
psychiatric help there."

Then one day Betty received a ducat, a blue-
slip invitation from the prison staff, to go to
Mothers Anonymous. She had never heard of
M.A., and she didn't want to go.

"I was afraid if I went that somebody would see me—the *real* me, what I felt inside. At that time, I still didn't like the person I was seeing when I looked at myself. I could barely stand in front of a mirror and comb my hair straight back into a ponytail. Makeup? Not a chance—I couldn't stand to look in the mirror that long. I was afraid I'd see myself and all the ugliness I'd known was there throughout the years.

"I finally had three ducats, and someone told me, 'Well, Betty, you're never gonna get outta this trap unless you go there. They send you the invitation, and you know it's your choice, but you'd better make the right choice.' "

May 1971

Ray Helfer is a smallish, natty, soft-spoken man who at first glance would seem more at home on the society page than on the frontier of the country's most distasteful social problem. As coauthor with Henry Kempe of *The Battered Child*, he is also one of the "bigwigs" in child-abuse research. After the Child Welfare Conference in San Francisco, Jolly and the two group members who had been working on compiling M.A. literature had sent out letters to Helfer and other researchers in the field in the hope of gaining credibility for the organization and ultimately putting together an advisory board. In March of 1971, Helfer had written back:

Dr. Theo Solomon has told me of some of the most interesting and exciting aspects of your Mothers Anonymous program. I'm very interested in hearing more

57

regarding how the women in your program are helpful to each other.

As you may know, I have been involved for some time in the problems relating to child abuse. Dr. Kempe and I have recently finished a second book on this problem entitled Helping the Battered Child and His Family.[8] *We have been trying to develop a reasonable and practical therapeutic approach for some time. Your efforts in this area are most encouraging.*

Do you feel that you and some of the women in your group would be willing to talk with me if I were to come to California to visit with you sometime this spring? I would consider it a privilege to have the opportunity to spend a few hours in discussing similar interests with some of the members of your group.

His visit was scheduled for May, and arrangements were made for him to interview five or six members who wanted to "go public." The rest, as they wished, would remain anonymous.

We were jubilant. It was one of the first indications that M.A. wasn't going to be regarded as another bunch of "California kooks" who would pass from the scene in a year or two.

One of the women who volunteered to be interviewed was Ginny; by that time, she had been with the group for almost a year.

Ginny: I'm twenty-three. I was nineteen when Brett was born. From the time he was born, I just didn't feel anything for him. I never gave him the attention I gave my daughter. I just felt like he was an intruder. I resented him.

I was in therapy at the time I had Brett, but whenever I told the therapist I was having trouble feeling anything for my son, he would just shift the attention back to me.

I got into therapy because I was really screwed up—my marriage was a mess. I was a disturbed child, really, from the time I was about three years old. For years I took out my anger and frustration by ripping up my clothes. I was depressed all the time, I never felt good. I was seventeen when my oldest child was born—I got into trouble when I was seventeen.

I was very close to my mother, but my dad was a tyrant, an alcoholic, and I was the one he picked on and blamed for everything. I don't remember him ever telling me he loved me. He was verbally abusive, whether he'd been drinking or not. My mother was very withdrawn around him; they got divorced when I was fourteen. He died when I was nineteen, when I was pregnant with Brett. I didn't feel any sorrow when he died. I felt he must be happier dead—he was so unhappy when he was alive.

I don't know exactly when the actual abuse started. If Brett and the older girl were having a fight, I'd blame him. I left marks, but to my knowledge, I never broke any bones. Then one day I saw a TV show that showed abused kids with the marks all over them, and I felt guilty. Even though I tried to rationalize that Brett deserved it, that he was an unruly child, I knew deep down that he wasn't; he didn't deserve me being so hard on him. My husband tried to tell me not to be so hard on Brett, but he'd never discipline the kids at all. And when I was uptight, he'd make jokes about what a mean mommy I was. That made him look like a great guy.

One day I had Brett right up against the wall

59

with my fist drawn back, and I knew if I hit him,
I'd really hurt him, and it scared me. My mother
wasn't any help because she had picked up on my
bad feelings and treated him the same way. She's
changed now since I've been in M.A.—because *I've*
changed. One day I saw an ad in the paper, "for
moms who blow their cool," and I called the
Mothers Anonymous number.

Dr. Helfer: Was it hard for you to go to M.A. the
first time?

Ginny: Yes. I called Jolly that first time—I got her
number from the ad—and talked to her on the
phone. She wanted me there at the next meeting,
but I couldn't go—I was going on a vacation. Then
after that Brett got pneumonia, and she kept
calling me all the time saying, "When are you
coming to our meeting?" Finally I thought, "Oh,
I'll go to one of the damn meetings just to shut her
up, so she won't keep calling me." So I went, and
I've never missed one since. And I think that to *not*
miss a meeting has a lot to do with recovery, or
not losing your cool with your kids. You can keep
your head together from week to week, but if you
miss a few meetings a month, it's too easy to slip
back into your old pattern. We've been under a lot
of financial pressure—my husband was sick and
out of work for a long time, and there are a lot of
day-to-day stresses still going on.

Dr. Helfer: How does M.A. help that?

Ginny: Just letting it all out helps—being able to go
in there and say how I feel, to release all my
hostility. The times I've gotten upset with Brett
since I've been in M.A.—the few episodes—I've

slapped his face. Afterward, I felt bad and I sat down and talked to him about it. In M.A. we're taught that: to sit down and talk to our children, tell them we're sorry—"Mommy just got angry; I'm sorry"—let them know it's *our* problem, not theirs. Before, when I blew up at Brett, I'd never tell him I was sorry or talk to him; I'd always just leave him kind of hanging there. I couldn't talk to *anybody* about it. I was close to my sister, but *nobody* knew I had an abuse problem until after I got into M.A. *I* didn't even know it; I just knew that something was wrong.

I had been in M.A. one week when I could see changes. Everybody there was in the same boat as I was. I had always known that what I was doing was wrong, but here I had somebody telling me in no uncertain terms to *stop*. I needed somebody to say, "Stop! You can't go on treating your children like that." At first I stopped everything cold; I was afraid to discipline the kids at all. That happens with a lot of the members; then you sort of get back on an even keel where you can discipline properly without abusing.

M.A. helped me learn to let people around me know when I was uptight and to let them step in and handle the kids. Sometimes when I needed help, I'd go to the phone and call one of the other girls. I've had only two or three episodes since— and I've been in the group almost a year.

Dr. Helfer: Do you feel comfortable when members call you?

Ginny: I'd been in the group about two months when somebody called me. I feel comfortable, depending on the problem. Some of the problems I can't handle—for instance, when I feel people aren't facing the fact that it's their abuse problem, not the kid's problem. But I'm getting more comfortable telling them right out when I think they're not facing their abuse problem.

Dr. Helfer: Do members bail each other out by helping out with their children—by baby-sitting, for example?

Ginny: I don't encourage them to drop their children off if they're feeling uptight. It's too easy to use that as an excuse. It's okay if they come over with the kids and talk about what's bothering them.

Dr. Helfer: How often do you call another member?

Ginny: Recently my older girl got me so mad—she needed discipline, but she got abuse, and it really made me feel bad. I called one of the girls, and she got me calmed down so I could go in and talk to my daughter. I was afraid that I had hurt her. I told her it wouldn't happen again, and I don't think it will.

December 1971

Several months after the interview with Ray Helfer, Ginny decided she'd grown strong enough to leave M.A. She had contributed a great deal during that year. She was one of the dedicated parents in the original group who had helped put together literature for the members and had given numerous speeches to help promote M.A.

The second year had seen growth and change for many members and for the organization as well. Jolly and Leonard had felt for some time that since child abuse involves the entire family, the fathers ought to be encouraged to participate too, and the chances of this would be better if the organization weren't called Mothers Anonymous. By late 1971, Mothers Anonymous had officially become Parents Anonymous.[9]

During some of our long weekly drives up to the prison at C.I.W., I had watched and listened as Leonard and Jolly tossed ideas at each other, hacked out solutions to immediate problems, rejoiced in the progress of some of the members, and worried aloud about a few of the others. They still didn't know where P.A. was going, but they were giving it everything they had, and there was the ever-mounting feeling that they must be doing something right. Leonard has his own recollections about that time.

"The best teacher I ever had in graduate school, John Milner, once told us that even with all the education we might be picking up, we really weren't going to be worth a damn unless we were decent human beings first and skilled people second. I've never forgotten that, and I've tried, failing sometimes, to give service recipients a sense that I was a good person who, by the way, had some skills.

"I'm remembering back to a summer evening when our first group was meeting at the little house in the back of the church lot. Attendance was down, as it usually is in the summer. I got there a little before seven, but I didn't have a key to the building. I noticed a woman drive up in a fairly large pickup truck. I sat in my car waiting for somebody else to show up. Nobody did, and this woman was still sitting there in her pickup truck. She had a sad look on her face, and I had a feeling she was a brand new member—certainly I hadn't seen her before. I went over and introduced myself. She seemed fearful and defensive, but after a while I realized that she, like anybody else, merely needed somebody to care about what was going on in her life.

"Since nobody else came that night and we couldn't get into the church room, I proceeded to have a P.A. meeting with her on the running board of her truck. I stood there and we chatted, but she was still so fearful that she wouldn't even get out of the truck.

"Whatever went on between the two of us must have been positive because Wilma came back the next week. She later developed a fairly close relationship with Jolly and began dealing with a lot of things in her life—in particular her abandonment of a child six years earlier in Missouri. She spent a couple of years in our P.A. group and finally developed the emotional strength to return to Missouri and claim that child whom she had abandoned six years earlier.

"This experience had a profoundly strengthening effect on the group; it allowed us to see the enormous influence that human beings can have on each other.

"In the spring of 1971, Jolly and I were asked to be interviewed on the Bob Abernathy segment of the KNBC (Los Angeles) evening news.

"Afterward, while we were driving home, I turned to Jolly and expressed a very strange feeling. That evening, I felt that we had embarked on a very special course. Jolly's vision of P.A. reaching many people, one that I hadn't really taken too seriously before, was becoming a real possibility.

"On another occasion during that time, Jolly and I were asked to participate in a phone interview with Bernie Herman, a radio talk-show host in Philadelphia.

"It was an evening show, so Jolly brought her two girls over to my house, and Faith and Roz entertained Michael for the two hours we were being interviewed. Jolly was on the upstairs phone, and I was on the downstairs phone. Toward the end of the show, we answered questions from listeners who called in. One of the calls was from a seventy-year-old man in Philadelphia who began to tell us, haltingly at first, about his own experiences as an abused child. He said that because people hadn't talked about abuse until very recently, he had never felt able to tell anybody about his experiences until that evening.

"I think I went to bed that night feeling a lot less lonely because an old man didn't have to take a buried hurt with him to the grave.

"That experience and many others like it became emotionally addictive for many of us because we began to realize that we provided a means of allowing people to rid themselves of some very painful kinds of things with people who cared. And this was the backbone of our whole program, the thing that made it so special to us."

2
P.A.
Grows Up

Keeping Parents Anonymous alive during those
early years wasn't easy. Jolly and a growing
number of parents and volunteers scrounged for
money, answered emergency calls, and occasionally
rushed off in the middle of the night to help a
troubled parent, if that was what was needed.

Jolly kept the program going, and Leonard
kept Jolly going. Often unsure about some course
of action she had taken or was about to take, she
would call him at 2:00 or 3:00 A.M. with, "Did I do
okay?" "Did I goof that up?" "How should I
handle it from here?" Leonard's reassurance that
she was handling things very well indeed gave her
the confidence to reassure other parents that they,
too, had the strength to get a positive hold on
their lives.

Donations trickled in, along with the continuing evidence that the program was on the right
track: group members *were* learning to live with
and enjoy their kids, and kids were changing in
front of our eyes because their parents were
changing.

Several new chapters struggled into existence
across the country, and though P.A. didn't exactly
become a household word, there were a number of
people who helped to make it better known.

In August of 1971, we hosted a very special
visitor—Judy Kinnard, who was doing an article
about the P.A. group at C.I.W. for the *New York
Times.* Her story was picked up by other newspapers throughout the United States, Canada,
England, and beyond.

Like many others who got involved with P.A.,
Judy found that her interest became more than just

professional. She was deeply touched by the women at the prison; it was obvious that they weren't simply a group of "losers." As Leonard remembers it: "Judy had a soft, fawn-colored suede coat. One of our prison members had admired it, and when this member was about to be paroled, Judy presented it to her as a wedding gift. At the end of a meeting, she just took it off and put it around the woman's shoulders. It was a very special gesture, one that many of us will never forget."

In autumn of 1971, Ray Helfer and Henry Kempe were finishing their second book on child abuse, *Helping the Battered Child and His Family*. Helfer's enthusiastic report on P.A.'s program was included in it, along with these words: "With the proper support and nurturance, this youthful program could have as significant an impact on child abuse as A.A. has had on alcoholism."

Between Christmas and the New Year, C.I.W. Superintendent Virginia Carlson paved the way for the filming of an ABC special on our P.A. group at the prison. Marlene Sanders brought her crew in for an evening, and the group appeared in her program "Children in Peril," which aired in early 1972. The holidays are an especially tough time for inmates, and this evening was no exception. The cameras framed some beautiful, painful interchanges between members, the prison nurses who served as the group's sponsors, and several of us from the outside. "Children in Peril" was the first show specifically dealing with child abuse to get national exposure.

In January, an article in the *Los Angeles Times* by Arlene Van Breems (now a producer at KNXT in L.A.) further heightened P.A.'s image. A lot of people were starting to get the message that child abuse was a problem of major proportions and that something could be done about it.

* * *

Early in P.A.'s history, Jolly decided that it was going to be a real organization and as such should have a real board of directors. Dr. Roland Summit seemed like a good person to start with. He was then (and still is) the Head of Community Services in the Department of Psychiatry at Los Angeles County Harbor-UCLA Medical Center. Jolly had first heard of him through Leonard, and one day she and Wilma went to see him and asked him to be on the board. He was immediately supportive of her idea and has given generously of his time and talents since then.

In February of 1971, Parents Anonymous held its first board meeting at Harbor Medical Center. At that time, the board consisted of Jolly, Leonard, and Roland Summit. I attended the first meeting in order to tape it. Between 1971 and 1972, four more people joined: Gary Faber, Helen Boardman, Jean Matusinka, and Jerry Tarlow. These four, along with Roland Summit, formed the core of stalwarts who have seen P.A. through its preorganizational phase to its present-day challenges and are still going strong.

Dr. Gary Faber is a psychiatrist. He and his wife, a teacher, have five children. In 1970, he was dividing his time between the Community Services Division of the State Department of Mental Hygiene and South Bay Mental Health Center.

"I was working in the same office as Leonard," he recalls, "and I was also seeing some patients who had abuse problems. My background is in public health, and I very much approved of self-help. I was happy to join the board when Leonard asked me; I regarded parents with child-abuse problems as people who had to be educated, informed, and given social support; and I saw P.A. as being supportive.

"Those early board meetings were so informal that they seemed like ladies' sewing circles; there was virtually no organization. One of the big problems was trying to keep parents on the board. They came and went. I think they were so overawed by the professionals that they tended to self-eliminate. But the big problem was money. I'd had several years of experience in getting federal grants, and at the meetings, we spent a lot of time talking about federal grants—where to get them, how to get them. We talked about big grants while I lent them money for postage. We had many screwed-up fund-raising ventures.

"My association with P.A. has certainly made me a more reflective parent, but professionally it has made me an evangelist about getting parenting education in schools and getting day-care centers for respite care, for primary prevention of child abuse.

"My hope and goal is to get the public to realize that we have to have better parenting education. I would like to see every junior high school also functioning as a child-care center, with the students—both boys and girls—caring for the little kids and using the class as a lab to find out what little preschoolers are like. Because of the isolation of the modern nuclear family, thousands of kids are growing up having no idea what babies are like and how small children act."

Helen Boardman is a former social worker who coauthored one of the first child-abuse reporting laws in the U.S. in 1965, participated in the White House Conference on Families in 1950, and is generally regarded as a pioneer in the field of child protection. She is married to a retired psychologist for the L.A. County Probation Department; they have no children. Helen had been the Director of Social Services at Children's Hospital of Los Angeles for thirty years when she first heard about Parents Anonymous in 1970; today, she is the president of the P.A. board.

"I was aware of the growing epidemic of child abuse. I had been Director of Social Services at Children's Hospital since 1941, and there were these children being brought in who had been injured. Occasionally, they were identified as 'non-accidental injuries,' such as the two year old whose mother, in a fit of anger, had turned the gas up high and set him on the flame. Some of these were the very grossest kinds of injuries. From 1958 on, after we could see the X-ray evidence of injuries in infants and young children, it became very obvious that this was a common occurrence. About the time I was working on the material for my paper,[1] Henry Kempe in Denver wrote to the hospital because he had started doing a survey around the country on child abuse, and we were already a little bit ahead in that we had figures to send to him. By 1970, from *our one hospital*, we were reporting approximately 100 cases a year. Well, that's too many for one hospital.

"In the early 1970s, I had seen *no* evidence that psychiatry, psychology, or social work had a basic understanding of the problem so that they could be of any appreciable help. Even when I had thought that I could personally be of help, I had realized that this was beyond my area of competence, too, as a social worker. When I said, 'Yes, I understand' to a parent, I felt that parent had every right to say to me 'The *hell* you do. How can you understand how I felt and what prompted me to do this or what precipitated that?' One psychiatrist told me that a mother had been referred to him without any background information, and he had seen her several times before he found out that she had killed a child. After that, he had to stop seeing her, because he couldn't deal with his feelings about it.

"As a social worker at Children's Hospital, it took a lot of effort to try to maintain as objective a point of view as possible. At that point all we knew how to do was to protect the *child;* we had the capacity to request a court order to remove the child from the parent. But we didn't yet have any idea what we could do to help the *parent* who would lose control to the point of injuring an infant or a very young child. I used to see great swings of sentiment on the part of the staff in the hospital. Nurses would come up to me on the floor and say, 'Oh, Mrs. Boardman, how I'd like to do to the parents what they did to that child!' Then the parents would come in to see the child that evening and the next morning the same nurses would say, 'Oh, Mrs. Boardman, don't you think you're making a terrible mistake? These parents are so nice!' Nobody had the ability to recognize that at that point we had to put the welfare of the child first. We also had to protect the parents from going on and on inflicting injuries.

"Leonard first called me back in 1970 and asked if we would make referrals to a group that

Jolly was trying to set up for abusive parents. There were only two people in her group at that time, and I said, 'Leonard, this is ridiculous. These parents won't admit to *anything*. Sometimes they won't even admit that there *are* injuries, or they'll try to accuse the doctor in the emergency room of inflicting the injuries during the examination. How can we get them to a service voluntarily when they won't admit there's anything they need help for?' Then Jolly came to my office one day with the first pamphlets about Mothers Anonymous and left them with me.

"I met Jolly again at a legislative hearing in 1971. I remember being very impressed when she stood up in that hearing and loudly said, 'I was a battering parent.' This was the first time I had *ever* heard a parent admit to being a person who could injure a child. Then Jolly called me in January of 1972 and asked me if I would be on the board of P.A., and I was very pleased to be invited.

"I felt at that time that P.A. offered the most positive kind of approach; I'd seen *nothing* going on in the helping professions that was really getting to the basic kinds of problems. Of course, by that time, there were a few other parents who were beginning to admit that they, too, had these feelings that exploded. I didn't believe then, and it's hard to believe now, that the climate could change to the point where so many parents today are willing to admit that they need help in this area. It's an absolute phenomenon to me. I couldn't have anticipated that there would be thousands of parents who could say, 'I have these hostile, angry feelings that I express in such unhealthy ways!' P.A. has demonstrated that parents can respond when they realize that they're not alone in this, that there are many parents who have these feelings, even if they don't act them out. Before that, the community attitude was, 'Oh, abusing a helpless infant is the most horrible of crimes.' I think that the community has a better understanding today of child abuse because of Parents Anonymous and other sources of education. Now it's time for P.A. to put its greatest amount of effort into prevention and try to reach more parents who haven't yet acted out their negative, hostile feelings.

"I'm also very interested in how we can help teenagers to recognize the responsibilities of parenting. I think that once they're aware of this tremendous responsibility, the number of unwanted pregnancies might be reduced. If a pregnant teenager decides to keep the child, then she'll have to be given a great deal of help so that she can meet the responsibilities of parenting. Of the 500 cases that I was personally familiar with at Children's Hospital, I was very concerned by the fact that so many of the parents of the abused children were either teenagers at that time or had had their first child when they were teenagers. It was close to 70 percent."

Jean Matusinka was (and is) a deputy district attorney in the Los Angeles trials division. She got her law degree from Brooklyn College and is married to a supervising parole officer for the State of California; they have no children. Jean is a past president of the P.A. board.

"Back in 1970, I didn't know how widespread child abuse was. There wasn't much being said about it at that time, and I think that most of us are very much sheltered from the whole area unless we're directly involved in some way. I first began to find out about it when I was a deputy DA in juvenile court. At that time, I was handling quite a few dependency cases—cases that determine whether children should be made wards of the court for protective purposes—and Dino Fulgoni, who had been a deputy in the office for many years, took me under his wing. He's our medical and psychiatric expert, and he'd been interested in the area of child abuse for a long time. Whenever there was a meeting of one kind or another relating to child abuse, he would ask me to go along with him. I first met Jolly when she, Dino, and I were on a panel program together on KHJ radio in 1970.

"Before I met Jolly and started learning more about child abuse, I couldn't believe that parents would actually *do* the things that I saw they had done to their kids. I found it very difficult to understand, and I still do; that hasn't changed. I think I can understand the dynamics more, but I haven't really changed my attitude in many respects.

"In the DA's office, we seldom came into contact with the *less* serious kinds of abuse, only the *very* serious types. And we usually found with these people that there'd been a history of abuse. We would go back in the records to when the abusers we were dealing with were juveniles and find that they'd been juvenile offenders. It was almost like a lifestyle of violence toward everybody, but especially toward people who were vulnerable. It was as if they had developed a 'pack mentality' early in their youth, directed toward those who were younger, weaker, more vulnerable—similar to a gang rape attitude.

"I first heard about P.A. when I was on the

radio panel in 1970. Sometime later, Jolly contacted me, and I became curious about P.A. I asked her what went on at the meetings, and she invited me to come to one. I said that I wanted to come but I didn't want to make the group members ill at ease. If they knew I was a DA, I was sure they wouldn't want to talk freely. So Jolly told me to introduce myself anonymously, to give only my first name like everybody else.

"I went to a meeting and found it very interesting, very enlightening. But I was a little concerned that someone would blow my cover or, if I were found out later on, would never again trust any new face coming into the group. Later, I went out to the P.A. prison group with Jolly and was introduced up front as a DA. For the first thirty minutes, there was a lot of silence until Jolly broke the ice and began talking about her own background.

"Later, she asked me to be on the P.A. board, and I agreed. I felt that P.A. was a great thing; I think that there has to be someplace for people to go who recognize that they have a problem and really want help and really want to change. A self-help group seems to be the most effective setting for this kind of growth. I also believe in *coercive* self-help, which works and doesn't work, depending on the individual. There are some people who need to be prodded and coerced into getting counseling. Then they may sit there and think 'Why am I here? I don't abuse my kid, I *discipline* my kid.' Or they'll think '*They* took my kids away, and I can't understand it; *they* must have it in for me; *they've* gotta have it in for me because *they're* doing rotten things to me, and I didn't do anything to my kid.' That's often the initial attitude of the court-referred parents. They may take longer in a program like P.A. because they didn't have the initiative to go on their own to begin with. Some of them never realize that they have a problem.

"When I first joined the board, there were a lot of problems. Chapters would begin, then fold up again. It was hard to keep a chapter going. One of our early goals was to keep a chapter alive once it got started, but the main problem was usually getting enough money. I was a latecomer. Roland, Gary, Jerry and Helen were already on the board when I joined, plus several P.A. parents who came and went. It was about 50 percent parents and 50 percent professionals. I spent a lot of time just listening and trying to orient myself to what was going on. Jolly had a great deal of influence over the board, but it was clear from the beginning that if we were going to be a board then we were going to have to work together. And we have.

"The evolution of P.A. isn't surprising to me; I feel it's gone its natural course, and I'm delighted about that. I have no doubt that it's prevented a lot of people from even starting to abuse their children."

Jerry Tarlow, immediate past president of the board, is a Los Angeles attorney. His wife, Ellen, is a licensed marriage, family, and child counselor, and they have two little girls. He was thirty years old and had been practicing law for three years when he first became involved with P.A.

"My first contact with Leonard was when a client of his was suicidal and a judge we both knew referred the client to me for legal help. Then one day Leonard brought Jolly in to meet me and asked me to be on the P.A. board. I was really turned on to the idea. I attended two or three meetings, and then Ellen and I went to a P.A. party at Leonard's house. Before I became involved with P.A., I was aware of some child abuse because I had handled some cases, but I had no idea how widespread it was.

"I remember one neglect case I defended. The child had cystic fibrosis, and the mother was divorced. She had done what she could for the child, but she just couldn't cope. The father sued to regain custody and got it. I really felt empathy for what that mother went through. And I felt great empathy and admiration for Jolly, who was running this thing out of her kitchen with no money and helping so many people. Joining the P.A. board gave me a chance to do something, to contribute something as a human being that the law simply doesn't address. And I trusted Leonard; I trusted what he was doing. I contributed administrative and legal help that just wasn't there at the time. Somebody would have done it, I'm sure, and I consider myself fortunate to have been given the opportunity.

"I remember when I lent Jolly the funds to go to Detroit. A little girl had been killed there; this was before there were any P.A. groups in Detroit. She was able to stay a week, and when she left there were five P.A. chapters. To be a part of that is ego-satisfying, of course, but it's much more than that. No organization I've ever been involved in has been as rewarding as P.A. It has contributed so much to *me*.

"Being in P.A. has raised my level of awareness about my own childhood; I hadn't looked at my childhood before in any evaluative way. I began to realize how better parenting could have helped me a lot. Even more important, though, the quality of my own parenting has improved. There have been times when Lisa has awakened at five in the morning, and I've wanted to let Ellen get her sleep; Lisa won't tell me what she wants, and I've flown into a rage. I can see how a parent could hit and could kill. And I *have* spanked her, but I'm able to back off, to separate myself from my rage. I've gotten an insight into parenting I wouldn't have had. And when I feel myself lacking as a parent, I know more about what I'm feeling; I'm more in touch with my emotions. I've learned a lot about child abuse, and my awareness gives me more control. Ellen and my relationship has been more satisfying, too; we've used the concept of P.A. for ourselves as people as well as parents."

Mary Y.'s story

Mary Y. is a "graduate" of the original Redondo Beach Parents Anonymous group and was one of the first parent members of the P.A. board of directors. After regular chapter attendance for two years, she moved to Dallas, Texas, and started P.A. there. She is now living in Sherman, Texas, with her second husband and three children, working and majoring in agriculture in college.

"I was nearly twenty when I married. I had my first child at twenty-one, a girl, and about three years later, I had another girl. I was nearly twenty-four when I joined P.A.

"When I first heard about P.A., I was in counseling because my marriage was such a mess. I had married to get away from home, and my husband didn't want children. Most especially, he

81

didn't want girls. But I got pregnant for *myself*; I wanted someone to love, something that belonged to *me*."

Mary's childhood was typical of many P.A. parents: an alcoholic father whose own father had been very abusive; a mother who screamed at her and called her names and let Mary know that she couldn't be trusted.

"Whenever I was the least bit affectionate with my father, she accused me of trying to take him away from her. I just remember that my home life was terrible most of the time. My mother and father fought constantly and finally got divorced after we grew up. They'd stayed together for the sake of the kids. I had three sisters. My father was unhappy about having all girls; he felt his manhood was threatened.... We weren't bad off financially; my father made pretty good money. He hated my younger sister, though, and I remember I picked up his feelings and treated her the same way. I turned against her. I was really cruel to her and locked her in the bathroom just because she hated it.

"After I had my first child, my husband just wasn't there. He was very nonsupportive. I felt deserted, that this kid was solely *my* responsibility, but I had no knowledge of child care or child development. I didn't even read anything. That was frowned on in our family—nobody should need any experts telling you how to parent; it's supposed to be a natural instinct. And I had such unrealistic expectations of how my daughter should behave. I thought she should act like a lady by the time she was two."

Everything was fine for a while. As long as the baby was young enough to stay quietly in her crib, Mary could pretend she was a toy. When she was ten months old, though, the baby began to get more active, and Mary found that hard to deal with. In addition, money was tight, and Mary had to get a full-time job. The baby started sleeping in the afternoons and staying awake during the nights. Mary wasn't getting enough sleep, and the stress was building.

"The abuse started out verbal and emotional. I was cruel; I would yell at her and call her names—*'Bitch, I hate you!'*—I would withhold love. As she grew older, she was very thin and nervous, just as I was, and that's why she made me so mad—because she reminded me of myself. She was so thin I would try to force-feed her. Then I'd scream at her because she wouldn't eat. One day I got myself really worked up and slapped her face pretty hard. I put her in bed and went out of the room, and she started screaming. I went back in and discovered I'd broken a blood vessel in her nose. It really scared me and it scared her, too. Then she broke out with chicken pox. I took her to the doctor, and she said to me in front of the doctor, 'You hit me in the nose, didn't you?' I thought he was going to pick up on it, but he didn't say anything. He just ignored it."

Mary joined an outpatient therapy group at Harbor General Hospital, and one day a social worker there suggested that she try Parents Anonymous. At first, Mary didn't want any part of it.

"I thought it was going to be a bunch of weirdos sitting around telling horror stories about what they did to their kids, and I didn't feel I belonged in a place like that. And I was also convinced that my problems with her were *her* fault, that she was an impossible kid.

"But then one day I had a really bad time. I had applied for a job I was sure I wasn't going to get, and our money situation was really bad. Tammy started in about something, and I threw a toy gun at her. I threw it so hard it broke the door. I realized I was so out of control that if I'd hit her with it I might have killed her. I called the woman at the outpatient group and told her what had happened. She gave me Jolly's number. I called and talked to Jolly. She sounded friendly, so I thought it would be okay.

"I went to the meeting that night. Jean Matusinka was there disguised as another member. It turned out she was very favorably impressed with me for joining, luckily for me—because the next day the child welfare people came out to the house to take my children away because of a report they'd gotten from the lady at the hospital. Jolly called Jean, and Jean said she'd help. Jolly and Jean somehow convinced the social worker everything was under control, but of course this really made me lose faith in the hospital people.

"I felt pretty strange when I walked into that first P.A. meeting, but that feeling didn't last. These people *weren't* just sitting around telling horror stories. There were a lot of ideas and solutions and feelings and support. I started really using what P.A. had to offer right away. I called other members and took my kids over to their houses, and I took care of their kids when they needed help. I attended regularly. I began to relax more, but it still took a long time after joining before I could learn to stop calling Tammy names. What made it worse was that Tammy was so *forgiving*; she was always so sensitive to my needs. When I came home from work she used to say to

her little sister, 'Be quiet now so Mama can rest.'
After I joined P.A., I talked to her about the
changes I hoped to make, and when I did slip and
lose my temper I apologized after the incidents. I
let her know it was my problem, not hers. And I
never did abuse my second daughter; most of the
abuse had been directed at Tammy.

"I was in that first group in Redondo Beach
for two years. I even went up to the prison group
with Leonard and Jolly several times. I remember
feeling sure I was going to hate Betty Lansdown;
I'd read those articles in the Bakersfield papers.
Then I met her up there at the prison, and, as it
turned out, she became one of my best friends."

Following a move to Texas in 1972, Mary
managed to get a P.A. chapter started in Dallas.
Then another move, to Sherman, Texas, where
Mary's efforts to start yet another P.A. group were
unsuccessful. In 1974, she went back to college and
was divorced during that same year; she remarried
in 1975.

"My relationships with my kids and my
second husband are better today than they've ever
been. We have really open communica-
tion—everything that's bothering anybody gets
talked over. We've had counseling, too. It hasn't
been easy, but I feel we're reaching the kind of
living situation we all want.

"Today I'm very close to the one sister I was
so cruel to when we were growing up together. We
talk about what happened, and I realize now why I
treated her that way. My parents felt very
threatened when I joined P.A., though. My father
literally disowned me, and I can't discuss it with
my mother. She's said she feels that the group did

me some good, but she doesn't take any responsibility for my getting to where I had to join a 'group like that.' So I don't try to discuss anything like that with her; it's as though *I'm* the parent now, and *she's* the child.

"I haven't been active in P.A. for four years. I don't really need it anymore, although there are still times when I feel bad about myself. But when I do, I see these feelings for what they are, and I can work them through."

Bobbye G.'s story

In 1972, Bobbye G. was twenty-two years old and had two little girls, ages three and five.

"A friend of mine saw the ad for P.A. in the Dallas paper, and she called me and said, 'Come on, I'm going. Why don't you go with me?' But I didn't want to admit I was one of 'them.' I used to read in the newspaper about those horrible monsters who abused their children, and I used to tell my husband that those people should be strung up. I just couldn't relate to 'them' at all. I'd be telling myself this while my own two children were locked in their rooms, sitting in wet diapers that hadn't been changed all day. I tried to tell myself *I* was okay, even when I went to their room with a plate of food that I just put on the floor, letting them crawl through their own filth to get at it. I was so afraid of them, of myself, of my parenting, and of what I might do to them that I would leave them locked up in there for hours, sometimes whole days; they were screaming and crying and crawling around like animals. Then I finally admitted that I was just as bad, that what I was doing was just as bad, and I *was* one of 'them. That was hard—to admit that.

"I especially neglected the older one. I just didn't want to be around her, and when I had to be around her, I called her names. I really let her have it. I found excuses to punish her.

"When I went into that first meeting, I felt very defensive. I was going to go in there and tell them how bad my kid was and how she deserved everything she got. But when I got there, Mary Y. was helping a new chairperson take over the group, and she seemed to know so much. I saw her as being up there on a pedestal. Looking back, I realize that was my own insecurity. Anyway, for the first few meetings I just shut up and listened to everybody. After about a month, I realized it wasn't my daughter's problem, it was *my* problem, and I hadn't been taking any responsibility for my own behavior.

"I'll never forget one of the things that happened when I went into that first group. They said I was pretty! I had always thought of myself as ugly, and that really touched me."

Not long after Mary Y. left Dallas and moved to Sherman, the group folded. Bobbye felt so desperate without the group that she called the director of social work at Children's Hospital and then took part in a panel about child abuse at the Child Care Association. Finally, Rosemarie Biggins, a social worker, offered to sponsor a group, and Bobbye wound up acting as its chairperson— because, as she recalls, "nobody else wanted to."

"I felt so unworthy of being a chairperson. For the first three meetings I just sat and cried. I still had so many problems of my own; how could I sit up there and lead a group? I even got sick thinking about it. When I went to the doctor and nothing was wrong, I realized I was making myself sick. Then somebody in the group said to me, 'Bobbye, if you have the power to make yourself sick, you have the power to make yourself well.' That's when I started to get in touch with my power and take responsibility for my actions.

"I had a really bad relationship with my mother. She had beaten me about every day of my life and constantly abused me verbally when I was growing up. She stopped beating me after I got married, but the verbal abuse continued. Every time I went over to visit her, I wound up in tears. The group members said, 'Bobbye, quit going over there and letting her do that to you.' But I wanted her to love me. When I finally started to feel better about myself, I could handle her better, and I hung in there until I got her love. We have a good relationship now. P.A. has rubbed off on her, and she's improved her relationships with my younger sisters, too. She even goes with me on speaking engagements sometimes. I also realize now that my father had been passively involved in abusing me all those years. He just let it happen.

"Six months after I was in that second group, I was starting to get my act together. But the verbal abuse has been really hard to stop. I have a good relationship with my kids now. The other day I got mad and really let loose with my bad mouth, and I was so pleased when my daughter spoke right up to me. She told me off, but not in a mean way—she just set me straight. For a long time after I got into P.A., I still wasn't able to talk to my kids at all; I didn't know how to communicate with them. Now we have very open communication. I know when my girls need to talk, and I know how to draw them out. I'm tuned in to where they are.

"My husband hated the thought of P.A. at first, and he never would go to a meeting. His behavior began to change, though, because mine was changing. He stopped his severe punishment of the girls; when he saw me doing a better job of being a parent, he realized there were alternatives.

"I still don't enjoy being a chairperson; I still feel scared about beginning a meeting. Now the group has *me* on a pedestal, just like I used to do with Mary, and I'm uncomfortable. I don't like being up there with everybody thinking I have all the answers. I talk about my weaknesses and faults a lot so the new members know I'm human."

Bobbye G. has been chairing groups, giving public presentations, and doing P.A. media work continually since 1973. She is currently employed in the state office of P.A. of Texas.

"I was really scared to do public speaking that first time, and I still am. But I just take my guts out and lay 'em on the podium. Afterward I sometimes go home and think, 'Oh, Lord, what'd I say?' "

Rosemarie Biggins's story

Rosemarie Biggins is a social worker and state coordinator of P.A. in Dallas. She is married, has a six-year-old son, and has been a group sponsor since December of 1973.

Rosemarie first heard about Parents Anonymous when she was with the Child Care Association. One day, a panel came in to talk about child abuse, and one of its members was Bobbye G., who was looking for a sponsor for her P.A. group.

Having just been promoted from a direct-service position to an administrative job, Rosemarie decided that P.A. was a way in which she could again work with parents.

"For several meetings there was just Bobbye and me and Bobbye's friend Mollie. Looking back on those early days, I realize that I was learning everything I could from Bobbye and Mollie. Bobbye and I were cementing our relationship as chairperson and sponsor. We were fortunate to have that kind of time alone to get to know each other before we got into a larger group.

"We met at one of the day-care centers, so we had facilities for kids. After a general parent meeting there, we added a few more members, and we published a twenty-four-hour Hot Line number and got still more members.

"When I first got involved in P.A., my son was about six months old. He was one of those perfect babies who ate and slept and rarely cried. Once he started moving around more—climbing the furniture and coming close to being a problem—I could identify with the feelings of anger and frustration that group members were experiencing. I began to realize that you *can* get angry enough at a child that you want to pitch him or her through the window. After a while I could say, 'Yes, I know what you're talking about. I have those feelings too sometimes.'

"By 1974 we had enough people to split into a second group, and soon after that we had three groups going all at once. I was feeling really good about it, but after a year, I felt like I'd had it—I was just so tired. So I found another sponsor, somebody the group already knew, and that worked out well. I stayed involved in P.A., but I took six months off from being a sponsor. After that Bobbye and I started up another group. I went for about six months; then we got another sponsor, and I rested again. This process worked for me.

"I was learning more each time I went at it. I am, by nature, a controlling person; I have a tendency to take over, so I try to keep away from that. My style has changed every time I've sponsored a group. I see myself in the role of a *clarifying* person. I observe what's happening and give feedback if something needs to be clarified. Sometimes, if I see somebody cutting someone else off when that person needs to finish, I'll say, for example, 'Jane, did you want to say more about that?'

"We have more men in the group than we used to, but not as many as I'd like to see; it's still 80 percent women. Men *do* have more trouble expressing their feelings, so I try to encourage them more. Usually there'll be one who's more verbal than the others, and we'll do some role playing; we don't *make* anybody do it. We'll say something like, 'I'll be your father, John; tell me how angry you are.' If we can involve just one guy, that helps the other men feel more comfortable. If a parent brings up a parenting situation I'm familiar with, I'll share the way I handled it with my kid, whether I did it poorly or well.

"Just last week I was having a little problem with my son, and I didn't know what to do about it. Afterward I called a child psychiatrist I know, and she suggested how I might have handled it better. Then I went into the group the next week and said, 'I'll tell you how *she* said I should have handled it.' So we learn together."

Parents Anonymous sparked the interest and curiosity of the media people from the very beginning when Jolly first put an ad in the local newspaper inviting "mothers who lose their cool with their kids" to call her. Feature stories written in the *Long Beach Press Telegram* and the *South Bay Daily Breeze* ultimately resulted in the second P.A. chapter starting up in Long Beach, California. After Ray Helfer visited us in May of 1971, he and Henry Kempe began to make referrals that resulted in new chapters in Michigan, Boston, and New York. Other chapters began because of members like Mary Y. who would move and start P.A. in another town or state.

Sometimes it was relatively easy to start a P.A. chapter; at other times it wasn't. Many new chapters folded within weeks or months. This was especially true in the years before P.A. was federally funded. Some appeared to die altogether before rising again out of the ashes.

Throughout the ups and downs, the stops and starts, Jolly was tireless. In a Detroit suburb, the strangulation death of a three-year-old girl in a nice, middle-class family so shocked the community that a committee was formed to study child abuse and determine how and why such a thing could happen there. When they turned to Ray Helfer for guidance, he was involved with another commitment and referred them to P.A. They contacted Jolly, and in March of 1972, she journeyed from California to Michigan. One week later, the *Grand Rapids Press* carried a feature story on P.A., and five new chapters sprang up in her wake.

A social-services supervisor named Ed Welz and his wife, Marilyn, were involved with the formulation of the first group that got things off the ground. With so many chapters beginning almost simultaneously, the problem of finding enough sponsors became a major concern. One of Ed's early letters to Jolly said, in part:

I am aware that the sponsor should be at the meetings in order to prevent any possible destructive exchanges, among other things. Now, the problem is where, and how, do we get sponsors? Some of the people who would make good sponsors won't come forward, due to the commitment. What kind of sponsors do the chapters have in California? I'd like to know what kind of background the California sponsors have and how successful they are in being sponsors. We may have a consulting psychiatrist who called today and is interested. I'm sending him a booklet and asking for a commitment. If he commits himself, when and how do we use his services?

Ed solved part of his problem in the next few weeks by becoming a sponsor himself, and later he became a member of the P.A. board.

The chairperson/sponsor concept has long been a mainstay of P.A. organization. It more or less evolved naturally because the first group in Redondo Beach was the result of Leonard and Jolly's joint efforts—Leonard being the professional, or sponsor, and Jolly being the parent. As Leonard remembers it, "Everyone else who became part of that group was new, and Jolly and I were looked upon as the old-timers, the 'crazies' who put the thing together. It just seemed natural for us to assume responsibility for the communication and other kinds of things that were necessary for the group process. As time went on, it became obvious to us that what worked well was a parent leading the group, knowing that someone with extra skills was there to chime in when necessary. It was also helpful to know that the sponsor was available as a backup to the chairperson, who sometimes needed to lean on the sponsor for support and nurturing.

"When people wanted to duplicate the concept elsewhere, they just took a look at what seemed to be workable in our group and set it up so that a volunteer professional assisted the group, which was led by a parent. For whatever the reasons, this has been the best system in P.A. Groups led by professionals without parental leadership are not as creative for the members. The same is true for groups led by parents without benefit of the sponsor. In the latter case, the group is on very shaky ground because they don't have any professional expertise available."

June 1972

With help from the Pacific Palisades Junior Women's Club and other dedicated volunteers in the Los Angeles area, money was raised for printing and distributing P.A. literature and a newsletter called "Family Chatter," which Jolly sent out two or three times a year to all chapters. In it, she pleaded for the chapters to keep in touch and send monthly reports. These reports—when they were sent at all—were often no more than sketchy, handwritten progress diaries. Sometimes they were submitted by chairpersons, sometimes by sponsors. This one, which was sent in by a Michigan chairperson in June, was typical:

Dear Jolly,

I received your newsletter recently. Here's the information you requested. I am the new chairperson, as D—— went back to work. You have my correct address. My phone number is——.

Our group seems to be getting smaller. Our average is down to about nine. I can't pinpoint a reason. I think maybe some are losing interest, and some husbands might be objecting.

We'll be putting some advertising in the local papers after we establish an evening meeting. We're having trouble getting a sponsor. I was invited to do a half-hour radio program on a black radio station. We didn't get much response—probably because it was aired at night and there was a lot of static. We did get two calls about the new central city chapter. No information about how it went yet.

I am eagerly awaiting the posters, although it might be a problem getting them up because most of the women don't have cars or babysitters. I was thinking maybe the women who didn't have cars could babysit for those who did. If you have any suggestions, let me know.

As soon as one group gets too big, we split. We are trying to keep it as personal as possible, so as not to "get lost in the crowd." Then, too, we'll have chapters in as many areas as possible, which might help to hold our members and perhaps bring in new ones who might not want to travel too far.

Well, we have $36.15 in the kitty, so I am enclosing a check for $11.15. I hope it helps. If there is anything else I can do, please let me know.

Sincerely, Judy L.

In April of 1971, *Coronet* magazine carried an article about Parents Anonymous. On April 19, 1971, Leonard received the following letter from the Chairperson of the Citizens' Committee on Child Abuse in Binghamton, New York:

Dear Mr. Lieber:

At Dr. Ray Helfer's suggestion, and after reading an article in Coronet *magazine, I decided to write you for information.*

We are in the process of starting Doctors Helfer and Kempe's "Plan for Protection" for battered and neglected children in this area. It is taking time to get off the ground, and we are in need of something like Parents Anonymous to help the parents now. Could you send us the available information, such as approach, recommended size of group, how often they would meet, etc.

Subsequent letters from organizers of the Binghamton chapter revealed the typical time lag and problems that were encountered before a chapter actually got under way. As a January, 1972, letter to Jolly reported:

In your letter of July 2, 1971, you stated that when we are ready to start a new chapter, we should contact you for mailing literature for the members. Also, could you instruct us on the role that the professional counselor would play within the group? According to the article in McCall's *(January, 1972), they are to be present at each group meeting, but after that it is a little vague. We have someone who has agreed to work with our first group. Enclosed is a check...*

P.S. I caught the coverage CBS did for you and

noticed that a few fathers were beginning to attend the meeting.

In February of 1972, Jolly wrote back:

About the literature for the members, it seems that although response has been overwhelming, the finances have not been. And unfortunately printers cost money. We think that we can have some literature available in the next two or three weeks, but in the meantime, I'd like to suggest you continue with plans to meet and let us know approximately the number of pamphlets that you'll be needing to start with. I'll see to it that you receive some of the first batch. I don't mean to sound funny about this, but it has been such a big headache for so long that if I don't laugh about it I'll cry a lot. Thank you for the check you sent. It will help go toward the printing fund. You noticed correctly on the CBS program; we have about six fathers attending regularly at the present time. Please keep in touch and let us know how you are doing with the new chapter.

In September of 1972, the acting secretary sent a letter to Jolly indicating that the chapter was under way, had twelve members, and had held twelve meetings.

October 1972

In Tacoma, Washington, a social worker named Noel Hagens of the Pierce County Legal Assistance Foundation was trying to put together a treatment program for abusive parents in late 1971. She began corresponding with Jolly in December and over the next six months used the information she gathered about P.A. to help shape her program. In

June of 1972, she asked Jolly to come to Tacoma and introduce P.A. there.

It is approximately 1,500 miles from Los Angeles to Tacoma. To save money on hotel bills, Jolly fitted out her Dodge van with a mattress and lashed an old trunk inside to hold her clothes. She slept in the van for three nights, with a gun and an axe lying beside her. When she arrived at Noel's house at two in the morning, she spent yet another night in the van parked in front of Noel's house, not wanting to disturb her.

On Sunday, June 11, the *Tacoma News Tribune* ran a big feature story on Parents Anonymous. During the five days Jolly spent there, she had twenty-seven speaking engagements. It was an all-time record, even for her.

By June 27, Noel had become the sponsor of that city's P.A. group, and she wrote back to P.A. "headquarters" in Redondo Beach:

Greetings from the Pierce County chapter. I am replying to the newsletter, and the chapter will soon send you the first of the monthly reports. We had the fourth meeting last night, and eleven people were there, not counting me! Seems like we finally got some response to the publicity. It was a very lively discussion, and I was really happy about it. The "old members" show some real leadership and often quote "Jolly says" as they make some of your suggestions and comments.

We still have no chairperson, but I believe that will come very soon, along with a permanent meeting place.

By October, a report had come in from the new chairperson, a woman named Marty:

I thought we'd let you know we're still alive and kicking here in Tacoma. Boy, our growing pangs are fantastic.

One of our members voluntarily placed her children in a foster home a little over two months ago, and she now has her two lovely girls back home with her. Great progress.

We've also been on television in a program called "Law in Action." It was great publicity, which we were happy to receive. Now it looks as though we'll have a documentary on a local channel about P.A., very tactfully done with anonymity remaining foremost. One of our other members has been doing some public speaking at local high schools. We're really happy about what's happening with us.

November 1972

In the summer of 1972, P.A. got started in Canada. A coordinator of the Parent Child Concern in Burlington, Ontario, and a parent from Toronto who had met Jolly in Detroit both sent for P.A. literature and began strong groups in their areas. The parent was a woman who had sustained a great deal of emotional abuse as a child and was terribly unhappy about the quality of her own parenting. An excerpt from a letter she wrote to Jolly in November speaks of the group's progress and her feelings about herself:

We have increased our membership considerably since I saw you in Detroit. Some of our members do not have telephones due to extreme poverty. How would you suggest that they handle a crisis when there is no phone, no car, and tremendous family problems?

The more I get involved with P.A., the more I realize how fortunate I was to escape reasonably well. I have my bad times—mostly with my lousy image of myself—but I'm even working on that. I relate extremely well to the group. I told them all about Detroit and meeting you. How I wish we could get you to Toronto; it would give our group a big kick where it's most needed.

We now have a sponsor for the group. She is a social worker in a hospital here and is a warm, lovely individual. I think she will do very well.

Around this time, we also heard from Tacoma; they, too, had been having phone problems:

One of our members who was in dire need of a phone has been issued one due to the efforts of our sponsor, who arranged a loan for the deposit. Results have been great. Now the member has been able to curb her abuse-crisis problem by communicating with fellow P.A. members. Membership is climbing slightly, with some prospective parents still thinking things over. We hope they decide soon before it's too late.

May 1973

While 1972 was a banner year for Parents Anonymous, 1973 saw a number of these early groups become even stronger. By April, there were forty-seven P.A. chapters in thirty-five states.

Sharon Pallone served as sponsor for the first P.A. chapter in Arkansas, which was formed in early 1973 in Little Rock. She was also Executive Director of SCAN (Suspected Child Abuse and Neglect), a private nonprofit agency contracted by Arkansas Social Services to provide assistance to abused children and their parents, with emphasis on helping the parents through the use of trained lay therapists. Fran Millard, State Coordinator for SCAN, soon joined Sharon as a cosponsor. Group attendance in those early days averaged approximately ten people. A note from Sharon to Jolly on April 17 read in part:

Sure enjoyed your visit to Arkansas. I, for one, learned a lot from you. Parents Anonymous is growing—eighteen members last week and each one gaining new insights. Can you send us forty P.A. pamphlets?

P.A. slowly began branching out into other counties, and new chapters were formed, largely due to community awareness and support generated by SCAN. There are currently seven active P.A. chapters in Arkansas.

By May, a second group in Binghamton, New York had gotten under way with fifteen to eighteen people attending regularly. During that same month, the Toronto chapter managed to gather enough money to fly Jolly to their city. She stayed for a week, talking with P.A. people and doing media work.

And so it went, small scattered brush fires all over the country, some burning out, some igniting others.

July 1973

Long-time sponsor Michael Turner remembers the beginnings of P.A. in Boston:

"The idea of starting a Parents Anonymous chapter in Boston took shape in the spring of 1972, after a visit to Boston by Dr. Ray Helfer, who was at that time writing his book (with Dr. Henry Kempe) *Helping the Battered Child and His Family.* Dr. Helfer talked about Jolly K. with a great deal of enthusiasm for her work. At first we were somewhat intrigued with the idea but questioned how effective such a group might be. Nevertheless, we presented it at a Children's Advocates meeting and received approval to see what we could do about starting a chapter in Boston. Fortified with the Guidelines from the Parent Chapter, we set about preparing publicity. Joan Wheeler, a nurse who was a board member of Parents' and Children's Services, became interested in helping get a chapter started.

"We wrote a number of stories for city-wide and local newspapers. We set up a target date of June 27, 1972, to have the first meeting. Notices were sent out to all agencies that might have potential referrals.

"The first few meetings were very disappointing; although we had received calls from many of the agencies inquiring about referring some of their clients, no more than two or three parents showed up at any meeting. Parents would come to one meeting and then not return, and new members would come instead. We also had several people who were so afraid that they left either in the middle of meetings or before the meetings even started, without finding out what was going to happen. It became clear to us that having more than one professional advisor at meetings was a real deterrent and that a parent who was interested in recruiting others and acting as organizer or chairman of a group would probably offer more effective leadership."

Turner hung in there with incredible patience and tenacity until the parent leader the chapter needed emerged. Then the two of them went through another year of sporadic attendance until the group gelled. By July of 1973, it had become one of the P.A. strongholds on the east coast.

Around this time, the Senate passed S. 1191, also known as the "Mondale Bill." This was an omnibus bill aimed at focusing federal attention and action on child abuse and neglect through the states; it included the establishment of a federally operated national center on child abuse and neglect that would coordinate federally funded services, research, and informational projects. The passage of this bill was a real cause for celebration, and we heard from the Tacoma chapter, among others:

We hear that the Senate passed S. 1191. Good news. Our chapter is planning our one-year anniversary celebration for August 27. It is our way of saying "look at us now" to the community. We plan lots of publicity for this and will need some funds to pay for cardboard, construction paper, etc. We plan a car wash and/or garage sale to raise funds for these materials. We may also include a raffle as part of these. If we need written permission from the parent chapter, as the manual suggests, please send it to us. We will keep records on what we take in and what we spend, and we will send you the excess, if there is any.

Cathy M.'s story

In late 1973, the Tacoma parents came to the rescue of Cathy M.

Cathy was born in Denver, Colorado. Because her father was an Army officer, their family moved around a lot. She remembers feeling overprotected, even smothered; but she can't remember ever feeling loved. Her father dictated to her much as he did to his troops.

"When I rebelled against the authority in my teen years, I was verbally abused. When I was late coming home from a date, I was called every name in the book, and this happened time and time again. I was made to feel like a terrible person—and I proceeded to live up to the image.

"I was still in my teens when I gave birth to an illegitimate child, a boy. I was never allowed to decide for myself what I wanted to do with this child; my father said to give the baby up or he and my mother would disown me. I needed my parents; I didn't want to be rejected by them. So I gave up the child for adoption and never even saw what he looked like.

"I left home then and went from one job to another and from one man to another. I was looking for love, and to be loved and needed. Nothing worked out the way I wanted it to until I met the man I married."

A year and a half later, Cathy had a baby boy. When the child was a year old, her husband—who was also in the service—was sent to Viet Nam. Two years later he returned and a year after that Cathy gave birth to a baby girl. Following a transfer to Tacoma and growing financial problems, Cathy had to go to work when her daughter, JoAnn, was only six months old.

"I needed a 'You're okay, Mom' message from this baby, but I never seemed to get it. She began crying more and more with me. I was really having trouble with my feelings and thinking, 'If she doesn't like me, I won't like her, either.' Then I lost my job, and I really began to strike back at her. It was as though I was blaming her for everything. One day I was getting ready for a job interview. She cried and screamed when I picked her up, and I lost control. When I realized that this time I'd *really* hurt her, I called my husband and the ambulance."

The baby was on the critical list for a week. During this time, her doctor told Cathy about Parents Anonymous.

"I called, and they came to my house; and for the first time, I was able to talk about what had happened without feeling judged or condemned. My husband and I began to go to their meetings every week. These people were able to talk about what was going on inside of them with the parent-child relationship. I began to get some insight into myself.

"After JoAnn was released from the hospital. P.A. people were there helping. On the day of my arraignment, P.A. was there with support and encouragement. I was given three years' probation with the stipulation that I attend P.A. meetings, which I had planned on doing anyway.

"My daughter and I began rebuilding our relationship slowly. By the end of that year, she was back in our home full time. By the following April, I had it together enough to start a P.A. chapter back in Colorado Springs, where we'd been transferred. Then, in October, I started another one across town. I want to reach as many parents as I can to prevent them from having to go through what I've been through. Being a parent is one of the toughest jobs in the world, and we need to help each other."

Cathy's tireless work in Colorado Springs paved the way for the present P.A. organization in Colorado. In 1976, she and her husband and children left Fort Carson for Wiesbaden, Germany, where he had been transferred. She helped to organize a Parents Anonymous group there, too. It is one of several groups operating in Germany today.

August 1973

It was fast becoming time for Parents Anonymous to go national. Jolly had visualized early on that the effectiveness of P.A. was not going to be limited to a few people in a few cities around the country. In fact, she saw no reason why it couldn't become worldwide—which it eventually did.

P.A. continued to be Jolly's full-time nonpaid occupation. She kept things moving, kept making people listen. For her own sake, she needed people to listen to the "kid" in her that needed attention, affection, and nurturing.

In early 1973, then-Senator Walter Mondale and his staff of the U.S. Senate Subcommittee on Children and Youth organized public hearings on child abuse in this country. Jolly had become fairly well-known by that time, and she was invited to testify. She asked Leonard to accompany her for moral support. As he recalls:

"This was a big step up for her, and she felt it. Her testimony before the subcommittee was filmed by network news teams. Jolly became heralded as the first child abuser to publicly admit to the problem on national television—the Walter Cronkite News, no less.

"The Senators were duly impressed with her; they should have been. She broke the stereotypes about child abuse. She was articulate, forthright,

106

middle-class, bright. She was worth their time and commitment.

"We experienced the support of the subcommittee after this. Ellen Hoffman was particularly encouraging; she was the subcommittee's chief aide through Mr. Mondale's ascendancy to the Vice Presidency and is now a staff member of the Children's Defense Fund.[2] Ultimately, the 'Mondale Committee' hearings led to Senate Bill 1191's enactment into Public Law 93-247, which eventually established the National Center on Child Abuse and Neglect in Washington.[3]

"The positive publicity we received in Washington wasn't enough, though. There was talk of money becoming available, but the Mondale bill wouldn't take effect until late 1974. In the meantime, the P.A. 'kitchen table' was creaking under a heavy demand for services.

"The money problem was so acute during the summer of 1973 that nobody quite knew where P.A. was headed. The only thing we knew for certain was that P.A. would fall apart if we didn't get help from somewhere fast. We simply couldn't deliver any more information or consultation. When Jolly heard of some federal funding that was available for a small number of special programs, we decided to apply."

On the fatal night before the government proposal was due to be sent off to Washington, Jolly and Leonard were hammering out final draft revisions on my kitchen table while I sat grinding out dumb one-liners for a political gag column I was writing. I had been divorced for a year by then, and like millions of other divorced women, I was trying to make a living and spending whatever time was left over figuring out how best to help myself and my half-grown children through a very tough period. The column was one way of making some extra money.

So there we all were. Jolly and Leonard were pounding and arguing, crossing out things they had just written; I was bent over my typewriter trying to make jokes. It was late at night. We were all exhausted, and the strain was showing. We were convinced that if the proposal wasn't accepted, P.A. was pretty well down the drain. When they asked me to type up one more change, I burst into tears for some reason—fatigue, I guess. Leonard sat clutching his head with one hand and absently patting my shoulder with the other.

Jolly left abruptly and was gone for about ten minutes. When she returned, she was carrying a bouquet of asters in green paper. I didn't know where she'd gotten them at that late hour, and I was afraid to ask; but I was touched. She stuffed them into an empty teapot that was sitting on the table and gave me a big hug.

"I've never seen you cry," she said.

"No," I answered, "I mostly cry alone."

"Don't cry alone," she said.

I looked over at Leonard. There were tears running down his face.

"What are *you* crying about?" I asked him.

"The asters," he said. "I'm allergic."

February 1974

While our grant request was being reviewed in Washington, we received some out-of-the-blue help from a very special person, Dr. Leonard Borman. A cultural anthropologist and an expert by trade on groups and self-help, he had called from Chicago months earlier. Representing the W. Clement and Jessie V. Stone Foundation, chaired by Donna Stone, he wanted to determine how that organization could be of service to P.A.

Just as everything was looking sick, Dr. Borman delivered a care package of $12,000 in "seed money" to keep P.A. afloat. The money came through in late 1973 and provided for office space and support for a couple of warm bodies to keep cranking out the coordinating work across the U.S. Leonard was hired as administrator in February. We had been reprieved once again.

June 1974

When the federal grant came through, the P.A. "staff" had 36¢ between them.

Secretaries were hired and equipment was purchased. There were manuals and pamphlets to be written and a newsletter to be gotten out on a regular basis. I became the staff writer and editor of the fledgling P.A. periodical that we decided to call *Frontiers*. Margot Fritz, a former caseworker and then chairperson of a P.A. group, came aboard as director of training.

Margot's story

Like many other P.A. parents, Margot's motivation for getting involved was guilt. Unlike most P.A. parents, however, her abuse problems were pretty much behind her when she joined.

She was working for the Department of Public Social Services when she heard about P.A.

"One day I opened a case file, and a cheaply printed pamphlet fell into my lap. It had the words 'Parents Anonymous' printed on it in large black type. I opened it, read the brief description of the program, and noted the names of two persons listed as board members: Leonard Lieber and Dr. Roland Summit.

"I had never heard of Leonard Lieber, but Roland Summit's name was familiar. He had come to the district office where I worked to train social workers in dealing with the problems of incest and sexual abuse. The calm, equable manner in which he handled this loaded subject, coupled with the humanity of his approach, had impressed me at that time. So when I saw his name on the pamphlet, my immediate thought was, 'This must be a good organization if he's associated with it.' I took the pamphlet home and put it away in a drawer."

Margot left the Department of Social Services in August of 1972. Along with 1200 other county social workers, she had been demoted at the beginning of that year.

"It had meant a reduction in salary as well as in status, the latter being the harder of the two injuries to sustain. Like so many women of my generation, I had returned to school in the mid-sixties to finish my bachelor's degree. I loved school and worked hard to make good grades. My children were all school age but still young enough that they required a lot of my time and energy. Keeping house, worrying about child-care arrangements, trying to meet the expectations of

110

my children and my husband, and, for two semesters, working part time as well, made for a heavy load. I was exhausted but very proud of myself when I finally graduated in June of 1968. I went to work for the county the following month, full of hope and idealism.

"I know now that my wet-behind-the-ears notions of eradicating poverty and racism are often shared by people going into the helping professions, especially if, like me, they have had very little practical experience of the world. My four years as a worker in Compton were an education of a different order and just as valuable to me as the time I had spent in college. When the Department demoted me as one of the casualties of the county's welfare-reform plan, I was devastated. I knew that if I quit, it would be impossible for me to find a job as a social worker without a master's degree. The only work available to me would be secretarial work—something I had done on a part-time basis all the years of my marriage and felt I had escaped by finishing my degree and going to work for the county.

"In August of 1972 I did quit, however, and took a part-time secretarial job. I tried to convince myself that I wanted to be home with the children, to get into the routine of housework and cooking, but I knew I was lying to myself. I was bitchy, uptight, and very unhappy.

"One morning several weeks after I had quit working for the county, I got up and went into the kitchen to fix myself a cup of coffee. The house was empty except for me and Tina, our Samoyed. There was a piece of cherry pie sitting forlornly on top of the coffee can on the stove. I looked at it and started to cry. I suddenly felt that I couldn't

111

go on, that if I stayed there and faced another day of feeling helpless and defeated I would die—or, more important, that something in me would die. I ran into the bedroom, got dressed, and started throwing clothes into a suitcase. Then I ran out to the driveway and threw the suitcase into the back of my old 1960 Corvair. When Tina tried to get into the back seat and I pulled her out, I knew that this was for real—I was leaving.

"I backed the car out of the driveway and headed for the freeway. I had absolutely no idea where I was going; I just knew I had to go. I stopped at a filling station, and while I was waiting to have the tank filled, it came to me that I was going to Yosemite. We had camped there twice in recent years with the children, and it seemed to me to be the most beautiful place on earth.

"I stayed in the park for a week—alone, but only occasionally fearful. For me, it's impossible to look at the magnificence of Half Dome and not know that God exists. At first, I had intended to leave home and never return. When I got to the park, however, I saw some children about the ages of my own, and I knew that while it might be possible to leave my husband, I could never leave my children. I wrote them a postcard to tell them where I was and when I would return."

The week before Margot left home, she had written a letter to Roland Summit describing her social-work background and volunteering her services to Parents Anonymous. When she returned from Yosemite, there was a letter from Roland Summit waiting for her. He had referred her to Lynn Bunje, the P.A. volunteer coordinator. She called Margot about a week later to tell her that a woman named Aalsa Stieber had just started a P.A.

112

chapter in her area. Would Margot be interested in acting as the group's chairperson?

"I had never had any prior experience leading a group of any kind, and I was terrified at the thought of accepting that responsibility. I went to Aalsa's home one evening, though, and the two of us got on so famously that I agreed to join the chapter as the chairperson. This was the beginning for me and, as it turned out, one of the most significant crossroads of my life.

"During that first year, the group grew from a few parents who came sporadically to eight or ten who attended consistently. I leaned on Aalsa a lot back then and can remember being terrified most of the time. I would sit there and be grateful that we sat at a table because it covered my trembling legs. My mouth would go dry and my voice would shake. It took me a while to realize that I was constantly afraid I wouldn't measure up as a chapter leader and would be cast out, expelled. Once I got in touch with the fact that my own fear of rejection was giving me the shakes, the tension began to ease.

"A few months after I joined the chapter, I was asked if I would become secretary to the board of directors. Aalsa was already a board member, and she had suggested me because she knew I could type. I accepted and for the first time in my life, I found myself in a peer relationship with professional people.

"I had spent several years in therapy and was in awe of any human who bore the title 'psychiatrist.' They were godlike creatures; one could gaze up to them but never hope to be on an equal footing with them. Working with Roland Summit and Gary Faber, both psychiatrists, Jean Matusinka and Jerry Tarlow, both lawyers, and Leigh Colitre, an administrator for the ACTION program at Pepperdine University, gave me an opportunity to view professionals from a different perspective. Before, my relationship to people of professional status had been a 'one down' kind of experience—either I had a problem and they had the answer, or I was a subordinate and they had the power. At P.A. board meetings, we were just a small group of people trying to further the aims and goals of an organization we believed in. Nobody was addressed as Dr. or Mrs.; nobody had special status by virtue of his or her education or earning power."

After a year, Aalsa chose not to continue to be a P.A. sponsor, and Margot was left as sole leader of their group.

"Those months were good for me; I found out I really didn't need to lean on anybody. Chairing a chapter is a heavy responsibility, and that's one reason why P.A. prefers that each chapter have two leaders. Doing it alone helped me to grow up, but it also made me keenly aware of the fact that some kind of training was needed for group leaders.

"I felt that my chapter was successful, but I had no idea why. So I decided to find a way to get training for group leaders in Los Angeles County. I wrote a proposal for state funding that would have provided training through the Thalians Community Mental Health Center. This was the first proposal I had ever written, and I invested a lot of myself in it. It was 'my baby,' and its success meant a great deal to me. At about the same time, Jolly and the board were involved in writing a proposal to H.E.W. for a large grant that would establish a national office and staff for P.A.

"I was surprised when Jolly approached me about the possibility of my accepting a staff slot if the grant came through. I was certainly interested, but I told her that it would depend on whether my own training proposal was funded. The truth is, I was scared. I didn't feel qualified to handle a job that was national in scope. I much preferred to stay with my own smaller and less ambitious proposal.

"As things worked out, my training proposal wasn't funded, but the H.E.W. proposal was. I was asked to be director of training—not because I had either the educational background or the experience for the job but because Jolly and Leonard trusted me and felt I had the potential.

"I had never in my life had a position of so much responsibility. I was no longer a worker toiling in the vineyards. I was a boss. It was a funny feeling. I needed a model of how to be both a boss and a supervisor, and I found it in Leonard. In his relationship with me, he neither bossed nor supervised. Whenever I went to him with a question or a problem, he answered me evasively or simply threw it back at me and told me to figure it out for myself. At first this frightened and infuriated me because it meant that I had to make my own decisions and live with them. Little by little—and after overhearing Leonard in conversation with P.A. people all over the country—I came to realize that this is how he operates. He really believes in allowing people a maximum degree of freedom to find their own answers and resolve problems for themselves. After a while, I became more comfortable with my ability to make good decisions; and I recognized that even when something didn't go well, I wasn't going to be attacked or blamed. The P.A. office is an incredibly comfortable place; I've never worked in an environment where morale was higher.

"The past six years have been the best and most fulfilling years of my life. It's ironic that something which caused me great pain—the abuse of my children—should have been the stimulus for so much of my own personal growth and happiness; but that's what happened."

July 1974

The federal grant was exactly what was needed to save P.A., but we all knew that there were strings attached. First, it was only a "demonstration grant": during its three-year span, we would have to prove that our program could demonstrate effectiveness in the child-abuse arena. Second, we would no longer be strictly on our own: along with the grant came government supervision.

One of our biggest allies in Washington was a man named Duane Ragan, who became our government project officer. He's a military person now—an Air Force colonel. Duane is opinionated, has a loud bark, and is incredibly supportive. Margot best summarizes the way we all felt about him:

"When Leonard announced in May that our H.E.W. project officer, Duane Ragan, would be making a site visit, I was immediately thrown into a state of panic. I had never met a 'Washington bureaucrat,' but I was quite sure I knew what one would be like. First of all, he would be very medium—medium height, medium weight, medium hair. Nothing would distinguish him in any way. He would be dressed in a conservative business suit and carry an attaché case. He would arrive, ask a few pointed questions, make mental notes of all deficiencies and discrepancies, say very little, and leave. Shortly thereafter, I would receive a detailed memo that would document the ways in which my performance of my duties fell short of the mark, followed by explicit instructions as to how—and how soon—I was to mend my ways. My failure to comply would result in immediate dismissal. My terror at the prospect of this approaching visitation was made more extreme by my personal knowledge of the fact that I didn't have the foggiest notion of how to go about being, acting, or looking like a director of training. There was no doubt in my mind that the project officer would realize immediately that I was a fraud and an impostor.

"The first disparity between my little fantasy and the reality was Duane's physical appearance. He's about 6'3" and has the bearing of a career man in the military, which is what he had been. 'Medium' he ain't; imposing he is. His face in repose has a no-nonsense severity, which could be misleading to people who don't know him.

"Jolly, Leonard, Diana Shea (then executive secretary of P.A.), Roland Summit, and I were all in attendance at the first meeting with Duane. Business proceeded in an orderly and subdued fashion for about fifteen or twenty minutes, with Duane saying little and looking severe.

"I had about made up my mind that even though I was off the mark insofar as his physical appearance was concerned, the rest of my little fantasy was right on target. Then Duane said something perfectly outrageous; we all broke into

117

peals of laughter, and relief swept through the room like a forest fire. There was an almost audible sigh, which expressed a unanimous feeling of 'thank God he's someone we can be real with!' "

Beth's story

Beth was twenty-three years old when she joined an L.A. area P.A. group in 1974. Her two boys were ages four and three, and her little girl was a year old. She had been attending a group regularly for two years when its sponsor moved to the east coast and its chairperson stopped attending meetings.

Realizing how much she still needed P.A., Beth started another group on her own and kept it running with herself as chairperson. The group had no sponsor until Beth did her first public speaking engagement at her children's school. After hearing Beth's story, her son's teacher offered to sponsor the group. With additional support from the school principal and a local minister, the group gained strength and is still flourishing.

Her story, like those of most P.A. parents, is both typical and painfully unique.

"When I was growing up, my dad was kind of cold and he just wasn't there most of the time, both emotionally and physically. There were four kids—my three brothers and me—and my brothers were always getting in trouble. Getting them out of jail and prison was a continual thing, and I was kind of pushed into the background. My mother was warm to me at times, but she was busy, too; taking care of my brothers and doing all of this bailing out of jail just drained her emotionally. When I was fourteen, one of my brothers went into prison for the last time, and we packed up everything and moved out here from the midwest."

Beth was a frequent witness to physical violence between her father and her brothers.

"I remember he'd come home late at night after he'd been drinking—all three of my brothers drank, too—and they would just get into a fight. I would happen to walk in sometimes, and my dad would be on the floor with my brother towering over him; or sometimes it would be the other way around. I just kind of withdrew. My dad would come over to me and say some little thing, and I would just shrug my shoulder. I didn't want anything to do with them; I didn't want anything to do with being beaten up, so I tried to be the good little girl. I tried to be the one they'd be proud of. I thought I could earn their love by being good. I just never got it, though, so finally I gave up and thought, 'Hell, I'm never going to get it.' I decided to get it in other ways, with other people.

Although Beth managed to escape the beatings her father and brothers dished out to each other, she suffered another form of physical and emotional abuse: both of her older brothers abused her sexually, as did a next-door neighbor. She was only six years old when the neighbor began giving her orange soda pop to win her "friendship." Like most victims of this kind of abuse, Beth had no one to turn to for help.

"I couldn't tell anybody about it. I was afraid. We never talked about sex, and if we did bring it up, we got a look like, you know, *shut your mouth.*'

So it was kept in the closet for years. I grew up thinking sex was something dirty; I was caught saying *fuck* once and my mouth was washed out with soap and I was slapped and I never mentioned that word aloud again. Even when my husband and I got married, I thought I could mention it in the privacy of our own bedroom, but I never dared."

As a result of the sexual abuse Beth experienced as a child, she had problems in her marriage. Finally, she told her husband about her brothers and the neighbor.

"At first he was shocked, but then after the initial shock wore off, he was more understanding of why I had problems in our relationship— sexual problems. I didn't want his sympathy; I just wanted him to know where I stood and where he stood, what I felt comfortable doing and what I didn't feel comfortable doing. Some of the scars that are left I still feel today. But it helps to talk, and we can communicate. We've been married now for ten years.

"I was eighteen when I got married, but I had my own apartment and a job before then. I guess I just thought that I should get married, and I wanted kids real bad. I wanted kids ever since I was about eleven. A month after we got married, I got pregnant. I had high expectations that I was going to be the perfect mother—I guess because my mother wasn't. I wanted to make up for everything I didn't get. I was going to show my mother that I had it all together. Boy, did I have it all wrong!"

Beth started abusing her first child two weeks after he was born.

"He had colic, and I didn't know how to

handle that. He just cried all the time, and it seemed like it never let up. My husband was working nights, so I was getting very little sleep. My mom stayed with me for the first week, but I couldn't relax and let her take over; I felt this responsibility very heavily, and I guess it was because of the expectations I had about mother-hood. When my mom went home, I felt as if I were doing something wrong. I did all the usual things—checking his diapers, seeing that the pin was closed, taking the temperature, and everything like that. Then one time I was up all day and all night; I fed him and put him back to bed and changed him—the whole thing. I was crying myself because he wouldn't go to sleep, and so I went in and picked him up. But the more I rocked him the more he screamed, so I just threw him over to the couch.

"I felt guilty thinking about what I did, so I went over and checked him, and he seemed okay. He stopped crying for a few minutes, though. Next time it happened, I thought afterward, 'He'll stop crying for a little longer.' I just got into this cycle, going round and round. It seemed at the time there was no way out."

Two months after her first son was born, Beth got pregnant again. The delivery was extremely difficult, and Beth was kept under sedation for three days after the baby was born. There was no opportunity for the initial mother-child bonding to take place, and at first Beth rejected the child.

"When they did bring him back to me, I told them to take him back. 'I don't know this kid,' I said. 'Get him away from me.' I blamed him for the fact that I almost died, I almost didn't make it. I hated him. I couldn't stand him. When I brought him home, I tried to make an honest attempt—and that was where I made my mistake. I tried so hard to love him that I got exhausted physically and emotionally. I went into a depression that just wouldn't go away. Finally, I got into therapy.

"The therapist and I hit it off really fast. She was real understanding, and she suggested many times that I get into Parents Anonymous. She knew I was scared, though, so she fed it to me slowly at first, saying, 'There's a place where you can get help for what's going on.' She could help me with my depression, but it was like I needed someplace else to go to get the child abuse under control. I was getting worse instead of better, so I finally decided to try P.A. I called the office, and they referred me to a group. Millie was chairperson at the time. I talked to her, and she was very warm. It was as if she understood everything I was going through, and that made me feel good. When I told her things like 'I threw a glass of milk at my son,' she'd say, 'Why, I've done that to mine, too. Let's talk about what led up to that. Can you give me a call before that happens again, when you feel like that?' I wasn't sure I could do that; but she got me into the first meeting.

"I was scared, really scared when I walked in there the first time; but I didn't deny anything that was happening. It takes a lot of parents time before they'll admit the things going on at home, but I was at the point where I just didn't want to beat around the bush. It was like, 'Here I am. Fix me! What does it take—a day? a week? a month?' I wanted to get right to the problem. But it took a year before I quit the physical abuse. I had to go through so many things before I could get to that point. I went over my background, talking in the group about the sexual abuse and everything else in my childhood. I had to go through a lot of backtracking, and it seemed like Millie and Leigh[4] could bring things out of me that I couldn't remember on my own. It took a while before I could set those things aside, let them go; I wanted to hold on to them so bad."

Although Beth's husband didn't attend P.A. meetings, he encouraged her to go and even handled some of the P.A. calls that came to their home. At first, Beth was afraid to tell him about the extent of her abuse problem.

"You know, you have that fear that they're not going to understand, so I never came right out and told him, 'I'm beating the kids and I have to go to Parents Anonymous.' I just said that I needed some help with handling the kids and that P.A. was really helping me.

"It took time before I learned how to use P.A. I would hit one of the kids and call Leigh; and Leigh would say to me, 'Next time, you have to call me *before* something like this happens.' I'd think, 'Yeah, I'll do it, I'll do it.' Then Todd would spill his milk, and he'd be right there, and I'd be right there, and I'd tear into him. I'd always think about calling afterward, and that made me mad. I was angry at myself for not being able to call beforehand. I thought there must be some magical thing that the group could sprinkle on me to make me call *before* an incident instead of after. It took a while before I could think to do it on my own; it's like I had to be trained in the group. Millie would yell at me sometimes and say, 'You *have* to call, you *must* call.' Then Leigh would throw a scare into me. He'd say, 'One of these times, you're really going to hurt him. *One of these times, you're going to*

123

land in jail. Knock it off!' Then I'd leave the group, feeling a little rejected and afraid. But I think I needed that scare."

Not long after Beth joined P.A., two court-referred parents came into the group. One of them had been in prison and talked freely about his experiences there.

"I used to think, 'I'm not like that. I'm not that bad. I don't do that. I don't abuse my children to the point where they end up in the hospital or have to be taken away.' But the more I heard him talking about prison and really sharing what he had done, the more I realized I wasn't that much different. The only difference is that he was caught. This made me take a harsh look at my situation because by then the thought was always there, 'What if I *really* hurt my kids?'

"There were times when I felt like P.A. wasn't doing me any good or when things were going okay and I would stop attending meetings for a while. Then I would have an incident with one of my kids and run back into the group. I found myself needing it, as an alcoholic needs AA."

In 1976, when Leigh moved away, the group fell apart. Beth plunged ahead and started up another group—without a sponsor. Then came her speaking engagement at her children's school and an offer from a teacher to sponsor the group. Not long afterward, a local minister let them have a room at the church to use for their meetings. Both Beth and the group have come a long way since then. She said she has never had any abuse problem with her daughter.

"I feel that I abused the boys because they were boys. With Dorrie it was just never there. I had good feelings about her. I delivered her naturally. I was wide awake, and there were no drugs. I felt really good, and the bonding was there. We didn't have rooming in, but the nurse would come in and leave the baby and then just conveniently 'forget' that the baby was there; so I'd have her for two hours.

"I still worry about getting angry at the boys, though—especially Todd. I found the more I was trying to keep my anger under control, the more things he'd do. He knew the things that could push my buttons, and he'd use every trick in the book. He still does today. But since we started going to Richstone Center[5] three months ago, there have been a lot of changes and improvements. It seems as if there was something we just didn't quite get to in P.A. It was helping me understand feelings I had that would lead up to abuse, and I was using the phone more, but I really wasn't getting any good suggestions on how to handle a problem the minute it came up. When we go to Richstone, Todd and I are seen together—something that never happened when I was getting therapy before. And I feel comfortable talking about the past child abuse.

"The first thing Elaine [a therapist at Richstone Center] taught us was how to deal with Todd's whining. When he was younger, that always set me off, and I'd be hitting him and yelling at him. First, Elaine told Todd that he could whine five times for whatever he wanted but after that he had to go to his bedroom—he couldn't ask a sixth time. He had to go to his room, hit a pillow, or throw something soft against the wall. That worked pretty well. Then we graduated to the check system we have now, and

125

that's worked fantastically. We have two big charts on the refrigerator. The kids get checks for bad behavior and stars for good behavior. They have certain chores they have to do each day. Todd can get a star just for not whining. Whenever I feel a star should go up, I also give the kids verbal praise and a hug. Todd doesn't like to be hugged that much, though, so maybe I'll tousle his hair a little bit.

"I really like the program at the center, and I wish there were more programs where parents and kids were seen together for therapy. I've learned more about Todd since we've been going to Richstone than I have since he was born. Before, Todd clammed up and didn't say a word if someone asked him something. But the very first time we went to Richstone, he started talking. Now, we go in, and Elaine says, 'How did things go this past week, Todd?' and he responds. He feels safe and secure just being able to talk.

"We're coming along. Things aren't perfect, but when we get into problems that are hard to handle, we usually sit down and try to figure out a way of compromising—making alternative suggestions and things like that, not just making snap decisions."

As Beth's relationships with her own children have improved, her self-image has, too. This has allowed her to take a closer look at her family, including her brothers and her parents, and to work on better understanding those relationships.

"My two older brothers are in AA back in the Midwest, but my younger brother is out here. We have a pretty good relationship now. We don't talk a lot about the things in the past; he's trying to build on today, as I am. He's getting some help, too. My mom and I are getting along better. She knows all about my being in P.A. She's here on Thursdays when I have an appointment at the Center, and she handles some of the P.A. calls, too. She's very supportive.

"My dad and I aren't that close; it's more or less the same relationship we've always had. He's always been cold, and he never showed his feelings of love. He never asked 'How are you doing in school?' or the kinds of things I wanted to hear when I was growing up; that hasn't changed. It's more like he'll say, 'How are you?' and I'll say, 'Okay,' and that's it. I've never talked to him about P.A., but I have with my mother. I think she's grown with P.A., too, because I've mentioned some things to her, and she's said, 'Oh, I never really realized that.' Or we'll get to talking about my brothers and what could have led up to what happened there, and she'll say, 'Well, I didn't realize that.' I try to talk to her in a way that I'm not blaming her. I guess they did the best they could with the information they had."

February 1975

Along with our federal grant came a request from Washington that P.A. expand its services as quickly as possible. Leonard reasoned that the most efficient and effective way of doing this was to bring interested professionals and community workers together to meet with P.A. staff, regional coordinators, and sponsors and parents from around the U.S. It took nine months of intensive planning, but in February of 1975, P.A. held its first National

Conference on Child Abuse in Long Beach, California. By that time, the nationwide P.A. chapter count stood at approximately 150.

The night before the conference began, I finally met Betty Lansdown. I had seen her before in the C.I.W. prison group, but this was our first real face-to-face encounter. She had been on parole since mid-1972, working in L.A. as a nurse's aide.

The smiling thirty-one-year-old woman who stood in my entrance hall bore little resemblance to the seemingly dumb, scared blonde in the old newspaper clippings and that first P.A. prison meeting.

"Betty?"

"Yeah." Her voice has a chronically hoarse quality; her eyes and face have been to hell and back. Old-young, smacked around, able to reach out, warm, yet vulnerable—a survivor who has triumphed.

"Patte," she said. We hugged, and that's all the introduction we needed.

"You like cheese omelettes?" I asked.

"I love cheese omelettes."

After dinner, she curled up on the couch with a glass of wine. Four other P.A. members would be sleeping in the living room.

Three hundred people representing thirty-six states attended the conference held at Long Beach Memorial Hospital from February 13-15. Many came with sleeping bags and little money; P.A. chairpersons and sponsors came bearing the good wishes of their spouses and instructions from their chapters to bring back everything they could. Some chapters had managed to raise only enough money for one person to attend. Some people doubled up in staterooms on the Queen Mary; some stayed in private homes; some camped out.

On Friday, Valentine's Day, Sergeant Jackie Howell of the Los Angeles Police Department asked the attendees in her workshop, "Child Abuse, The New Look in Police Work," to talk about what they were seeking and what they wanted to take back with them. In her audience were police officers, nurses, judges, social workers, filmmakers, a priest from Alaska, a correctional officer and P.A. sponsor from a California prison, a policeman who was a foster father of two children who had been mentally handicapped because of abuse, P.A. parents, sponsors, regional coordinators, and some parents who had been convicted of child abuse. They stood together, introduced themselves, sat down together, and talked. We had come a long way from that evening in early 1971 when a young policeman had suggested to Jolly and me that the panicky lady who didn't show up at Morningside Hospital should help herself off the nearest bridge.

Jolly had come a long way, too. When she had made the keynote address the night before, she had appeared self-possessed, handsome, and comfortable in her role as program director of a national organization.

At lunch, I sat next to a pretty, vivacious girl with long, curly black hair and merry eyes. She talked so knowledgeably that at first I assumed she was a P.A. sponsor or a volunteer. Then she introduced herself: She was Bobbye G., the P.A. parent and chairperson from Dallas.

We were just finishing lunch when a very overweight young woman approached our table and smiled in recognition. She was a P.A. parent who had met Bobbye for the first time in one of the workshops that morning.

"Everything's going to be all right when I lose this weight," she said. Then she looked at Bobbye with friendly envy. "If only I had a figure like yours."

Bobbye stared up at her with compassion, unsmiling. Her face had the look of a small child who has known too much suffering too young.

"Lose the weight," she said simply, "but that isn't the answer to your problem. My good figure doesn't keep me from being unhappy with myself. If we don't like ourselves, it doesn't have anything to do with our figures or faces."

That night there was a P.A. party—a no-host get-together aboard the Queen Mary in the Flamenco Room. A huge, three-tiered cake stood on a corner table. It was decorated with the P.A. symbol, three interlocking rings proclaiming "Parents Anonymous, Family Love, Family Unity, Stops Cycle of Child Abuse." In the middle of the cake were the words "Happy 5th Anniversary Parents Anonymous."

Somebody was taking a picture of the cake, moving around it to get just the right angle so that both the symbol and the "5th Anniversary" would be clear. A lot of pictures were taken throughout the course of that evening, but no mere photograph would ever capture what those five years had meant to the people who were there that night.

*   *   *

On the last day of the conference, P.A. members from

130

the California Institute for Women at Frontera presented their program "From the Inside Out." The panel consisted of five women who were at that time incarcerated on felony child-abuse convictions, plus Betty Lansdown, former chairperson of the P.A. group at C.I.W., and Lt. Jean Land, Correctional Officer and then in-house P.A. sponsor for the prison groups.[6] Dr. Brandt Steele, a professor in the Department of Psychiatry at the University of Colorado Medical Center, in Denver, acted as discussant. Leonard, as master of ceremonies for the Conference and former outside sponsor, introduced the women. The following are excerpts from that presentation.

Brandt Steele: Either failing to do the right thing or doing the wrong thing leads to the parental behavior of punishing the child, and it is this belief in the educational value of punishment that has been present in our Western culture and maybe in all cultures since year one.

Two years ago, one of our Denver papers reported that the town council and school board passed a resolution that rubber hoses could no longer be used for disciplining the children in school there. Henceforth, only leather straps and paddles would be allowed. We still believe in the educational value of punishment; this pattern is built in and taught in our Western culture to a very high degree.

Another manifestation of this educational value of punishment is what we call our prison system, our penitentiaries, which were basically designed not only to get revenge on people but, theoretically, in more recent centuries to rehabilitate people. To put them in a punitive institution was supposed to make them better, teach them how to shape up....

Leonard Lieber: The first five years of my work in the field of child abuse as child welfare, protective services, and mental health practitioner and supervisor taught me little about the subject. Compared to my experience in working with inmates sentenced to prison for child-abuse offenses—including murder—that half-decade had been an exercise in a textbook.

It wasn't until I started spending time with the women in the Parents Anonymous group at C.I.W., when I was locked in with them for two hours every week, that I began to know the anguish and sense of loss that a child abuser could actually feel, having physically and emotionally brutalized her own child.

Hearing them tell their own life histories of abuse and neglect, listening to them sobbing and calling out for a healthy parent of their own, I was taught only too well how we all pay mightily when children are destroyed. It became clear to me that the destruction or the killing of one's own offspring is as much an act of suicide as the taking of one's own life.

Yet that individual who has destroyed her child, a literal extension of her own personality, has died too. But out of a gross need to self-punish, for reasons that have taken root long before, the child destroyer lives on, crying every night in her tiny cell, calling for love and hate from us all at the same time. . . .

Jean Land: I worked with the psychiatric unit for two and a half years. I met Betty, Wanda, Holly, and Sara during the first few weeks they came to the institution, crushed, broken, so torn with guilt that they could hardly talk. They were afraid even to admit what their charge was. I've held some of them in my arms, and we've cried together because there's nothing else to do.... So I go to them individually and say, "Hey, this is what we have: we have Parents Anonymous. This is what we can do." I assist them with that fear of even admitting why they're there, and sometimes I can help them to put together the pieces of identity and self-esteem and growth. Yes, some of our ladies are in danger from other inmates. And we have a lot of staff that are prejudiced. They pick up the files and say, "Oh, that's a juicy case!" I'm trying to train them. We're going to go back, and we're going to tell those people what we are and what we mean to do....

Wanda was on the panel; she had written a poem. She didn't read it aloud at the conference; she probably couldn't have gotten through it. She had sent it to me a year before from prison, and I had run it in the first issue of *Frontiers*:

INSIDE

December 27th is the day.
The Day I love and fear.
For, on this day, I remember;
Spiritual joy of my daughter's birth,
Bright moments when we were near,
And the body-shuddering agony of her death.

    I think of her alive and vital,
    An extension of myself really...a tiny twin.
    We spoke without words, loved without
        doubt.
    Truly we were two children as one.

133

Her beauty moves me still,
Her voice...as sweet as any angel's song.

Wise she was...in her eyes I saw it.
The wisdom in those eyes tortured me.
Mother? Drunk, whore, broke, scared.
A poor mother was I, in every way but Love.
But my pitiable efforts to survive held me rigid.
It would have been better simply to scream; for
  Help.

Too many motels, too much booze, too little
  warmth.
Too many nights with a car as our only home.
Too many hungry times, and times beaten and
  raped.
I told myself it was all for her.
She was with me...she saw it all.
I thought she understood the ugliness...
And her eyes were Wise.

     With such a beginning, how would she be?
     Would she be defeated and without...like
       me?
     I loved her so...my Soul cried no;
     And when she died there was relief in grief.
     It seemed that she had escaped and was with
       Light now.
     My love, warm as ever, wished her peace and
       pride.

     One by one, the women on the panel passed
the microphone to each other with shaky hands.
They shared the parts of their own lives that had
led them to prison and talked about how they had
grown through P.A. They also spoke about what,

134

in their opinions, families in trouble needed from professionals and the community at large.

• "My daughter and I had a very loving relationship, but I was without money, unable to provide materially. Without the love and nurturing needed to fill me as a human being, I was unable to give the full measure of my love. I was without family or friends to provide emotional support. I was very guilty about not being a 'good' mother."

• "An already guilt-ridden parent will rarely ask for help from the traditional sources. In fact, I felt the need to hide because my behavior was 'unacceptable.' Abuse was only a small part of the relationship between my daughter and me—but, it was large enough that, in days when life was hopeless and nights were fearful, I ended her life and very nearly my own. How many times I've wished I were dead."

• "Welfare? Federal programs that are designed to 'mount a comprehensive attack on the national problem of child abuse?' What did any of that have to do with me? I needed help. I would have felt safer if 'helpers' had no agency connections—no connections with the system. That is threatening to me. I needed somebody to talk to me as if they *wanted* to know what was wrong, without backing me into a corner and being horrified. I needed somebody to *let* me ask for help."

• "In the medical field, there is a need to end the horror stories and provide service to heal abusers physically while referring them to parent groups to heal them emotionally."

• "Teachers are finally beginning to provide the

invaluable service of informing teenagers and young adults about the realities of parenting. It's not all baby powder, sweetness, and cuddling. There's education in the tense, all-night vigils and sickly, smelly diapers as well."

• "I hope that legal people are beginning to end their track-'em-down and lock-'em-up kind of treatment of child abusers. There *must* be alternatives to imprisonment. Diversion programs begun in Los Angeles and San Francisco are pretty good alternatives—leaving the parent in the community, provided that he or she begins and maintains involvement with parent groups. Creating foster children or wards of the court is *not* the remedy for most abusive situations. Vital to healing (both emotional and physical) is the reuniting of the family, and such reunion is possible in 80 percent of the cases. It is imperative that we overcome our false belief in the value and education of punishment. Those who prescribe prison for child abusers must learn that the isolation and degradation is neither a cure nor a deterrent. Prison is punishment —only that—and for an already tormented parent it is downright damning. We will not stop abuse by abusing."

• "We need people helping people, willing to share fears, families, triumphs, humiliations, and realities. We need to decide for ourselves what kind of parents we want to be and then support one another so we can develop the power and self-control to be as we've chosen. Even though my child is dead, it's not too late—if I can save others and, by so doing, grow myself. I'm going to try."

Betty Lansdown: So I went into that first P.A.

136

meeting feeling like, "Hey, you guys, I'm here, but only because I have to be, and I know you can't help me because you don't care enough to really help me. You're a bunch of phonies." But somehow I got some good vibes from 'em. Then I said, "Hey, you know, maybe they care."

But then I remembered, *I'm not good enough. No one could care for me.* I went to the group every week, hoping that I would find out one thing good about myself. The group pushed me into starting back to school. I asked the principal how long it would take to graduate; he said three years. I said to myself, "Let's see where it's really at with you, Betty. Find out if you're still stupid."

I started in the school in June. One year later, in June, I graduated. But I still didn't like the person that I saw inside. I wanted to bury that person because that person had almost buried me. So one day I made a list of pros and cons about myself. What are the good points about me? What are the bad points about me? The list of bad points was really a long one. The good points? I had one: *I'm trying.*

I kept building on that list. I began to put more things down about myself that were good. When I made an evaluation one year later, I thought, "Wow, the good outdoes the bad. I'm worth something!" Most important of all, I was worth something to myself.

Now I finally feel worth something to someone else. Valuable. I couldn't have done that if there hadn't been people around me saying, "Hey, we care about you. We see good things in you that you can't see yourself. We're willing to help you bring those good points out." To accept this wasn't easy; it was a hell of a lot of hard work. But I finally did it, and I'm asking all of you to help all of those other parents out there who have a really low picture of themselves, who are purposely trying to destroy themselves because that's what they feel they should do. That's what they've been trained to believe.

I have a lot of feelings for the parents out there, the ones that you *don't* see in prison, the ones that you *don't* see in the hospital waiting room. How long are they going to go on destroying themselves and others? Those are the persons that I really hurt for. Because I know what it is to be isolated and unable to look at myself in the mirror and say, "Hey, you're okay."

Betty's story concluded the prison presentation. When she finished speaking, several hundred people slowly rose to their feet, applauding the group. Betty regarded them with tears in her eyes. Stupid, ugly Betty was receiving a standing ovation. She'd come a long way, but she still had a long way to go. She had six children she hadn't seen or talked to for years, and she didn't even know where they were.

* * *

The four P.A. members who had been my houseguests took a great deal back home with them, but not quite everything: one left a towel, one a mascara brush, another a comb. They left by plane and by bus; two of them hugged me good-bye, one stood back shyly, and one left a note and two dollars for gas tucked into the steering wheel of my ancient Buick.

The conference was over, and a few hundred

evaluation sheets pronounced it an official success. But behind those evaluation sheets were people who went back to their communities eager to use what they had learned during the three days they had spent in Long Beach. One of them, Betty Stratigos, returned to South Bend, Indiana, convinced that she would now be able to do a better job at the scary task to which she had recently committed herself: sponsoring a P.A. chapter there.

Betty Stratigos's story

Betty Stratigos is an RN who specializes in rehabilitation nursing. She first became interested in the problem of child abuse in 1973 when a young South Bend boy died because of neglect and an overdose of medication. At that time, she was a volunteer board member for the Mental Health Association. The child's death so moved her that she suggested that the MHA study the emotional needs of children with the aim of fostering education. In particular, she wanted to find out what had happened to Johnny and his mother. This led to the development of a child-abuse and neglect organization in South Bend, which eventually became an agency all its own.

In 1974, Betty volunteered to organize and lead a two-day conference on child abuse—something that had never before been done in that city.

"I was very ignorant about what I was getting into; I had no idea of what child abuse and neglect were or the extent of the problem. In my naiveté, I invited all the big shots in the child-abuse field I could think of. The conference went very well, and other organizations got on the bandwagon with us.

"I became one of the charter members of our child-abuse and neglect organization. Each of us assumed responsibility for certain activities. I decided that I wanted to get more intimately involved with families who were having these kinds of problems. I had heard of Parents Anonymous on TV and thought, 'That sounds like something I'd like to be involved with; I'll offer to sponsor a group here in South Bend.' After I had committed myself, I really began to shake and wonder, 'What in the world have I done? What do I know about this field?' So I begged and borrowed the money from various interested people in the community to go to that first Parents Anonymous Conference in Long Beach.

"That experience—hearing Jolly K., hearing Leonard, meeting them and shaking their hands, and especially hearing those women from the prison—touched me in a way I can't describe. I have four daughters who were in their teens and twenties then, and I thought, 'My God, these women from C.I.W. could be my children!' They were sending out their message to us in the audience: 'Go back to your communities. Tell it like it is. Do what you can. Prevent what has happened to us.' I came home realizing that I had made a good decision in getting involved with P.A., and I let the word out that P.A. was starting up in South Bend."

Three months passed before Betty received any response from the community. Meanwhile, the child-abuse organization had printed up posters, and Betty had convinced a public library to donate a meeting room. When she realized that the public library might not be the best place for a P.A. meeting—"Why would any parent want to go to

140

the information desk and say, 'Hey, I'm looking for Parents Anonymous?' "—the location was changed to the YWCA, which had both ample parking and facilities for child care. The Y helped to spread the word that P.A. meetings were being held there.

"The first mother who came forth had heard about P.A. at her Head Start meetings. One of the child-abuse workers there had been letting the mothers know that verbal abuse was something they should guard against, and that mother had gone up to the speaker and said, 'That's me, and I want to do something about it.' She was a Hispanic American, and we don't have many Hispanic Americans in South Bend. She brought her sister to P.A., and then pretty soon a third sister came. I had these three in the group for over a year. It was the best kind of beginning.

"Finally the group began to take hold and more people came in, but they'd stay maybe one or two meetings, and then they'd be gone. I was going through all the growing-up processes, thinking, 'Well, I must not be functioning right; I must not be doing something I'm supposed to be doing.' But that wasn't it at all, of course; the community was only *beginning* to think about the problem of child abuse and ways to help with this problem. I stuck with it, and I got volunteers interested. Then reporters started calling, asking if they could interview the parents. A few chairpersons had grown to the point where they were willing to be interviewed on TV, and that's where the trouble would start. The families of these chairpeople climbed down their necks for going public like that. They really suffered, and I'd lose them.

"But we have three good groups now, and one mother has started a fourth one in Niles,

Michigan, just across the state line. We have one black minister who's an asset to the whole program because the black families feel better about having a black leader in P.A. And we have a retired senior minister who's seventy-five years old and a doll. They love him."

Betty gained something from P.A. she hadn't expected: the realization that she herself had been an abused child. She also acknowledges that even though she's in her fifties, she must still work on the relationship she has with her mother.

"She still abuses—not in a battering or verbal way, but in a psychological way. She rejects us all. But I can see that there's a time in our lives, if we allow it to happen, when we grow beyond what our parents did; and we become, in our education and our emotional growth, a parent to our parents.

"My mother came over from Europe, single and pregnant; I think I was an unwanted child. She went to live with her brother on his farm in Illinois, and even then I guess she was difficult to get along with. So after I was born, her brother said, 'There's the door; you've got to go out on your own.' She tried being a domestic for a while with me along, but it just didn't work, so she placed me in a foundling home.

"I went into the orphanage when I was sixteen months old, and I stayed there until I was five and a half. It was run by a church order. I remember that this strange woman would come to see me there every once in a while; she would bring me cookies and candy and fruit, and I'd have to dress up in my best dress. She would swing me on the swings; then all of a sudden she was gone.

"I have happy memories of my childhood during these years. The people at the home were very good to me, very kind, very loving. The other children there were like brothers and sisters to me; I never felt lonely. Then my mother and dad decided to get married, but he wasn't allowed to leave Czechoslovakia until his military service was over. That took a long time, so I was almost six years old when all of a sudden I was plucked out of that nurturing place and found myself in a strange home with two people who spoke a language I couldn't understand. And I didn't know who the man was. I remembered having seen the woman occasionally, and they said she was my mother, but I had never seen him before. Their cooking and language were different. I felt so displaced; it was horrible. They tried to be parents and didn't know how. When I did things like not eat, their attitude was, 'You're going to eat or else.' Then the punishment began—the big thick razor strap, the battering, the verbal abuse, and the hate that came out. Whenever my mother was in a bad mood and I did something naughty, she would strip me of my clothes and make me kneel on popcorn kernels on a wood floor. I had to kneel there all day long. If I had to go the toilet, I did it there. If I cried, I got the strap across my back. I remember praying, 'My God, who is this woman, and why is this happening to me?' I could feel the pain in my heart like a two-edged knife. I remember saying to myself, 'When will all this stop, and what do I have to do to avoid this kind of thing?'

"I learned to adapt. I'd realize that there were times when her temper was worse than others, and I spent a lot of time playing outside with my friends. I would avoid coming home. But then a very special person came into my life. Dr. Rose was a friend of the family; she was a young woman when I knew her and was engaged to one of my dad's friends, who was also a doctor. Her fiancé died suddenly, and she, in her grief, dedicated herself to staying with the Czechoslovakian people in that particular neighborhood in Chicago. Somehow she must have spotted me as a child in need because she kept me with her when she made house calls from morning till night. She would feed me, buy me clothes, nurture me. I can still hear her saying to me, 'Betty, you will meet nice people. You are good.' She gave me all the positive feelings that we want children to have about themselves. She convinced me, somehow, that I should go into nursing. When the time came for me to choose a nursing school, I selected one where she was on the staff.

"I was accepted, and I was so relieved to get out of that house and be on my way. I think my mother was relieved, too. It gave her an opportunity to try to work out her own problems with my dad, which she is still trying to do. She would never seek professional counseling, though. She had so much pride. I can still hear her saying, 'Don't ever take your troubles out of your home. And always, 'A child should be seen but not heard,' and 'Shut up! Who do you think you are to talk? You're just a child.' That kind of downgrading constantly.

"I got through nursing school, and World War II broke out. I went into service like most of the other girls. That's where I met my husband. Joe came from a very loving family, and his mother became my mother; we're like mother and daughter even to this day. I saw how she treated her son, and I knew what the word *mother* means. We've had a very beautiful, warm, understanding relationship. She's been a model for me of good parenting. Of course, we have our ups and downs like any other family, but we discuss them, we talk about them, we get angry, and we make up; but we have good times together, too.

"Joe is very, very pleased that I'm involved with P.A. My children know a little about my background, but I've spared them some of the most painful episodes. They, too, are suffering because they see that they don't have a loving relationship with their grandmother, my mother, and they don't know why. They also see how Joe's parents treat them as compared to how my parents treat them. It's a learning process for the whole family, and we're very fortunate, I think, because Joe's parents came from strong ethnic backgrounds—strong religious backgrounds—where the family was the core around which the members fanned out. And we all, as family members, draw upon this strength.

"Our parenting doesn't stop at any certain point. It becomes easier to handle, though, as we allow ourselves to study and grow, to listen and to maybe not be so hard on ourselves if we make mistakes, to level with young people and to be encouraging and enthusiastic. I get calls from the community hotline. They don't know what to do with some of the parents who are having problems with their teenagers, and they want to know if P.A. handles things like that. I'm in a very unique situation; I live across the street from a runaway shelter for teenagers, and I've made it my business to meet them—have them come to mow my lawn or clean my house or have a cup of cocoa with me because it's cold outside. These runaway teenagers tell me about all kinds of abuse they've lived through, and it's like an echo of the same stories that the people in our P.A. group tell. Sexual abuse is very, very common. Very little about this comes out in group meetings, except mention of funny grandfathers and such; the heavy stuff gets dealt with over the phone."

Being a P.A. sponsor isn't easy; sometimes Betty goes through periods of being burned out.

"Then I say to myself, 'Maybe I've given until the cup is empty, and now I have to fill it up again.' So I back off a little bit, and I read, and I turn to religion for strength, just to keep me going. I'm not a fanatic about religion, but I do know that my strength has to come from a source higher than myself or more powerful than myself."

She has her own personal sponsoring style; P.A. encourages this individuality. She attempts to contact every new member by telephone before they come to their first meeting in order to prepare them for what they will find in the group. If she doesn't hear from older members, or if they don't attend for several meetings, she makes it a point to contact them, too, if only to say hello.

"And if some of the members say, 'You know, I'm over my problem now,' or stop coming to the group for whatever reason, I get back in touch with them every six months or so. We have a very unstructured group; I spend a lot of time encouraging people to seek help and to seek it from each other.

"By the way, we also have a very special volunteer—my nephew, who is a combination artist and social worker. During the day, he works with teenagers in the criminal-justice department, and in the evenings he gives his time to the young children of our P.A. group members. He relates to them in a kind, calm, encouraging way, and they just eat it up. He shares himself with those children, who need a stabilizing force in their lives. Because of him, the children encourage their parents to keep coming to the P.A. meetings. It means that they'll get to see Johnny and play."

* * *

Betty is a prime example of an "invulnerable." "Invulnerables" are children who are able to overcome the effects of abuse because of nurturing they receive from other sources. By the time Betty was put back into her destructive home environment, she had something better to compare it to: the love she had received while in the foundling home. Later in her life, she experienced support from Dr. Rose. As a result, she never felt she deserved the treatment she got from her mother.

Too many other children never have the chance to find this out; they spend their whole lives ignorant of the fact that there's something else out there besides abuse and neglect and punishment. Betty was lucky. As a child, she found love outside her family; as an adult, she developed a relationship with her husband's mother that has helped to make up for the one she never had with her own mother. Today, as a P.A. sponsor, she is spreading some of her luck around.

March 1975

Like Betty Stratigos, we all learned a great deal from the Long Beach conference. Margot Fritz has her own special memories of the days leading up to and following it:

"As director of training, I was responsible for planning and implementing training for those who had been selected to act as P.A. regional coordinators in the ten H.E.W. regions. The training was scheduled to take place at national headquarters three days prior to our first national conference. Almost all the regional coordinators were parents like me who had come out of the program. They had no idea what they were expected to do as R.C.'s; it was my job to get them ready for their roles as administrators of the P.A. programs in their regions.

"Following the training session, I went to Duane Ragan, our project director, and said, 'Duane, I goofed. I made a mess of it. I think I made just about every mistake possible. I could write a manual of don'ts on training. You'd be within your rights to fire me.'

"He listened, put his hand on my shoulder, and said, 'Margot, learning takes place best when it's needed.' He went on to encourage me to use resource people to help me get a handle on training concepts; and he approved the expenditure of grant money so I could attend the National Training Lab workshop. This made it possible for me to design the one-day P.A. training workshops, which have since met with such great success.

"Duane's attitude and support were critical to my growth and development as a trainer. It wouldn't have taken much criticism from him at that point to convince me that I really had no business trying to train anybody or anything. That's how he functioned with all of us. He never asked me nosy questions about how I was doing or how anybody else in the program was doing; that just isn't his way. Duane likes people, and he makes it his business to get to know them so that he can assess their strengths and weaknesses without having to go behind anybody's back to get the information he needs.

"Most important, Duane believes in the program and in what we're trying to accomplish. That belief is not attached to any one person or group of persons but is based on the premise behind what P.A. is all about.

"Never once in the two and a half years he was our project director did he criticize, interfere with, or in any way undermine anything we tried to do. He's left us now to return to military life, but at his own request, he continues to be involved with P.A. as a member of the national board. His stewardship of P.A. at the federal level made it possible for the program to keep growing and thriving."

*   *   *

On March 12, Leonard, Betty Lansdown, and I drove to C.I.W. and met with Lt. Jean Land and the Parents Anonymous group there to ask the women if they wanted to contribute their stories to the book I was putting together about P.A. Most of the women knew Betty; some knew Leonard; none knew me. It had been four years since I'd been to C.I.W., and none of the old group was left. I recognized the five women I'd seen on the podium at the Long Beach conference, but of course, they didn't recognize me. They had read *Frontiers*, though, and they had learned to trust anybody connected with Parents Anonymous.

149

The verdict was an overwhelming yes. The women who decided to talk to me wanted very much to participate in a project that might help to keep other parents from winding up where they were. Betty planned to accompany me on the first few interviews, mainly to provide support if the women broke down emotionally. It was agreed that we would begin as soon as I received official permission from then Superintendent Brook Carey.

Later, when we had been checked through the main entrance, Betty stood in the parking lot and shivered in the weak spring sunlight. She looked out over the cow pastures that surrounded the prison and said, "You know, someday I'd like just to walk all around the outside of this fence, now that I can."

* * *

Brook Carey gave us permission to talk to the P.A. members at C.I.W., and we drove down for our first visit two weeks later.

As I walked down the shining corridor once more with a cup of machine-made chicken soup in my hand, I began to feel strangely at home.

Sara's story

She was pretty and bright, with a look of sad irony when she smiled—a little uneasy, but straightforward and willing to do what she'd set out to do.

The small boardroom at C.I.W. was bare except for polished wooden chairs and a table. I bought coffee from the machine, and the three of us—Betty, Sara, and I—sat in our little circle and made ourselves as comfortable as we could on the hard furniture.

Sara was twenty-eight years old and a former school teacher. She'd had one child, a girl.

"I came from a middle-class family. My father's a boss in a steel mill, and my mother doesn't work. I guess they were typical parents. I've heard a lot about child abusers often having been abused as children, and in my case that's not true—not in the physical sense. I've really thought about whether they abused me in any way, and the only thing I can say is that they were very unaffectionate. I don't recall any 'Honeys' or 'Dears'; I don't recall walking down the street arm-in-arm with anybody, or being hugged. I think that was an abuse to them as well as to me because they didn't know how.

"So my needs were never expressed and never met; we all lived in isolated shells. But everything else was okay. I had clothes, and my mother was interested in grades, school, social events, and all that. My father was an intellecutal man with a lot of hobbies. He spent a lot of time by himself, but he brought in the bread and gave me advice—in a nutshell.

"I went to college and studied to be a teacher; and then I was a teacher, which drove me crazy. I like teaching, but I found it difficult working under a really strongly bureaucratic kind of system. It was the same thing again: 'Keep your respect; don't really communicate with the kids.' I just felt as if I were hemmed in in a lot of ways with that kind of lifestyle. And I didn't quite know what was wrong because it seemed like everybody lived that way in Ohio at that time. But I knew something was wrong, and I was really unfulfilled;

151

'over there,' somewhere else, people were different. I had seen families that *could* relate to each other; somewhere, things *had* to be different."

After teaching for a year, Sara left her job and spent about three years traveling. She finally ended up in New York City, where she became involved with drugs and prostitution.

"I felt up until then that the traveling time was really good, but I felt extremely guilty about the drugs and prostitution.

"I went back to Ohio and got pregnant. After the baby was born, I moved to northern California, where I met another man who had just come back from Viet Nam. He had a lot of the same problems that I did—jumping around many different places, trying to find something. But he had a stronger family core. His father had died, but he had a strong religious thing about his mother. He had a lot of religious confusion but a very spiritual background, and I needed that feeling of strength and family.

"This didn't work, though, because underneath that facade were a whole lot of problems—his guilt from Viet Nam, my guilt from prostitution, the fact that it wasn't our baby together, our use of drugs. I wasn't hooked on anything; I didn't even take much of anything at that time because I'd gone through a kind of cleansing. But in our encounters together, it all started to come back to the surface. He had been on alcohol, and I started drinking a bit. I can't say what actually happened because I don't know. All I can say is that between the two of us we were having a lot of struggles, and the baby was somehow the *new me*, the better me. But I wasn't a very good teacher for her. And what if she rebelled against me? She was my only lead-in, I thought, to a really good, pure life, and *he* had me kind of afraid that she would rebel against me. He was very much afraid of not fathering right. When she cried, he felt that she was doing it against us as a partnership and against him as a person—that we weren't doing it right. And this was always combined with some confusion about the 'enemy' hearing us; he always had that Viet Nam thing.

"He refused to seek psychiatric help because he saw psychiatrists as authority figures, self-righteous. And you know how psychiatric help is. I went once, and it was kind of shabby. All they did was what you're doing right now: listening. And then I walked out and felt better because I at least got to talk to somebody. But big deal; I could have hired a taxi driver.

"I left him several times because what was happening was no good. He also hit me a lot of times. In a way, I felt I deserved it. I still had a real guilt thing. And I thought, 'This poor man is suffering; look at what everybody has done to him. He's had to go to war; he's had to develop a strength, which is also his pain.' I had never fought in a war, so I thought I had to feel that pain, too. When he walloped me one, I felt it was my obligation to be strong and take it. I had no place to go, anyway. I didn't know too many people. It was pretty obvious when I'd come out with welts all over my face that something was amiss, but there was nobody who was going to do anything about it. You know, some people would say to me, 'You really should put a stop to that,' and I knew they didn't understand anything and probably wouldn't do anything, so I'd just say, 'Yeah, you're right. Good-bye.'

153

"I've thought a lot about whether I would have gone to Parents Anonymous at that time. I might have, but he might have stopped me because he would have seen it as threatening. So anyway, I was getting hit, and then the alcohol came on, and the baby would cry, and he would hit her too. She was ten months old, and it just didn't seem right. On the other hand, though, his reasoning was that she was going to go wrong if she didn't get it. *He'd* gotten it, and that was the only thing that had helped him to make it through this cold, hard, terrible world. If she was going to be different from me—and I was totally convinced that I was flimsy, spineless, and weak—she needed to have discipline. He rationalized it as 'character building.' And somehow that struck a chord in me. I believed it, but I couldn't do it. I was ashamed of myself for not being a good disciplinarian; but I didn't want to hit her. I thought there must be a better way.

"So we had this pattern. I was carrying her around all the time to compensate for what he'd done. It became a matter of him hitting her and me picking her up and saying I'm sorry. Sometimes, rather than letting him hit her, I'd spank her a little bit because it was better than the way he did it. Then *he'd* feel sorry and pick her up. I began to believe that she knew we really didn't mean to hurt her, but that she had to take it in order to live in this cold, hard world.

"Things were really bad at that stage. She never showed any signs of abuse. But in court I found out that she had fractures I didn't even know about; old breaks that had healed over. She'd been taken to a couple of pediatricians for colds and things, and they didn't see anything either.

154

"The abuse wasn't really that frequent. I remember two times when she had some bruises and some marks, and I hid them from people; I put long clothes on her because I didn't want anybody to see what had happened. I knew that they wouldn't understand that it was necessary, and I really felt at that time that it *was* necessary. Yet part of me felt it wasn't right, and I didn't want to admit that we were doing something that wasn't right because I wanted everything to *look right*. I'm really good at camouflaging things. I've been doing it all my life. It might have been better if I'd been really dumb and hadn't known how things were supposed to be.

"I was really wary of people—distrustful of everybody. I was on welfare; I wanted to be with *her* instead of teaching or working anywhere. I didn't know anything about child-care centers. I thought that even if they worked, I would have had to give her to some other people for the day, and I felt sure they'd want to take her away from me."

* * *

We were interrupted by the sounds of a door clanging shut and footsteps echoing down the corridor toward us. Our door opened, and a head popped around the corner.

"Just taking the count," the woman said.

"I'm here," Sara said.

"Very well, all right. You may skip lunch." The head disappeared, the door shut once again, and Sara went on with her story.

* * *

155

"So I wasn't working, and the man I was living with worked sporadically. He was a musician. There was still a lot of drinking. We had isolated ourselves, and he was drinking more and more and wasn't providing for us in any way. There were two very bad incidents of abuse then, and that's when I tried to leave for good. I got all the way to San Francisco and got on another bus and came right back. I wanted our family to stick together. I was determined that we would override all our troubles, so I came back to talk about everything. That never got done. He wasn't able to talk. I kept hearing the same rationalization, about why it was right, and I knew it wasn't right.

"And then one morning after we woke up, I was cooking, and he was drinking.

"He started throwing the baby in the air and catching her. It was a playful thing.

"I'm grinning and everything is happy. But then he threw her in the air a couple of times and didn't catch her. I thought, 'He's drunk; he's gone and lost his mind, or he's doing it purposefully.' I freaked and went over and gathered her up again, which made him mad. He walked out; then he came back. I had finished cooking; I had held her while I cooked, and I was trembling. I fed him and fed her and we had this little meal together. And all the time, I was trying to figure out a way to get away and run back into the city; I was going to catch that bus again. We were tense all through the meal. Then he and I started arguing, and *she* came into the conversation again.

" 'She's not my responsibility,' he said. 'I've taken on this responsibility, but she's not my responsibility. I'm doing everything I can, and I've taken on something I don't even care about. You don't know how to take care of her. You don't know how to take care of me.' At this point something changed, and he gathered her into his arms as if he were trying to force us to stay with him. I wanted to leave. I said, 'I want to get out of here; I want to go!' and he answered 'Well, then, take *your* kid.' He threw her then, and she hit her head.

"She wasn't dead in the medical sense for a couple of days.

"I've been here for two and a half years now, and I suppose the worst part is deciding if I can have a kid again—if I *want* to have a kid again. I think the prison thing is very destructive. I'd like to see a special prison—a C.R.C. [California Rehabilitation Center for drug addicts] for child abusers—because drug abusers are different kinds of criminals, and I think we're different, too."

Later in the afternoon, Sara and Betty had a chance to talk.

Sara: What if you still have a child and you go out and the same problems are still existing? Those root causes have to be changed, and being here doesn't change anything.

Betty: The law keeps the kids away from you. Once you have hit prison, you're not likely to get those kids back—not when you have a child-abuse case. But if you don't get some kind of help while you're in prison, it's very likely that you'll go out and get into another destructive lifestyle, whether or not you ever get the kids back.

Sara: P.A. has helped me in some respects because it's a group of people that I can talk to. In other respects it hasn't helped because we tend to sympathize with each other and protect each other

157

a lot, especially in this environment. And there are a lot of things I don't talk about. There are a lot of things I know a lot of women don't talk about. We fight to stay kind of strong together in our heads. I don't really know of any woman who wants to send herself through the thrashing of going into detail about what kind of things she was doing, what kind of things were happening in her mind. And in this environment, those things aren't existing that much anymore. They seem long ago and far away. Here I'm not worried about whether there's food on the table, or how to get it on the table, because I know there's going to be food on the table.

Betty: The pressures are gone.

Sara: Well, there are some, but they're really self-imposed in here.

Betty: Yes, it's strange. I don't know whether you've felt this, but when I first came to prison I was super weak. God I was weak. But I realized that people in the institution who were not in on a child-abuse case were either going to beat you to death or put you down verbally until you *wished* you were dead, and I became strong against them. I said, "Well I did one thing, and I have to answer to that the rest of my life, and you have to answer for yourself."

Sara: When I first came through those gates, I was very defensive. But I still had a self-destructive kind of death wish, you know: "*She's* gone, *he's* gone." At the same time, I found myself saying, "I'm going to defend myself," which I've never done before. Because of a strong guilt, I'd never defended myself, and the guilt was now doubled. I didn't defend *her*, and that was one of my greatest shames—that I didn't stand up to him and say, "*You are not going to do that anymore.*"

When I came through those gates, I was kind of defensive; but there was also the feeling of "Do away with me; I don't care. What do I have to lose?"

Betty: It seemed to me that when I talked to some of the women and let them know I didn't give a shit what they did to me here—and I really *didn't* care—they didn't bother me. But if they saw that I was really super sensitive to everything, they would come on and really dig into my whole scene. They would want to know the whys, the hows—everything.

Sara: Maybe that's true. You know, I told you I had this pride before and I didn't trust people. I feel a lot closer to women now than I ever did. I used to believe all those things that were said about women being jealous of each other—that women are jealous because you have curly hair, women are jealous if you have a man, women are jealous period. I find now it's not so true. Women can be real good to each other.

Betty: I know. Whenever I came to the group, I wanted to be very honest and to dump everything that I felt needed to be dumped. But as soon as I walked back onto campus, I was like a different personality. My defenses all came right back up again. I really didn't have close ties with other women. With the women in the group I did, but mostly during group time. As soon as I got back on campus, I'd speak to the other girls; but it was in a whole different tone, even with the ones that were in the group with me.

Sara: Yeah, I've noticed that with a couple of other

women—especially one. She doesn't talk to any-body. She's really kept that defense high and strong and is really nervous around people. I sense that because I sense it in myself. I'm just not at ease a good percentage of the time, and I tell myself a lot that I'm phony and artificial. I don't want to be like that, but it's there.

Betty: Somehow it seems as if your only protection when you're out there on that campus is to be phony and artificial. I guess that's one reason why I got really involved with school and creative dynamics and lab technology—because I couldn't even feel comfortable sitting in another person's room and talking with them. I could be myself in group, but I couldn't do it on campus, ever. Some of the girls wanted to communicate with me; they'd come to my room, and I'd tell them, "Well, you'll have to excuse me because I have a test tomorrow; I've got to pass that test." I was lying.

Sara: I'm good at those things, too. I get kind of disenchanted with the group at times because we're really good at avoiding things, even with each other. We all seem to want to come clean with things, but somehow we slip into the bullshit. I guess we carry the bullshit seven days a week, and to just drop it all of a sudden and be sincere with one another is kind of difficult.

Betty: I wasn't sincere out of sheer desperation. I knew one day I'd be released, and I was afraid of that release.

Sara: Yeah, I'm getting more desperate as release starts to form around me. I've been thinking, "God, it's been two and a half years in here, and I've done almost nothing." Yet I've done a lot; I've run around and gotten *this* certificate and *that* class and *these* credits, and I've joined every club, and I've really gone frantic and learned some skills. But I don't know what foundation I can put those skills on. When my teaching certificate expired, I wrote to Ohio and told them I have a felony conviction. (I didn't tell them what it was for.) I asked if I could get my certificate back. They said that in order to get it back, I would have to meet with a board of directors of teacher certification and that board would decide whether or not I had a right to get it back. Once they found out that the conviction was for child abuse and child neglect, even if they did give it back, I don't think I could find a school that would want to hire me. But I'm not real distressed about that because teaching drove me crazy anyway. I was really afraid of having to discipline; it was something I never knew how to deal with. Corporal punishment was allowed in the school, so I countered with these fabulous lesson plans where everybody was going to be doing something all the time so no problems would ever occur. And I *worked*. The other teachers didn't seem to have to put out that much work. I kept the kids really active. They were sixth graders. To me, it was like a constant thing to keep the kids from confronting me in my weakness. I've never really seen myself as a good authority figure. I'd rather have a rapport. Back in school, when we were being taught how to teach, we were told that you *don't* say, "Class, will you open your books to page 46?" Instead, you say, "Class, open your books to page 46." If you ask the question, you give them the chance to say no. If I say to Johnny or Janey, "Drink that water," and Johnny or Janey says, "No," then I start to worry about how I'm

161

looking to other people, rather than communicating to that child. You know, I come from Ohio, and there if a child rebels against the parent's authority, people start looking at that parent as if to say, "Haven't you trained your dog right yet?" There have been kids coming here to picnics, and that's especially hard. You know that. Because the women know you, they know your case. They watch you very carefully when you're with their kids. If they know you well enough to know that you're not going to abuse them, they still watch you to see how you relate to kids because they're curious. So whenever I see a child here, it's hard for me to relax. Maybe when I get out, I'll need a group of women around, like P.A.

*   *   *

During the long ride back from the prison, Betty talked excitedly about the fact that her mother and sister from New York would be coming out to visit her in a few weeks. They would stay with her; she would provide for them; she would be in charge in her own place, her own apartment. She had scrimped to buy a new carpet, and she laughed at herself for making everybody take their shoes off at the door. But that carpet was *hers,* and for the first time in her life she could refuse to allow anybody to violate or ruin what belonged to her.

Betty's long struggle toward emotional health had reversed her role in the family; she had gone from being a "nothing" member to being the nurturing mother-figure. She had helped her sister through a crisis, and her brother had written, saying, "You're the only person I can talk to." But what she was most happy about was that her family members were reaching out not only to her but to each other. She had provided them with the catalyst that had enabled them to break out of the shells of their isolation.

April 1975

I had asked Betty if I could meet her mother and sister when they came to visit. As it turned out, not only did I meet them, but I picked them up at the airport along with their nine pieces of luggage.

Back in Betty's apartment, we were having a lunch of cold cuts and beer when the mail arrived. One envelope contained a newspaper clipping of an interview Betty had given in another city; it had been sent by a P.A. member. Her mother and sister both asked to read it.

When her sister had finished reading the article, she looked at Betty as though seeing her for the first time. "All those years, I never knew you felt the way you did," she said.

Her mother's eyes had filled with tears, and Betty gently took hold of the hand that was gripping the table edge.

"I wish I hadn't beat your brothers with my fist. I wish I'd done differently," she said.

"I didn't know you did," Betty answered.

"No," her mother replied. "Nobody did."

*   *   *

At the prison again. Diane, Holly, Wanda, Sara—fat, thin, brilliant, ignorant, eloquent, beautiful, homely. They seemed to have nothing in common except the hungry look they all gave

Betty and me when they caught sight of us walking down the corridor. Their stories, though, mingled into a single interrelated theme of isolation and abuse and emotional starvation.

Diane was big and overly affectionate. I felt little warmth toward her until we had shared a laugh at some goofy remark I made to the superintendent in the hall before realizing it was the superintendent. That was something we all had in common: we laughed about everything we could find, whenever we could.

Diane: "The first time I was sexually abused I was between ten and eleven. It was by my Uncle Harvey. I went to my mother, and she didn't believe it. I was shocked that she didn't believe me and shocked that she said, "You caused it; you brought it on." I was only a little girl, but she said it was because I was so developed. I matured physically early on, and she said I was promiscuous. She called me a tramp a lot—that and another term. I was sexually abused by that uncle, and it wasn't long after that that my second uncle, Art, started to go after me sexually. Then he got me alone. He would try to get me alone in the house, and he'd say, "You'd better not scream," as he put his hand over my mouth and around my chest. At that age, I remember I was frightened of being pinned in; it felt like being suffocated. Most of the time, I would get away from him, but he would frighten me. I was so scared and so paranoid of what he would do to me. They were my mother's brothers, and as I look back now, I guess that's one of the reasons she didn't want to believe me."

Betty: "My mom didn't want to believe me, either. When she finally did, it broke up the marriage, and I felt as if it were my fault. I really loved my father, and I wanted to please him. He used to tell me, 'Just a minute now, and I'll be through.' It hurt, and he was sweating, and I was only five. I didn't know what he meant when he said he'd be through in a minute. A couple of times, he heard my mother coming in the front door, and he shoved me in the closet. He told me that if I ever told Mama what he did, he'd call me a liar."

Diane shuddered and gasped, and Betty realized that they were both reliving their pasts too vividly.

"It's over," Betty said quietly. "It's over."

Diane mentioned that she was writing letters to her children, to her thirteen-year-old daughter in particular, to try to keep the relationships and the communication lines open until she got out. It wasn't until several months later that I learned she was in for putting her daughter into the hands of a boyfriend and allowing repeated sexual abuse. Not until she was due to be released could she confide—either to me or to her P.A. group—the extent of her shame and guilt.

*　*　*

Sexual abuse has always been the most difficult issue for P.A. parents to face. During the first year of the federal grant, it came to the attention of the national office that some of the P.A. people in Michigan were so uncomfortable with the idea of sexual abuse that they wanted to omit it from the P.A. program and had even left it out of their printed literature.

Jolly and Leonard flew to Michigan in 1974 to attend a P.A. function. They sat in on a board meeting that included a discussion of the controversy. In the middle of the meeting, Jolly got up and declared that P.A. had no right to further abuse and stigmatize people who needed to get rid of the garbage that had been dumped on them as kids. Instead, they needed help and understanding.

In 1975, Dr. Roland Summit, psychiatrist and longtime P.A. board member, wrote the following landmark piece on sexual abuse, which became part of the *P.A. Chairperson-Sponsor Manual* and was later reprinted in *Frontiers.*

"Many people, even those who have come to understand other forms of abuse, find they just can't tolerate the idea of sexual abuse to children. Anyone who admits to any kind of sexual feeling or interest relating to children is likely to be shunned and punished. P.A. groups may tend to say, 'That's not our problem.' But it *is* our problem.

"Many P.A. members describe memories of sexual abuse as children. Others feel guilty about sexual thoughts or activities, and they're afraid to discuss them in chapter meetings. If P.A. is to meet the needs of parents with abuse problems, every P.A. chapter must be willing to recognize, to understand, and to reach out to parents who have a capacity for sexual abuse.

"Part of the problem has been misunderstanding and prejudice. People imagine pictures of bizarre rituals, torture, or rape. They feel that children are pure and totally innocent, and they feel that only a beastly person could even think of violating that innocence. A better understanding of what sexual abuse is and how it happens will reduce some of the prejudice and open the way to understanding and help.

"Sexual abuse, much like other forms of child abuse, is a *frustration of love*. Sex at its best and most appropriate is an expression of love in the most intimate possible setting. Everyone has a need for being held, touched, and caressed, to be cared for and cherished, to be sure of being needed and very special. If people are free to experience and to express loving feelings, they will usually find someone appropriate to share those feelings. People who are frustrated and unsure of their sexual needs and feelings may seek out inappropriate partners. For adults the most intense feelings usually involve the sex organs and the more sexually sensuous areas of the body, so that every loving encounter carries with it some degree of desire to bring these areas into play. People learn through experience, tradition, and training to restrict the most specific sexual experiences to the most appropriate partners and to turn off, or repress, sexual feelings where they feel sex doesn't belong.

"One tradition is so practical and long-established that it has become an unquestioned taboo: never have sex with children. The strongest form of that taboo is: never have sex with your own children.

"People usually assume that these taboos are natural and that sex with children would be unnatural. Actually, the taboos have developed as a practical defense against a very natural experience: people who live together, who depend on each other for love and support, who have intimate daily contact with each other, will tend to develop sexual relationships with each other. *If it weren't for the rules, sexual experimentation among family members would probably be quite an ordinary experience.*

167

"Children are not completely innocent or inexperienced in sexual feelings. They respond gladly with their whole bodies to loving contact, and they have an intense curiosity to learn why their sexual organs are given such special rules. They want to be treated by their parents as something very special, and the sharing of forbidden sexual feelings can become very exciting. A parent who encourages sexual contact may find the child curious at first, then gratified and powerfully drawn to continuing contact. Once the taboo is broken, it may become easy for a parent to find reasons to justify continuing sexual activity: 'It shows how much I love the child, how precious he or she is to me; it brings us closer together; it's a wonderful kind of sex education; it's the only really tender, pure kind of sex I can enjoy; I deserve some outlet; it doesn't really hurt anyone; there's no way out; it happens only when I'm drunk.' All these arguments are twisted, just as the love expressed through sex with children is twisted and self-gratifying. Because premature adult sexuality can be disastrous to the emotional development of a child and to the survival of the family, it is the entire responsibility of the adult to protect the child from inappropriate sexual experience.

"It can be very confusing sometimes to decide when a relationship is too sexualized. Holding, fondling, kissing, mouth play to various parts of the body, snuggling together under the covers—all these are an important part of learning to trust and to love. Without them a parent may seem distant or too reserved, and a child may grow up insecure, cold, or sexually inhibited. These same loving gestures can be called sexual abuse if they become too lingering and seductive, if they are continued too long into adolescence, or if they become centered on the sex organs, anus, breasts, or other erotic areas. Far from being forcible rape, the most common forms of sexual abuse of children are gentle variations of adult lovemaking misplaced on the children of very needy, sadly lovestarved parents.

"Sexual activities with children are almost always destructive to the child involved, to the parents, and to the family. An adult who violates the taboos and yields to sexual desire is usually acting out of a disturbing inner need that denies real satisfaction in adult sexuality and compels him, or her, toward unusual, 'kinky' sexual outlets. The conflict between compulsion and taboo wipes out any really comfortable, rewarding parent-child relationship. The child is being used to meet the conflicting needs of the adult. The child inevitably feels betrayed, and the parent feels guilty and more or less depraved. Power struggles, blackmail, jealousy, guilt, and fear prevent normal personal or sexual development for the child, who finds severe problems trying to relate to appropriate sexual partners later on. Discovery of the sexual relationship may result in removal of the child, imprisonment of the parent, breakup of a marriage, and a lifetime of confusion, remorse, and lingering, guilty desires among the people involved. Everyone suffers, and the suffering is intensified by the repulsion and rejection of all the decent people who are afraid to recognize the problem as an ordinary, understandable, even natural human frailty.

"It is useful to have a firm taboo to serve as a clear guideline for family sexual behavior. Most people accommodate so well to the taboo against childhood seduction that they are not even aware. of the sexual potential of their love for their children. Some people, for a variety of complicated but very human reasons, find themselves unable to conform. These people slip into more or less sexualized, more or less destructive relationships with one or more of their children. For these parents, the taboo becomes a curse, taunting them to hate themselves, forcing them to hide their problem, and arming their neighbors and friends to punish them with contempt and public disgrace.

"P.A. has learned to help people who feel they must hide from public disgrace. We have learned to reach out and show people that self-hate only makes problems worse. We have learned to share with each other the problems and some of the solutions to all forms of child abuse. Within the supportive circle of the P.A. chapter, we can learn to understand and to help anyone who has trouble separating the needs and feelings of the child from those of the adult and who can't always control how those needs and feelings are expressed. Just as there is a fine line between discipline and destruction, there is an invisible border between loving and leching. Children need parents who can tell the difference. Parents sometimes need help in understanding the difference and in finding more appropriate ways of meeting their adult sexual needs."

*   *   *

Even though P.A. has officially accepted sexually abusing parents, P.A. groups have had relatively little success in handling the problem. The parents' sense of shame often makes the area an impossible one to talk about with others; there's too great a risk. Thus, P.A. recommends that parents with this particular abuse problem seek help from more specialized programs.

The Child Sexual Abuse Treatment Program in San Jose, California, is one such alternative. Hank and Anna Giaretto and their staff have developed what may be the most workable child sexual abuse treatment program in the world. It brings sexually troubled families (most often "nice," "clean," middle-class groups) into treatment, using couples, individual, teen-group, family-group therapy, and self-help (Parents United) in an attempt to keep families from breaking up or creating irreconcilable problems. The San Jose program is supported by the legal system there, and research has shown its effectiveness beyond a doubt.

In the future, we envision that parents from such specialized groups will come together with parents from P.A. groups to form a "seniors" group of paraprofessionals who would serve their communities on a reach-out basis. This type of arrangement would, we hope, help families to heal their own wounds and come to realize that they're people with solvable problems and not monsters.

3

On
the Road

At one time or another, we were all on the road in '75. One of the cities we visited would prove to be a kind of homecoming for me.

Leonard and I were planning a three-week P.A. trip to the east; his son Michael, who was eight by that time, would be going along. Our first stop would be a two-day conference in Dayton, Ohio, where my mother was born and raised. She had been wanting to go back again, but it took too long by car or train, and she was afraid to fly.

Mama used to run the name all together, and when I was a child I thought there was this place called Datenohio.

*   *   *

"Back in Datenohio when I was a little girl and Aunt Middy was just a baby ...." Thus would begin one of the stories she'd tell me while she was ironing. I'd be sitting near the basket of clean clothes on the floor, my arms around my knees, or lingering over Cocoa Malt at the kitchen table. Looking at Mama's feet in their sensible shoes, her legs disappearing up under the hem of her old print jersey dress, I could picture red lines running up the backs of her legs as she described the time she'd had blood poisoning from getting cut in a dirty creek. I could smell the spring violets she and her girlfriend picked; and I could imagine wild Aunt Middy running outside naked to chase off a dog that was after her cat; savage Aunt Middy, biting Mama in the stomach when she wasn't allowed to go along to a movie; hard-headed Aunt Middy, sliding down the levee at the age of four and taking all the skin off her fanny; clowning Aunt Middy, dancing and playing the piano; stubborn Aunt Middy, wetting the bed until she was thirteen, taking the beatings and hair pullings in stride; headstrong Aunt Middy, married at sixteen, annulled and aborted at seventeen, VD from another husband at twenty-two, hysterectomy at twenty-four. Aunt Middy in her flowered pajamas, sitting in our kitchen when I was four, showing me how to stick out my lower lip and blow the hair off my forehead, showing me so much love because she would never have children of her own. Aunt Middy, dead in a car accident at twenty-seven.

I walk down a street in Datenohio in 1975 and don't expect anything to be the way Mama described it. But then I see Rike's Department Store, and I recognize that name. My grandmother talked about buying all the latest things there for the big three-story house overlooking the Miami River, the house that was ruined in the flood over sixty years ago. My grandmother Grace had to have the best of everything; her home had to be a "showplace, a real showplace." She played a theater organ in the silent-movie house for $125 a week when most men weren't making half that much. By God, she would show everybody what she could do, especially her father, who demanded perfection and could never be pleased. A second husband, another showplace, then the talkies, and she wasn't needed to play the big organ anymore. California, a little restaurant that went broke, alcoholism, arthritis, and death in 1951 in a ratty downtown Los Angeles hotel. We found seven patchwork quilts in her room. They constituted her sole material legacy.

176

I look up at Rikes. It's big, but there's nothing I can see that sets it apart from any other department store. She'd made it sound so grand. Later, I phone a couple who had been friends of Mama's for years, and we eat lunch at Rike's. Gordon is just as I remembered him—sweet, funny, goofy. Dorothy is wise and understanding; she hasn't allowed the years to punish her too much. We talk about our common past, theirs and Mama's, which belongs to me because I've been living it vicariously for years and it's as real to me as it is to them.

When we return from lunch, Leonard takes a picture of me standing beside Dorothy and Gordon in front of the hotel. I send it to my mother as a memento of our visit. (She would have the snapshot enlarged and framed, and it would sit on her dressing table. She would die two years later; that picture would be the last she ever saw of Datenohio.)

* * *

The next day, a P.A. brunch—Sandy and Norma and Jim and Joyce and Sally and Tracy and Grover, and a lively discussion about sexual abuse. Datenohio had been replaced by Dayton, Ohio, and we had things to do.

New York

At Kennedy Airport, the first Eastern Airlines crash in thirteen years—this was the news on all the TV channels. There were reports of looting. As soon as some people heard about the crash, they hurried over there to pick through the luggage that was scattered all over the area. But it was also

177

reported that policemen and firemen who had been laid off and already had their pink slips were out there doing what they could to help. We left the TV set and went downstairs to have dinner with Helen Magnuson, who later became coordinator for Region II—New York and New Jersey.

Helen was divorced and had two grown children. She had spent many years as a volunteer on children's wards in a Long Island psychiatric hospital before getting involved with child abuse and Parents Anonymous. She had learned, from observation, how child abuse was often a precursor to the deterioration of a child's mental health. (In 1975, by the government's estimate, there were over sixteen and a half million children who were mentally or emotionally ill.)

Helen had no formal educational preparation for her work, but she had developed expertise in community organization and working with parents by simply getting very involved.[1]

Vermont

As we drove slowly past incredible old houses, our tranquility was shattered by Michael carrying on, complaining, tired, demanding. Although we had stopped, eaten, given him soda pop, he was being impossible—mouth, mouth, mouth. I fantasized about pulling over, stopping the car, and slapping his teeth down his throat. At the same time, I remembered my father threatening, "I'm going to slap your teeth down your throat." That must be why it was the first thing that came into my mind. "You hush up," Leonard told him grimly. "We've heard enough from you."

Before the public P.A. meeting, some

Vermonters who had been transplanted from California offered to take Michael for the afternoon. We went back there for dinner that evening and ate out on the lawn while the mosquitoes munched on us in the warm dusk. I watched the woman interacting with her children and wished that I had been more like her as a mother. She loved them unstintingly, without holding back; she was generous and obviously enjoyed herself with them. We talked about parenting and anger and child abuse. She spoke of the time when one of her boys became nasty coming home from the store; she pulled his hair and pushed him into the snow. She remembered wondering later why she had gotten that angry. As I looked at that gentle lady, it was hard to imagine her having an abuse incident, and I had to remind myself that it happens to all of us, all of us.

We left Vermont with good feelings about the people and the media groundwork that had been laid, but nothing much happened for over a year until Margot went back to conduct two of her one-day workshops. After that, chapters sprang up all over the state. At this writing, there are eight groups, one of which is in a town of fewer than 1,000 people.

Boston

Kay C. is a single P.A. parent who invited us to stay at her house during our visit to Boston. She lived in seven rooms, up three stories of peeling, reddish-brown wooden stairs.

"These are the houses the brewmasters built," she explained. "The front parlor was used only when somebody died or *very important persons* visited. The houses were built so that the back porches didn't face each other, the idea being that if the neighbors didn't see each other, they wouldn't fight."

We met her three children, and that night, we ate her special soup. It was made out of hamburger, onions, and leftovers that had been pulled indiscriminately from the refrigerator; it was delicious. Boston may be the cultural birth-place of the U. S., but for us, then, the most important place in Boston was Kay's house, with the radiator under the mantle, a lion mask over the bedroom mirror, and a fish named George, who made kisses at us through the glass tank.

The next day was the Fourth of July. Kay's daughter and her little friend Carmen were trail-ing a frayed jump rope behind them on the sidewalk. They pressed a bunch of badly squeezed flowers into my hand and asked me to come watch them swing at the playground.

When we got back, Kay told me that a boy next door had been shot in the eye when bullets from a .45 had been set off like firecrackers. The doctors wouldn't know if he had been blinded until the eye healed and they could examine the scar tissue.

The mother was inside the hospital with the injured boy, and the father was waiting outside with the other kids. He took off his belt and threatened to whip them if they didn't settle down. Kay talked to him and discovered that nobody in the family had eaten since the accident. We took sandwiches in to the mother, and Kay persuaded the father to take the other children home and feed them, too. He put his belt back on then and spoke more calmly to the kids.

We drove over to visit Megan. Her baby was a physical neglect case who is now a blooming and healthy little girl. Kay's long-term efforts with Megan and her daughter constituted a P.A. breakthrough in failure-to-thrive cases.

That night we watched the fireworks at Boston Harbor. As we were leaving, some kids set off their own fireworks on the pier, and a baby nearby began screaming hysterically. The parents immediately became angry and told him to shut up—they wanted their eighteen-month-old to control his panic at the loud, unexpected explosions and "behave himself in public." Kay's children were immediately concerned and upset over the parents' attitude. "The baby's scared," her daughter said. "They should take him home and let him go to bed, huh, Ma?"

Kay's daughter was nine then; her boys were seven and thirteen. I suddenly realized that they and hundreds of other P.A. children were growing up with a keen awareness—not only of what abuse was, but also of what nurturing and good parenting was all about.

We were a few blocks from Kay's house when we saw a strange creature emerging from a corner pub. "There's Fred," Kay said. "He has four beautiful sisters, but he was born with brain damage, and his family abused him. They pretended they didn't know him. He lives at Boston State Hospital. The whole neighborhood takes care of him when he goes to the bars. He dances all night, and the women all love to dance with him. He's quite an attraction." He was twenty-eight years old.

We put the kids to bed, and then Kay changed into an old, faded pink housecoat and began making her nightly rounds, talking to us, to the fish, watering the plants. Leonard lay stretched out in his trunks on an old boat mattress in the middle of the floor, staring at the TV. I sat on the bed just off the front parlor, reading, making notes, listening to Kay's stories about her family. The big fan in the bay window blew gentle night over us, and somehow it felt as if we'd all been together for a long, long time.

Maine

We drove into Portland in late afternoon. Portland is a wind-whipped town; the boards on the older buildings have been sandpapered by the elements to a satiny gray, and even in midsummer, there's a raw chill in the air. The Atlantic seacoast has a sweet-pungent smell that is unlike the plain-salt smell of the Pacific, and somehow this seems especially pronounced in Maine.

From the window on the ninth floor of the Holiday Inn, we could see the town all the way to the docks. With a population of approximately 70,000, it is the largest city in the state.

While Leonard was downstairs talking with two young parents who were trying to get a P.A. chapter started in Portland, Michael and I watched a huge, lighted ferry boat pulling slowly out of the harbor on its way to Nova Scotia.

*   *   *

Not long after we returned to California, the first P.A. chapter in Maine began in Portland. The parents who had met with Leonard had support from a potential sponsor: Betty Lennon, a social-work director in a Catholic child-care agency. Betty

182

went on to obtain assistance from the Diocesan Social Services in Portland. This enabled P.A. of Maine to put together a state office.

Linda W.'s story

Linda W. is now chairperson of the Augusta chapter and P.A. state coordinator for Maine. When she first became involved with P.A., she struggled to begin and maintain a chapter in Waterville, a town of approximately 15,000 people in the south central part of the state.

"I decided to have a baby for all the romantic reasons. I came from a middle-class family, and I thought I would automatically know the right things to do. I took good physical care of myself, and I took Lamaze classes so I could have my baby naturally. I breast-fed my son. I thought I was doing everything to make conditions perfect, and I was very much concerned with appearing to be the perfect mother. If my son cried and anybody asked, 'What's wrong with him?' I was really self-conscious about what I perceived to be criticism. I felt that people expected me to have the answers, and *I* expected myself to have the answers. When I couldn't do anything about his crying, I would get really frustrated—to me, it meant I wasn't a good mother. That's when I became aware that I had an abuse problem, that I was too immature emotionally to handle being a parent.

"I wasn't physically abused by my parents, but there wasn't much affection in my home, and I don't feel I was raised to have very much self-confidence or a sense of self-worth. When my sisters and I had squabbles, we were physically abusive to each other, and it got to be a habit for me to lash out that way when I became frustrated.

"My father molested me to a certain extent. We never had intercourse or anything like that, but he would fondle me when he was drunk. That was the only time I ever got any affection, when he was drunk.

"When my son was a year old, I thought I could solve the problem by going back to school. I put him in a good day-care program, but that didn't help me learn to be a better parent. I still had to come home and be with him, and I still didn't know any more about how to cope success-fully with a baby. But in the course of going to school and struggling to understand myself, I found out that Parents Anonymous existed. I read as much as I could find about it; it helped just to know that it was there. But we lived in New Hampshire then, and there were no chapters there. And the attitude towards parents who have this problem has been so bad that I couldn't admit it to anybody or feel comfortable asking for help. When I finally did tell my husband, he helped me as much as he could, but he didn't really know what to do.

"We moved to Liberty, Maine, when my son was four years old. I still lost control with him when I was under a lot of stress, though it didn't happen as often by that time. But I knew I still had the problem, and I decided it was time to stop trying to solve it all by myself. So I called up the P.A. national office, and they directed me to the Portland group. It was too far away for me to go to meetings, but I did get in touch with a parent who encouraged me to get involved with some people in Waterville and try to get something started there."

The P.A. chapter in Waterville began with three women, none of whom lived there. Each member was at least a half hour's drive away, and Linda was an hour away. There were other problems, too. A major one was that nearly every phone call throughout Maine is a toll call. In her early letters to the national office, Linda outlined the struggles and slow progress of their tiny rural chapter.

As of today, we have had no response (in the way of new members) to the article that appeared last week on the Waterville chapter. We still have an ad in the personal column of the Waterville paper, but we are thinking of revising it since it doesn't seem to be working either. Perhaps it just takes time. P.A. doesn't have a lot of support here. There is a cultural acceptance of familial violence in this state, which I think is true of a lot of other rural areas. Sexual abuse is very prevalent here, as is wife beating. Attacking the problems is a major task. We must adapt P.A. to meet people's needs and the realities of life in each area.

It's really difficult for parents who want to be anonymous in a place this small. Even if you're not known, there are usually relatives in common who know each other. I think the solution to that is, of course, education. We just have to keep trying to educate people as to what abuse is, to accept that we all have problems and that it's okay to ask for help for these problems.

Frontiers is our only tie to the whole of P.A. It helps eliminate part of our feelings of isolation. We are planning to visit the Portland chapter for a day because we need input from other chapters, ideas on different methods of outreach and morale boosting. I think the three of us feel pretty good about each other; in fact, last night all of us made a commitment that we would be available in our respective geographic areas to go to the house of a Child Protective Services family to talk to the parent(s) about P.A. when the worker determines that the family might benefit from involvement with P.A. Protective Services has agreed to pay our transportation and child-care costs, as needed. This is a big step for the group members, to be thinking about getting the word out to others.

The Waterville group later added two more members. The group was still small, however, and the sponsor was pressured to make better use of his time; so the group struggled to meet weekly without him.

A letter written six months later contained a five-dollar donation to *Frontiers:*

Dear Patte,

... P.A. isn't so unknown north of Portland anymore. Another chapter has begun in Rockland, which is on the coast about ten miles south of Camden and fifty miles west of Augusta. I was visiting a woman out there once a week for a while. She had no one else, and phone calling was ridiculous, so we decided we had to do something to establish a support system for her and hopefully other parents in her own area. We found some very receptive professionals (young, nonturf-conscious, caring.) These professionals are working in day care, a school for emotionally disturbed kids, protective services, community action, family planning, and hospitals; one woman screens kids who may have potentially handicapping problems. We have two cosponsors presently—a family day-care supervisor and a pediatric nurse—and we're experimenting with that. I guess each chapter has

to find out what works best for it. Last week I spoke to a group of about 100 doctors at a very posh resort a couple of miles from Rockland and quite a few from the area got your national toll-free number down. They were really pretty candid about their own parenting experiences. (Can you imagine how hard it must be for a doctor to admit he or she has an abuse problem?)

I told a group of social workers, homemakers, teachers, nurses, and policemen about P.A. at a conference on child abuse and neglect in Portland at the end of April. Betty Lennon, one of Portland's sponsors, answered many of the questions relating to her three years of involvement and was super-supportive to me (I was petrified). I don't want it to be just me doing all this talking, mostly because I just don't know very much except my own experience; and that's just one perspective. But P.A. has led me in a direction that is giving my life some meaning. There were times in my son's life when he could have been physically damaged. I consider us both extremely lucky that there was no damage, and I really want to encourage people not to wait as long as I did.

*   *   *

Because of parents like Linda, people all over the country weren't waiting as long to get the help they needed.

August 1975

Jolly had been thinking for a long time that it would be a good idea to set up a national telephone call-in service for parents who were in distress and needed brief counseling or referral to a local help resource. During the first year of our federal grant, there were no funds written in for a WATS line mainly because we were worried about taking on too much additional work at that time. We also figured that the government was taking a chance on us and probably wouldn't be too happy about investing even more money in a program that might not work out after the first year or so.

The period from May 1974 through April 1975 went very well, and finally we did put in a request for several thousand dollars to use in developing national and California WATS lines. We would service them during the day and employ an answering service in the evenings.

We had our hotline as of July, 1975. At first, all of us—including administrative support staff—answered the phones. We advertised the WATS line through our printed materials, and the various P.A. chapters worked with local media in identifying the P.A. WATS line as the only one of its kind in the country. It wasn't long before we realized that our hotline was the most comprehensive resource in the country for parents in distress. Through it, we were able to almost guarantee that within forty-eight hours, we would be able to refer any parent with an active or potential child-abuse problem to some source of help, no matter where he or she lived in the continental U.S. Today, the WATS line is still functioning and handling many thousands of calls each year.

A small group of people take the daily calls, and other staff members pitch in if we're hit by a large number of calls spurred by some radio or TV program or newspaper article. In the evening, several staff people are on call from just after closing at 5 P.M. until about 10 P.M. From 10 P.M. until 6 A.M. and on weekend days, Leonard and I are available to the answering service as the primary persons to whom fairly well-screened crisis calls are referred; and Michael helps by looking up references in the chapter books.

*　*　*

I continued going back to C.I.W. every few weeks for several months working the trips in between other commitments.

Sometimes Betty Lansdown went along with me; sometimes I went alone. The women's lives pressed eerily on mine—and their reality became my reality. I walked the streets of their nightmares until my own life became almost unreal, secondary. Thoughts flickered in the back of my mind of what might have been. What if my family's self-abuse had been more than half-hearted, if it had not been tempered by humor? In that close little boardroom at "the joint," I knew that a shift here, a shift there, and what had happened to them could as easily have happened to me.

Holly was tall and thin, with sensitive brown eyes behind her glasses. Her long, delicate hands were in constant motion while she spoke. She talked about finishing college when she got out, but she'd just heard that she wouldn't be getting out for a long, long time.... She was nineteen.

"My parents were in the Air Force, and the rules around the house were Air Force rules—yessir, nossir, that kind of thing. I never called them Mom and Dad. And I really didn't think much of myself. I remember the first time I ever thought about killing myself was when I was in fourth grade. I can't remember all the things that led up to it. I know I was restricted to my bedroom, and I was watching the kids playing ball out there, when I couldn't. I took a belt and wrapped it around my neck until I passed out. My parents never noticed it. They didn't comment about the marks on my neck, and so I thought they really didn't care. So I just built a bigger and bigger shell around myself. I felt alienated from everybody and more and more rotten about myself. I started getting loaded on drugs and staying away from home two and three nights a week, and finally, my parents kicked me out of the house and left town and wouldn't let anybody tell me where they were.

"So I got this job as a live-in babysitter, and I used to cry a lot because I felt like my parents had deserted me—I wasn't important enough for them to risk trying to take care of me. When I'd asked them for help, they'd told me they couldn't afford a psychiatrist and sent me to the base doctor. I went in there and he asked me, 'Do you have VD?' I said, 'No, I don't have VD. Why?' He said, 'Well, I just delivered this baby from this lady who had VD, and it almost killed her and the baby. So whatever you do, don't get VD.' I wouldn't go back to see him anymore.

"The two children I killed weren't mine. Their mother was a heroin addict and a prostitute, and I had it in my head the night I killed them that I couldn't leave them there alone; I would have to take them with me. I knew I was going to blow it, so I called the only person I thought cared about me—a poor old lady who lived in a trailer. She had been a sort of substitute mother for me.

But whoever answered the phone went to get her and nobody ever came back. So I decided that the kids and I should all die—they had nothing but a rotten life ahead of them anyway. I killed them and tried to kill myself, but I didn't succeed in killing myself."

* * *

Wanda, the woman who had written the poem "Inside" about the death of her daughter, had long black hair and green eyes—sometimes searching and lively, at other times blank, not wanting to remember.

"My mother and my father both believed in children being seen only rarely and never heard. As a result, when I was little I spent a lot of time locked in my room. I guess I never gave it any thought at the time. I just thought all families were that way. Also, my home was very undemonstrative—nobody believed in showing affection, and that more or less left me in the dark as to how to express feelings—particularly those of love. I didn't really know how to love anybody, but I tried hard to fall in love, mostly to get away from home. I got married when I was nineteen. I had a baby two years later, and the marriage collapsed. I had been drinking since I was seventeen, and I started drinking more and more; I attempted suicide a couple of times....

"My daughter and I had a very special relationship. We lived in a one-room place; we lived out of a car. I didn't have any friends. My daughter was everything to me. I didn't want her dead or physically damaged or emotionally damaged. I can barely even remember it happening. It

191

was almost like it wasn't me doing it; it was as though it was someone else. I had nobody to talk to until I found P.A. If I had had someone to talk to, my baby would be alive today."

There were so many times when I heard the same words coming out of different mouths, over and over: "I didn't know who to talk to, where to go; when I needed my family they weren't around; I knew something was wrong with me, but when I tried to ask for help. . . ." A jail cell was only a physical manifestation of the prisons they had been in all their lives.

* * *

In early 1975, a Santa Ana, California, newspaper had carried the following article:

BABY'S BRUISES NOT ACCIDENT

The pathologist who did the autopsy on a nine-month-old baby last June said in Superior Court here Wednesday that numerous abrasions and contusions on the body were not caused accidentally.

Dr. F. testified in the murder trial of Mrs. D., 20, the baby's mother, that the boy died of "massive hemorrhaging of the right side of the skull."

Mrs. D is charged with the murder of young ——. Her husband, ——, is standing trial on charges of child neglect.

On July 8, Ursula Vils had written an article for the *Los Angeles Times* entitled "Child Abuse: Turning Off The Faucet." On July 20, the following letter had appeared in the *Times*:

192

I highly commend Ursula Vils for her article "Child Abuse: Turning Off the Faucet" (July 8). I identified with it very strongly, as I am a child abuser. The public needs to know more about child abuse other than just reading about the case after it is all over. Perhaps through further understanding and compassion, society can begin to find ways of helping the child abuser instead of turning its back. There are two victims involved, the person being abused and the person doing the abusing.

As a child I was physically and emotionally abused from the time I was born until I was a teenager. No one interfered because they "didn't want to get involved." When I married at the age of eighteen and had twins at the age of nineteen, I had many emotional handicaps in dealing with marriage and children. I was abusing my children when I didn't want to and was trying to seek help in the many small ways that a child abuser who is trying to seek help does. Again, people turned their backs and didn't want to get involved and didn't get involved until after my son died. Then, they were condemning me and saying, "How could she?" just as I had said in reading of a similar incident a few months before. Now, I am considered an outcast from society.

In the past thirteen months since my son died, I have grown very much emotionally. In growing, I've suffered pains and heartaches. In jail, I gave birth to a son I had to give up for adoption along with my remaining twin son. I did it in order that they could have a new beginning. I have come to realize how very precious children are. I'm sorry that it had to take this experience to find out.

After I get out of California Institution for Women, where I am serving a five-years-to-life term, my goal is to help people who are in the same situation as I was and am now.

The letter was signed by Marcie D., the woman who had been charged with murdering her son.

Not long afterward, Betty Lansdown received a letter from Marcie. In it, she said that she'd been going to P.A. meetings in the prison ever since she'd been there and very much wanted to talk to us.

So we ended up back in our spartan boardroom at C.I.W., feeding quarters into the drink machine.

Marcie's story

Marcie had a round, pretty face and a short Dutch bob. At twenty-two, she still had remnants of baby fat, and she sat up straight, like a child at a school desk.

"I was born when my parents were middle aged. I was an unwanted child, and I was the only child they had. My father was an alcoholic and my mother was a very indifferent sort of person. In fact, a month before my son died, she told me that if she could have gotten an abortion when she was pregnant with me, she would have.

"My mother would verbally and emotionally abuse me, but my father would physically abuse me. I was afraid to let anybody know what was happening, but finally, when I was seven, my second-grade teacher came up with a theory that my father was beating me with a ping-pong paddle. Actually, he was using the floor tiling along the wall. He would fold it in half and beat me with it. They told him that if he ever did that again, they would call the authorities, so he kind

194

of lessened it. But he still did it. After they called him into the office, he asked me, 'Why did you tell on me?' I said, 'I didn't,' and he said, 'You're a goddamned liar. You *did* tell them.'

"In the third grade, he swung at me; I had turned my head, so he caught me right on the side of my face. I had a scab for almost a month.

"He was abused as a child, too, and my mother's family had been very cold and indifferent to her. Anyway, they separated when I was seventeen. I was strongly attached to both of them, even though they had done so many rotten things to me. I was caught in the middle—my mother was saying things about my dad and my dad was saying things about my mother. I left home then and got into relationships with guys where I was hurting them instead of letting them hurt me. But I wasn't happy. I was living with a guy when I met my husband, Wayne, and started flirting with him. He was a very sensitive person, and I really related to him, so we started spending time together. We met in June and were married in August. I was eighteen.

"I had problems from that day on because I didn't know what love was. I didn't know if I really loved him or not, but he loved me a lot. He's always loved me from the beginning. And so I had a lot of guilt feelings. We wanted a child, so I got pregnant, only to have a miscarriage. The day I miscarried, I called my mother and told her what had happened. She was happy about it; she was relieved that I wasn't pregnant.

"We had a fire in December of '72 and had to move. I was really depressed about that, and we were having problems with our marriage, too. I didn't know whether I was going to stay with him, and then I found out I was pregnant again. We were very, very happy about that. I wondered, though, if I was going to treat the baby the way I had been treated. I already had a fear of that.

"I had a lot of complications with my pregnancy, and I didn't find out until the end of August that I was going to have twins. They were born premature. Brian was the smaller of the two. He was born breech, and he had a dislocated hip. They looked so small, and I felt so helpless 'cause I couldn't do anything. Looking back, I felt guilty for Brian being born that way. I thought that maybe if I had done something different, they would have come later and this wouldn't have happened. I got to take Jeff home in two weeks, and Brian came home three days later.

"When I brought Jeff home, I just went to pieces. I didn't know how to diaper him; I didn't know how to feed him. I remember just standing there in the living room because I didn't know what to do. My husband had to show me how to fix the formula and how to give it to him. But when he had to go back to work, I was left with that baby, and I just sat there. I didn't even know how much they were supposed to eat. I'd call the hospital and ask, 'He only ate half an ounce. Is that enough?' I had tried nursing, but I was too nervous. When Jeff was three weeks old, I spanked him. I was just over the flu and having a lot of frustrations. I spanked him to the point where he was black and blue on his rear end. That was the first time it happened, and it really blew my mind. When Wayne came home, we were supposed to take the twins to the doctor for their first checkup. I said I couldn't take Jeff. I told him that I had spanked Jeff, and Wayne was really horrified that I had done that to a three-week-old baby. He told me, 'If you ever do that again, I'll take the kids and I'll leave.' That made me so afraid of losing him that I could never again talk to him about what I was doing.

"A public-health nurse was coming out to help Brian with his hip. I told her one time that I was afraid I would hurt my children, that I couldn't handle it. I was taking care of them all on my own; my mother wasn't helping; there were no relatives to help. All the nurse said was, 'Well, people who have their children naturally don't abuse them.' I'd had natural childbirth, and that was supposed to make me a natural mother! I was so floored I couldn't say anything.

"Then we moved to El Toro Marine Base. It's kind of out in the country. I would get the kids up at six in the morning and take my husband to work. We were having marital problems then, too, and things really started to pile up. I would abuse the children and feel really bad after it was over, but yet I could never admit what I was doing. I guess you could say I was selfish for myself or scared for myself. If I told anybody what I was doing ... Thinking back on what triggered the abuse, I remember that the children had very low birth weights, and when I kept trying to build them up and they wouldn't eat and wouldn't drink their bottles, I'd feel like they were rejecting me. I guess I just came apart because I couldn't stand being rejected by them.

"In December we went home to visit my husband's parents. I didn't want to go, but we went anyway. On the way home, the kids were crying, and I was upset. I kept yelling at them to shut up, and Wayne finally told me to stop yelling

at them. I don't know why, but I bit him. I bit
him, and he slapped me to bring me to my senses.

"In January, my husband's best friend was
getting a divorce, and Wayne was interested in his
wife. I was worried about losing him, and sometime during that month, I broke my son's arm. I
just twisted it to the point where it broke. I was
terrified to take him to the doctor, but I did. There
was a strange doctor on duty. He called my doctor,
and my doctor said, 'No, she's not that kind of a
woman. I don't think it was inflicted.' Later, when
I thought about it, I wished I'd been caught then.
But I got away with it, and things just kept going
downhill. I got pregnant again. It was my only way
of keeping my husband from leaving me. The
pregnancy *really* terrified me. I already had two
kids I couldn't control, and I couldn't control
myself with them. I didn't know what I was going
to do with another child.

"My husband wanted me to have an abortion;
but I felt very strongly that I didn't want to kill it,
so I kept it. Wayne had to take another job to bring
in more money. He was gone from home more and
more, and I was by myself more and more with the
children. I had no outlets, no way to get away from
them.

"Four days after my twentieth birthday,
Wayne was working late, and I was super, super
depressed that night. I read a book and cried; I
watched a movie and cried. And then I went in to
get Brian. When I went into the children's room, I
didn't know which one I was going to pick up; but
Brian's always been my favorite, so I picked him
up and brought him out. It was about eleven at
night. I tried to feed him, and he wasn't hungry.
He was tired. I was sitting on the floor trying to

feed him, and he wouldn't eat; so I slammed his head against the floor—I don't remember how many times.

"I can talk about it very coldly now, but it's hard for me to go back into it. He was quite messy by then, with cereal all over him. I had just knocked the spoon and the dish, and it was all over him. I had calmed down when I went to run the water and put him in the bathtub, but then I got scared that I might try to drown him or something. This part of it doesn't make any sense to me, but I put him in the bathtub and then I walked out into the kitchen. I realized that he could drown if I left him in there. When I went back to get him, he was unconscious, and I pulled him out of the water and pushed the water out of his stomach.

"I took him into the bedroom and was trying to dress him. He was real cold and clammy, and he passed out on me. I don't know how long I worked over him; I was doing everything I could to bring him back.

"I finally got hold of Wayne and told him to come home. By the time he got there, Brian had come out of it enough to look more normal or act more normal than he was. My husband saw the bruises on his face, and I told him he had passed out in the water and I had slapped him to revive him. He went for the story. Brian was very restless, so I took him to bed with us. He cried on and on throughout the night, and he was very warm.

"The next morning, when I fed the twins, Brian threw up his food; he was very still and quiet. I didn't suspect anything, or I didn't want to. I think that was it; I didn't want to. I kept asking Wayne, 'Does he look all right?' because I was starting to doubt that he was all right. I don't know if Wayne just didn't want to let it sink in or what, but he said Brian looked all right.

"Then Wayne went to work. I put Brian back in the bassinet and fed Jeff. After a while I played with Jeff; it was the last time I ever played with him.

"I went in to try to feed Brian again. When I looked down at him, I realized for the first time that something was wrong. Out of fear or anger at being rejected, I grabbed him by the throat and choked him, and he was unconscious again. My neighbor came to the back door to see if anything was wrong. We had told her that Brian passed out the night before, and when she came over, I said, 'Please help me; there's something wrong with him.' She looked at him and told me to take him to the dispensary; they transferred him to St. Joseph's. My husband had showed up by then, and there were people from the sheriff's department. They asked me if I would go back to the sheriff's station and answer some questions. They took me up to see Brian, and he was very, very still. I knew he wasn't going to make it.

"They questioned me and put it all on tape, and I was very scared. I just said that I had slapped him because he had passed out, and they got up to leave. I was going to tell Wayne what happened; I wanted to see him, so they let me see him. I told him that I did it, and when he came in I didn't know it, but Brian was already dead. I told him to take the kids and leave me, that I couldn't handle it. He said, 'Didn't they tell you?' and I said, 'Tell me what?' and he said, 'Brian's dead.' I just came apart. They had all that on tape, too. I just couldn't believe it then. Of course, I went to jail, and I was very terrified. I guess that's all."

Marcie stood up as if to leave the room, and then her face crumpled. I put my arms around her, and she hugged me almost fiercely. Betty wasn't there that day. Picking up the pieces and saying the right thing was Betty's job, because usually it was all I could do to hold myself together. I couldn't think of anything to say. There *wasn't* anything to say. So we just held on to each other for a few moments. She even smelled like a little girl.

Afterward, I asked her about her husband. What was happening with him? She told me that Wayne had joined a P.A. chapter in Santa Ana soon after she had gotten into the P.A. group at C.I.W. She gave me his address and telephone number, and I decided to visit him, too.

Wayne's story

Wayne's apartment was too warm—stale air, ashtrays filled with old cigarette butts, phonograph records lying out in the open, a thin film of dust everywhere. He had a two-day growth of beard, and he apologized absently for his apartment as we sat down.

Everything about him was thin, which made his eyes appear even larger behind the glasses. He looked like a man with a hangover, but there was no smell of liquor in the place, and the eyes that met mine were clear. He was temporarily jobless, a former operations clerk with the Marine Corps without the option to reenlist.

While he went into the kitchen to make

coffee, I looked through the small pile of newspaper clippings he had handed me—all the horror stories that had been written about the case. Among them was a letter he himself had written to one of the local papers after joining P.A.:

Late one afternoon, not so long ago, I sat alone in a small office, waiting for what would later determine my fate and the fate of my wife and family. At that time, my son was in critical condition in an Intensive Care Unit a few miles away. Two hours later, the wait was over, and my whole world had just come tumbling down around me. When the dust had finally settled, I had lost three children, my wife for some time, my freedom for a short period, and what little self-respect I had left. My son died from a severe beating.

I could never relate to my children. I had no idea of what a father should be or how to be one to my children. I expected too much of myself and my children; I expected myself to be a perfect father, and I demanded perfection from them. I didn't understand when they tried to show their love for me. Soon after the birth of the twins, I began to worry about my suitability as a father. As time went by, that worry grew. Coupled with that anxiety was the inability to express my feelings to my wife. I alienated her and then turned inward. Anything I didn't want to believe just wasn't there, and my mind wouldn't register the reality of what was happening in our home.

Our home life continued to deteriorate, and soon each new problem became an enormous crisis that neither of us could handle. Clear thought became impossible.

I love my children, and I always wanted the best for them. I'm still not sure why I was not capable of proving that to them. I didn't batter my children; but in many ways, my action or lack of it carried consequences just as grave. Worst of all, I helped to pave the way for the incident that ended in the death of my child.

There are parents who cannot control their actions around their children. And those, like me, who just do not know what being parents is all about.

Wayne returned with the coffee, sat down in an old chair, and, in a matter-of-fact voice, began talking.

"I remember being lonely as a child, keeping to myself. I was the middle child in a family of six kids, but my father always told me I was his favorite son and he expected more of me. He was in the Air Force, and we moved around a lot.

"I was aware that Marcie had been abused as a child when I married her, but she didn't really want to talk about it. The thing I couldn't understand was her drive to try to win the love of her mother and father. They never showed her any. She went to see a psychologist once. She told me a couple of times that she wanted me to go with her, but I didn't think there was any need for me to go. I just wasn't going to face things I didn't want to face. She tried to tell me what was happening to her, but I just wasn't going to see anything I didn't want to see. I did sense something was off, but I forced the feeling back to where I didn't have to look at it; so I didn't consciously suspect anything was going on. Even on the night when Brian died, I agreed that I was involved, but I didn't understand to what extent. Even then, I felt that I wasn't the one who needed help; Marcie did, but I didn't. For a long time, I didn't see my own need for help, even though I secretly thought I was a worthless father. I didn't know how to be a father to my children, but I wasn't ready to admit it—not to myself. And even at Brian's funeral, my father told me not to cry. The whole four days before my son's funeral, every time I would start to get emotional, my father would say, 'Control yourself.' My parents weren't very supportive of me. Basically, they thought I was guilty, and they didn't want me to go to jail. They totally rejected Marcie, though. The feeling I get from them is that Marcie did it and she's not to be forgiven, and that I should feel that, too. I should just want to kiss Marcie good-bye and go about living my life from here. I can't do that, though. When she gets out, I want to try to make a go of it again. I had as much responsibility for what happened as she did.

"Parents Anonymous has really helped. Since we've both been in it, I can talk more openly with her. I can tell her some of the things I feel. Learning to communicate is the biggest step either of us has taken since this happened. One of our biggest problems before was communicating, because I just couldn't. I was never able to tell her how I really felt about anything. Right now I'm able to see her only twice a month. She's been in for fifteen months, and she expects another two years.

"The other two children have been adopted. Marcie's lawyer, my lawyer, people in probation—everybody told me it was going to look worse for Marcie if there was any possibility of her ever getting near those children again. I have no idea where my children are now, and although I want to know, I'm afraid; I think I'd be tempted to interfere. I think I'd want to know if Jeff would recognize me, how he's doing, what he looks like. I didn't know Donny. He was only five days old when they took him away. It would be selfish for me to see them, though, and I don't think it would be good for Jeff, to drag him back from wherever he is. We've already done enough to him.

"Part of the problem was that we had no idea about how to go about being parents. We had a natural childbirth class, but the Marine Corps offers absolutely nothing as far as children are concerned. You still hear that old saying, 'If the Marine Corps had wanted you to have a wife and child, they would have issued them.' The first thing they do when you join the service is take you away from your family and friends and bring you into an area that's completely alien to you. There's nobody there you know to give you support. Then there's the pressure to conform to all of their standards all of the time. Then there's low pay, the long working hours, the separation from your family, the inability of the serviceman to put his own individual personality into his working situation or to argue with the system in any way. They're right, and you're wrong. You can't get mad, and you can't say no. You really marry the Marine Corps. As far as they're concerned, they come first. After Brian's death, I was so depressed I could hardly get out of bed in the morning; but I was pretty well told to be depressed on my own time.

"Even if Marcie and I had been able to talk about our problems earlier, there would have been nowhere to turn. They would have paid for Marcie to go to a civilian psychiatrist, but I would have had to go to a Navy psychiatrist—an officer—and there's a stigma attached to that because anything you say to them has to be reported to your commanding officer. You can go to the base chaplain, but until recently the chaplain here at El

Toro didn't know anything about family counseling or child abuse. If I had gone in there and said, 'Hey, my house is a mess, and my wife is having trouble with the children,' the chaplain would have given me some off-the-wall prayer. The attitude of the Corps is that we aren't supposed to need counseling anyway. A colonel informed my P.A. sponsor that there's no such thing as child abuse in the military. Of course, child abuse is *rampant* in the military. The reason it 'doesn't exist' is because it's unofficially condoned. If you go home and beat your children, that's natural for a Marine; that's what every Marine does. And physical and emotional neglect are everyday things because it's normal to go home and get drunk.

"At first, we decided that P.A. was out of the question in terms of sponsoring a chapter on the base; but my P.A. group has two Marines and one ex-Marine—me—in it. In the last year, there have been six deaths here in Orange County attributed to child abuse. Five of the six involved Marines, and the other case involved an army wife.

"I'm satisfied with the help I'm getting in P.A., except that it's going a little slow for me—I want to find out *why* I let the situation go as far as it did before I noticed what was going on. When I find out why, I can start really working on it. Right now, P.A. is the only answer. Maybe someday there'll be something else, but for now P.A. is the only answer to the whole problem, and I'd really like to get more involved than I am. I don't particularly want everybody in the world to know what happened with me and my family, because not everybody could handle it. But I don't have any objections to telling people I trust.

"I don't know what we'll do when Marcie

gets out. Maybe we'll go back to Canada. Marcie's originally from Canada."

* * *

Soon after I talked with him, Wayne became chairperson of his P.A. group. After Marcie was released, they worked actively in P.A. for two years and participated in the NBC special *Violence in America* which was broadcast in January of 1977.

October 1975

As early as 1973, it was obvious that with the help of the taxpayers' money and the staff's elbow grease, P.A. would keep growing. It was also obvious that the few of us at the national office couldn't begin to provide the technical assistance needed throughout the U.S. to get P.A. chapters started and keep them alive. The logical solution to this problem was to appoint regional representatives, or coordinators, in all parts of the country. They would be responsible for getting people interested in the program, recruiting parents and professionals for new chapters, doing correspondence and media work, and educating the general public about child abuse and P.A.'s approach. They would also serve as consultants to public and private agencies for P.A., follow up on the needs of new and existing chapters, trouble-shoot program "hot spots," and generally represent the P.A. national office and keep it informed about goings on in their territories.

By late 1973, several persons within the U.S. were identified as excellent prospects for the job.

When funding approval came through in early 1974, a recruitment and training strategy was planned that would provide R.C.'s in twelve designated regions of the U.S., following HEW boundaries, by mid-to-late 1975. Most of the potential R.C.'s were bright, committed parents from the program; some were dedicated community workers. Some were single; some were divorced; some were better off economically than others.

One in particular was an old friend. Betty Lansdown had been out on parole since mid-1972 and working, but she wanted to stay involved with P.A. in some capacity. During her stay in C.I.W., she had become chairperson of the prison group, and she wanted to continue helping parents. She became chairperson of another P.A. group in Los Angeles, began doing speaking engagements for donations, and proved so effective that she was given the job of coordinator for Region Nine (California, Nevada, Arizona and Hawaii).

By the fall of 1975, the regional coordinators had come together for training in Redondo Beach and were functioning nationwide; their "pay" was $300 a month. Linda Hayes of Birmingham, Alabama, was a community volunteer worker who became an R.C. and is currently on the Alabama and national P.A. boards.

Linda's story

"The first time I can remember hearing the words *child abuse* was, I think, around 1965. Channel Six did a documentary on it. It mostly consisted of interviews with pediatricians at the hospital and pictures of children who had been beaten. It started out with a dramatization of a mother losing her temper and hitting her child with a broom. I watched it, and it sparked my interest.

"Even then, I remember feeling sorry for the children *and* the parents and wishing there was some way to get help for families like that. Then I read an article in *Redbook* magazine about a little girl who had been horribly abused by her parents. I didn't hear much about child abuse for quite a while after that.

"Then, in 1971, I joined the Crestline Junior Women's Club. It was a fairly new club—it was just being organized—and I ended up as Project Chairman that year with instructions to find a service project that we could get involved in. I don't know why, but I immediately thought of child abuse, so I decided to go talk to Protective Services and the courts and different professionals in the community. I also went to Children's Hospital and talked to people there about child abuse to find out more about it and see if there was anything that we, as a club, could do. They all said, 'No, there really isn't anything you can do.' I guess they were overworked and honestly didn't know what could be done; they also couldn't afford to take the time to train volunteers.

"I went home and decided that it was going to be up to me and us to get involved. So I started reading everything I could find on child abuse, thinking that I'd find us a place somewhere. Of course, the more I read, the more interested I became, and then I attended a child-abuse conference in Charleston, South Carolina, that the American Humane Association was holding there. When I got back to Birmingham, I think I worried the professional people there to death because I kept going in and talking to them and suggesting things that we could do. At that time, it didn't seem that anybody was interested.

"I felt like giving up a few times, but I had this girlfriend, Barbara, who was a social worker in Children's Aid, and she encouraged me to keep on. Finally, we set up a program at Children's Hospital to detect child abuse, using volunteers that would come in. This was started in 1973; and it's still going on now.

"I knew, though, that there was so much more that we could do if we only knew *what* to do. Then one day I got a copy of *Woman's Day* magazine, and there was an article in it about Parents Anonymous. At the end of the article was a phone number. I picked up the telephone, called that number, and talked to Jolly. I told her who I was, gave her my address, and sent off a two-dollar check for a *Chapter Development Manual*. Of course, I could hardly wait to read it. Afterward, I was running around telling everybody about Parents Anonymous. I still couldn't seem to get anybody else interested, though.

"In the summer of 1974, I got a letter from Margot saying that she and Jolly were going to be in Montgomery, Alabama, on August 14. I rushed to put notices of their appearance in the Birmingham papers. Then I got a newspaper reporter, some members from another club in Birmingham, Ethel Gorman (who was at that time the Director of the Jefferson County Association for Mental Health), and several other people to go to the conference with me.

"A number of things about that conference impressed me, but there's one thing I'll never forget. Jolly was right in the middle of her talk when Margot went up to her and whispered something. Then Jolly excused herself, saying that they had to check out of their room or they'd be charged for another day—she promised to be back in just a few minutes. I remember the person sitting next to me saying, 'Isn't that something? I'm glad to know that they aren't wasting federal money.' Anyway, I jumped up and followed Margot and Jolly to their room and talked to them while they were packing. After they got their clothes together, Margot went to check out, and Jolly returned to the meeting room and finished talking.

"I was really fired up after meeting Jolly and hearing her talk; and I was determined to get a group started in Birmingham. One month later, we set up the first chapter there. I found a sponsor and arranged for baby-sitting and publicity, but the turnout was disappointing at first. Only one or two parents came, and we still weren't getting referrals from professionals. It wasn't until the end of the first year that we had ten or twelve people in the group. My friend Maezelle did the baby-sitting, and I provided transportation. Eventually we got a second group started.

"When Margot called me and asked if I would be a regional coordinator, I talked it over with John, my husband, and decided that I would. For several years afterward, my whole life was centered around child abuse. It became the state project for the Junior Women's Club. We had those bumper stickers all over Alabama that said 'Child Abuse Hurts.' I resigned as coordinator in 1976 because I was really exhausted, but I'll never forget those years and how rewarding it was for me to see it all finally happen."

Kay's story

Kay C., the single parent we stayed with during our visit to Boston in July, was a chairperson and a regional coordinator on the East Coast. She is currently on the P.A. national board.

"During a particularly rough period in my life, I voluntarily placed my children in temporary foster care and committed myself to a mental hospital. It was there that I realized that child abuse was a taboo subject. The hospital staff couldn't even talk about it with me. I remember one conference in particular—one of those show-and-tell things where I had to sit in front of the entire ward staff and tell why I was there. During this conference, I told about how I had nearly suffocated one of my children. In the following months of therapy, the subject was never mentioned again. I was encouraged to talk about my sex life, my early childhood, my recent hysterectomy (which had taken place four days before my commitment), the weather, my finances—everything but my real reasons for seeking help. By my show of compliance, I soon earned the privilege of leaving the hospital for brief periods.

"My child was admitted during this time to another hospital—for asthma. I was allowed to visit him there, always with someone in attendance, perhaps to protect him from me. At least *his* staff didn't ignore the problem. They met me with unabashed hostility; I remember being pointed at by silly, hysterical students.

"After a while I was introduced to a psychiatrist who was following my son's case. We met later at my hospital, where I released my records to him. He was genuinely interested in reuniting my family and explained to me that he would be responsible for determining if it was safe for us to be together. I trusted him, and together we worked out a schedule of appointments. Through him I met a lot of social workers, and it so happened that one or two of them were trying to get together a Parents Anonymous group. They reassured me that there were thousands of parents in the area who needed the help of such a group. I met Mike Turner, a worker at Parents and Children's Services. I'd left the hospital by that time, and together Mike and I distributed posters and publicized the first group meeting. No one showed up. For months we held planning sessions and meetings, trying to pull it all together. Sometimes one or two people would come once or twice and then not show up again. We'd get lots of calls, but none of the parents would come regularly.

"Then a parent came who was to become the core of the group. Now there were three of us. She hung in, traveling through snow and cold on public transportation, hoping her child would be returned to her if she worked hard, often not knowing what the social workers or courts wanted from her. She used the group meetings to sort out her problems and later became the chairperson of her own P.A. chapter.

"After several years, I went to the national office of P.A. to train for the role of regional coordinator. At that time, I wasn't sure what that would entail, but I felt that our chapters could no longer meet the growing need for more groups and more speakers to educate the public about people like me and other P.A. members. We met for ten days of extensive training. In many instances, we used our own experiences as training materials. We shared our feelings, often bringing out painful memories. It was during this time that I realized I wasn't allowing *my* needs to be met in my own group. All too often, my role of group leader got in the way of my sharing problems with the group.

"I went back to the group in Boston feeling elated. P.A. had developed some printed materials, too, and all of the groups pored over them. These helped us to understand ourselves better and to know that as parents we were not unique, that parents all over the country felt the same hurt, anger, and confusion over their roles as we did."

Marlene's story

Marlene and Frank Jones have been actively involved with P.A. in Norfolk, Virginia, since 1973. Marlene chaired their P.A. group for four years, and in 1975 the two of them were selected to be regional coordinators. They operated as a couple, and they appeared on TV as a couple who admitted to a vast audience that they had verbal and emotional abuse and neglect problems. The fact that a man was willing to be vocal about having had difficulty parenting was a significant breakthrough at that time.

Currently, Marlene is a P.A. state coordinator and a P.A. leader in the Tidewater area (Norfolk, Portsmouth, Virginia Beach and Hampton). Frank works with kids in Little League Baseball and Youth Football and is a member of the Volunteer Fire and Rescue Squad. Marlene tells their story:

"My parents were teenagers when I was born, and I was three years old when they were divorced. My mother married again within a very short time. My stepfather was in the army—I really remember him only after he came back, when I was just finishing the third grade. At some time during the next year, he approached me sexually.

"It was never a violent relationship; it was mainly lots of touching and caresses—and sneaking around. By the time I was old enough to know that 'all daddies' didn't act in that way, and that it was very definitely wrong, he was entirely in control of me. I was convinced that I was powerless and bad; otherwise, these things wouldn't be happening. By then I was in the seventh grade and trying hard to put a stop to it. I remember going to church (my family was *not* religious) and praying with everything I had in me for God to make him stop. I'd say things like, 'Make him leave me alone! I'll be good, God, I promise I will.' I felt like no one was listening to my prayers—and there was no one else I could talk to about it without hurting my mom. Finally, the army sent my stepfather to Japan—I was so relieved to be free of him. When Mom asked me if anything had been going on (she had begun to wonder before he left, but got even more suspicious from letters he wrote to me), I was so glad to be rid of that ugly secret that I felt as if a balloon had burst inside of me. She divorced him, but I still carried around a very guilty, dirty feeling for a *lot* of years after that. In fact, I didn't work on those feelings until after we found P.A.

"Frank's childhood was different from mine. His parents were poor, working-class people who were born and lived their entire lives in a very small North Carolina town. Despite that, Frank had the very best of everything—bicycles, ball gloves— but he also had the hell beat out of him when he lost or broke anything. One of the first stories my future father-in-law told me when we met was an illustration of 'Frankie's stubbornness.' It seems that one evening when Frank was two weeks old, he was fed and dry and warm and it was bedtime (his father's bedtime). But Frank was crying. There was no reason for his crying, so his father spanked him.

"Right after I discovered I was pregnant with my second baby (we had been trying for over a year), Frank decided on a job change, which meant our moving from Tennessee to Norfolk. I was sick from the pregnancy and sick about leaving. It took every penny we had to make the move. The job didn't materialize until six weeks after we got there—and we began to fall behind on the bills. We were also living near Frank's folks for the first time, and while Frank could laugh off all the unwanted advice I was getting from his mother, I couldn't. It only reinforced the bad feelings I was beginning to have about myself again. Our financial picture became worse, and I went back to work at a time when I wanted to stay home and take care of my babies. I was a good mother—and I loved my kids. I didn't mind dirty diapers, spitting up, or crying. The 'baby years' were the best for me, and I handled them well.

"I started the screaming sometime after Scott, the second baby, was born. The worse I felt about myself, the more miserable I made the people around me—the people I loved. If the kids bickered or teased each other, I screamed for them to leave each other alone. When they misbehaved, I screamed. If they were slow, or messy, or noisy, I screamed. I screamed like a crazy person and told them that they were driving me crazy. I realized I had a serious problem, but at first I never even gave a thought to finding help. After all, I was pretty sure that no one would or could help *me*. Then Frank's working hours were changed to nights, and things got even worse. I was working days and suddenly found myself alone with the kids with plenty of time to worry about money.

"As crazy as I felt, and as much as I knew I was hurting my kids, I didn't tell a soul until I flipped my lid one night. Scott (age three) had touched David's (age eight) record player—a no-no. I jerked Scottie up and began spanking him. It was the first time I'd spanked either boy in months, because I was afraid of my anger. I felt as if somebody else had stepped into my body and taken control of it. I began to hit him with both hands, and I kept on hitting him until I had no strength left. Then I sat him on the floor and screamed at him. When I regained control, I was horrified at what I'd done. I had to be crazy! A normal, sane person didn't act that way. I went and locked myself in my bedroom and was asleep when Frank got home from work. David apparently put his brother and himself to bed.

"The next morning I told Frank what had happened and what had been going on for the past year. I fully expected him to take the kids and run—I was sure that's what I would do if our positions were reversed. He surprised me by saying, 'Okay, if you've got a problem, we'll get some help.'

"He then spent two hours on the phone trying to find some help. We saw a psychiatrist twice, but he was expensive, and we were already having money problems. We stopped seeing him when he told me to think of myself as a computer and 'reprogram' myself. He never bothered to tell me how.

"A few weeks later, I heard about P.A. on a radio talk show. (This was back in 1973.) We managed to get some information about a group we could get into. The next week, Frank and I walked into our first meeting—only two other people were there. I was *very* nervous, and even though we talked about how 'we were all scream-ers,' it was several weeks before I felt safe. That was after another girl came in who turned out to be my best friend later on. When Jackie joined P.A., I had someone to call and someone I felt close to.

"The group met every Wednesday night, and that began to be the high point of our week. We began to notice the changes in our kids. By the time we got into P.A., we had David convinced that we didn't love him. Even worse, we had convinced him that no one else could, either—that he was unlovable. Inside of six months, we could see that he was finally convinced that we *did* love him. But it took two years before he was willing to believe that others could love him too—that he was actually worth loving.

"In addition to tearing down their self-esteem, my verbal abuse had scared my kids out of their wits. I still have two very vivid memories of this. One was when David was lying on the floor on his side, curled into a ball, with his eyes squeezed shut and his hands over his ears—and I was leaning over him screaming like a madwoman. The other time, I was yelling at both boys, and they had run around behind the table in the dining area. They looked like cornered rabbits who knew that a wolf was about to pounce on them.

They were trying to get away from me and at the same time to keep some physical object between us; and they hung onto each other for dear life.

"At first, Frank went with me to P.A. because I needed him for support. After several weeks of meetings, he began to see that he had contributed to the problem. For example, he knew our financial situation as well as I did, but he would go out window-shopping and see something he'd like to have. Then he'd call me and ask for permission to buy it, knowing full well (he finally told me this much later) that I would tell him, 'No. We can't afford it.' There were times when I felt like I had three kids instead of two. He quit putting that pressure on me after it was pointed out to him in P.A.

"Another thing he used to love doing was getting down on the floor and wrestling with the boys. They loved it, too—up to a point. Every single time this happened, a kid would wind up crying, and Frank would wind up angry. After playing for a while, the kid would begin to holler that Daddy was hurting him. Frank would emphatically state that he was *not* hurting him and would continue to 'play.' Eventually we learned that whether or not he was actually hurting them was beside the point. We were actually teaching the kids to think, 'If Daddy doesn't stop when I say he's hurting me, then he must *want* to hurt me!' Frank learned to let *them* call the shots, and when they yelled, he quit.

"Once Frank knew of the problem I had been having, he became very supportive. He started listening to me. He didn't step in and make the kids mind *for me*, which would have been no help at all. Instead, he would give me a pat on the leg and a gentle 'Easy, Mama.' Sometimes, he'd take the kids and go out somewhere so I could have some time alone. And when he realized that there were times when he got just as angry as I did, he was also able to admit the guilt he'd been feeling because of his own anger. He wouldn't admit that before because he was raising his kids almost exactly as he had been raised—except that his kids were never hit as hard as he had been.

"We told the kids why we were going to the meetings, and they got involved in the changes, too. For example, Scottie, at age three, would remind me, 'Mommie, you said you weren't going to yell at me anymore.' When we had been in the group for nearly two years, a new member asked if she should tell her kids, ages five, seven and ten, what she was coming to the meetings for. We all urged her to tell them the truth. The next week, she told us that she didn't have to tell them. They had told *her* on the way home that night because *our* kids had told *her* kids while they were all in the nursery together!

"Frank and I were pretty well on the road to a separation when we got into P.A. Since then, we've learned to talk to each other and to listen. We're happy together. We each have our own interests, but we each care about what the other is doing. We're partners and equals in our marriage. Ninety-nine percent of the problem is under control. I still have days (certain times in my menstrual cycle causes problems emotionally) when I lash out, but either Frank or one of the boys will let me know about it while letting me know they've done nothing to deserve it. My kids know we can discuss anything—all of us. And no matter what the problem is, we can work it out.

They know it's okay to have a problem and to get help for it. They feel good about themselves, and I think they feel good about their parents, too."

* * *

The current widespread acceptance of P.A. is due in large part to the efforts made by the R.C.'s. But the picture hasn't always been all rosy. Not all of the R.C.'s were able to handle success. Some of them with backgrounds of severe abuse reverted to self-abusive behavior, lost their grip on their work, and left P.A. It's pretty tough for people with a long history of low self-esteem to hold fast to the novel idea that success and the limelight are rightfully theirs.

Don's story

Columbia, South Carolina, is the site of the state capitol and the University of South Carolina. It rests at the center of a metropolitan area of 350,000 within the interior of an otherwise rural state.

Don Rosick is thirty-eight, divorced, and has custody of his ten-year-old daughter. He has been a training coordinator with the South Carolina Department of Social Services for six years and a P.A. sponsor since 1974. His chapter is one of many that P.A. regional coordinators have helped to launch and to keep going.

"When I first started reading about child abuse, I was really revolted. I thought child abusers should be locked away. But I did some more reading and met with some people who were involved—we had begun doing some training in the Department of Social Services and were identifying some people who came in as abusers. I realized, looking back over my own parenting, how easily frustration can get out of hand. Instead of concentrating on all the horror pictures in the book, I went a step further and realized that child abuse can happen anywhere, to anybody.

"I first heard about Parents Anonymous when Mike Corey, our state child protective service director, said that he was interested in getting Parents Anonymous started in South Carolina. He invited the regional coordinator, Kathy Jonas, to come down to talk to some of our county people. I helped him set it up, and when she came and talked, I was impressed. When they couldn't find a sponsor for this area, I decided it was something I wanted to do, so I volunteered.

"When we started out, we had one or two people, and that went on for a couple of months. Then we did some more advertising. Kathy Jonas made another trip down from North Carolina, and we did some TV and radio spots. We got four or five people into the group, and then in the summer of '75 it kind of dissolved again—P.A. was there in name only. In addition, I discovered I was just totally out of energy. My responsibilities at home as a single parent, combined with trying to keep the group going, just got a little overwhelming for me.

"Then the coordinator for the Council for Child Abuse put me in touch with Catherine Norris, a social worker at the Family Service Center, and she offered to be my cosponsor. Together, we got things started again. Having a cosponsor meant that I didn't have to feel responsible for the meetings every week. We're still sharing the responsibility, and it works beautifully. Sometimes we alternate weeks, and sometimes we do it together. This, I think, is where two sponsors can really help because one can kind of observe the group process and dynamics while the other is involved with a particular person.

"When I first started as a sponsor, I found it hard going until I realized that I was feeling possessive about the group. I was thinking, 'It's my group; I'm going to take care of it.' Then I began to realize that that's not what it's all about. Group members are there because they want to take care of themselves. When I learned to turn loose, the group began to blossom.

"We go beyond the group if we need to. If it looks as though members need some special kind of attention, we refer them to someone; we perform a kind of 'outreach' service. In many cases, we'll make the contact ourselves. We also use a good bit of what you might call 'gentle confrontation' to get our parents to do things on their own; we try not to jump in with immediate solutions. We confront a person in a fairly nonthreatening way if he or she seems to be avoiding the issue or playing games. A lot of times, people will play the 'yes-but' game. I guess we all do it sometimes. Somebody will make a suggestion, and a member will say, 'Well, yes, but that wouldn't work for me.' If this goes on long enough, we'll say, 'Hey, wait a minute. You're not listening. You're coming up with reasons why something *won't* work instead of being willing to try it. Why are you doing that?' We also use a lot of active listening and reflecting back, and there's an awful lot of support within the group.

"One thing we really need in this area is

emergency foster care, a kind of emergency foster home where parents could go and say, 'I've really got to have some help,' and the kids could stay there three hours or forty-eight hours.

"On the plus side the Council on Child Abuse has developed a parenting skills program and also a Welcome Baby project for mothers. The Welcome Baby project is set up in our local hospital. It's a group of volunteers who come and visit and talk with all the new mothers in the maternity ward and ask them how they feel about being a mother and offer them information on different things, especially things relating to crisis situations. It's really an outreach kind of program. It's been going on for about six months now, and I think they've gotten real good results.

"We try to encourage the husbands to come to the P.A. meetings, but right now, we've only got one man in the group. Men *are* more unwilling to deal with their feelings than women. I think that improves over a period of time as the man attends more often, but I don't see that problem disappearing very fast generally—especially not here. Maybe it's a Southern characteristic.

"I think my five years with P.A. have helped my relationship with my daughter. For one thing, they've made me realize that being a good parent takes a lot of work. But I've seen some really radical changes among our parents, and I know that the work can pay off. And I also feel that my daughter is learning some special things. She attends a lot of meetings and helps a little bit with the baby-sitting. It's been a fantastic experience. I recommend it."

*   *   *

224

In early 1976, Leonard and I were on a P.A. trip that included a child-abuse conference in Milwaukee.

Gwen is a P.A. parent who lives in a town about an hour's drive from Milwaukee. She had called Leonard during that year. When she heard that we were going to be in the area, she invited us to stay with her and her family. We were welcomed into their big, old house and accorded the family privilege of sleeping upstairs under heavy quilts with cats curled at our feet.

When I asked Gwen to tell me how she had become involved with P.A., she decided to write it instead. Over a period of several weeks, she put together the following chronicle, writing down bits and pieces late at night or when "the kid" was napping.

Gwen's story

"I had a very easy pregnancy—no morning sickness, no discomfort, no problems—except that my baby was born about six weeks too soon. For the first two days of his life, he was kept in an incubator. I didn't hold him until he was nearly three days old. I was there with my husband when the hospital chaplain baptized him, four hours after he was born.

"I brought him home when he weighed four pounds, eight ounces. We did fine for the first week—everything was peachy. Then came his colic and one sleepless night after another. My husband couldn't tolerate the baby's screaming, so he would leave the house. I couldn't tolerate the baby's barfing, but I couldn't leave the house. No one bothered to check out what the baby couldn't tolerate until he was about three months old.

"After two solid months of colic and countless calls and visits to the pediatrician, I spent an entire weekend without sleep. The baby simply would not *stop*. My husband is in the National Guard and he was gone, out of town, unavailable—as he frequently is—on some damn Army bivouac. It was bad. It was worse than bad—it was hopeless. At three A.M., you can't just pick up the phone and call a baby-sitter to come over for a couple of hours.

"I thought there must be something so radically wrong that I considered calling a cab and taking the poor kid to the hospital emergency room; but I didn't. Instead, I gave him an overdose of the medication he was supposed to get before each feeding. This was a potent concoction of alcohol, stropine, and God only knows what else. After that, he slept. Boy, did he sleep! I couldn't wake him at all. I still didn't sleep. I was afraid to go to sleep—afraid he might stop breathing.

"I called the doctor and told him what I'd done, making it sound as if it had been a mistake due to lack of sleep. The doctor checked him, and other than being knocked out cold, the baby seemed fine. I felt so guilty and so scared—I had really screwed up, and sheer luck had bailed me out. I knew all the time that if I'd done it once, I'd probably do it again, and maybe I wouldn't be so lucky then. All kinds of thoughts were running through my mind—'What if someone finds out what I did?' and 'What if they don't find out? What will my mother say? What if I get caught? What if I don't get some sleep soon?'—and on and on and on. I was driving myself nuts.

"It seemed it would start all over again, every time the baby woke up. Then it would be back to the doctor. Finally, one day, the doctor sits down and stares at the floor, and he makes a diagnosis. 'Can't be just regular colic,' he says. 'Maybe a milk allergy. Here's a couple sample cans of soy-bean formula. Try that. See if he gets better.'

"Thank God, it worked—no more colic, no more screaming, no more barfing. A normal baby at last! We bought soy-bean milk substitute by the case, and I was thankful to be able to sleep. I didn't realize, however, that those months of constant worry, anxiety, and stress had resulted in a lot of resentment on my part. The resentment didn't magically disappear in me as the colic had in my child. I was used to thinking of my child as sick, demanding, unresponsive, and ungrateful. I continued to think that way for almost a year. It was only when he really began to develop into a toddler and lost the cloying dependency of infancy that I began to accept him and respond to him. By the time he was two and a half, I really loved him, really enjoyed him.

"I do have one remarkable talent—the ability to see myself with 20/20 hindsight. I could admit to myself that I had experienced an episode of child abuse. I felt I could deal with that admission and do something about the problem if I could learn about child abuse. So I started reading. Between September of '74 and April of '75, I devoured Kempe's and Helfer's books; I read articles in women's magazines and health journals. One part of me was repelled and revolted by what I read and saw. That part of me thought, 'How can anyone *do* these things?' But another part of me found reassurance in those books—the reassurance to know and accept that I was not unique, that other parents had these episodes, and that there was a definite set of reasons why parents did these things.

"Throughout my reading, I kept noticing brief mentions of a group called Parents Anonymous. Mostly, the books related how a young mother, Jolly K., had reformed herself and socially redeemed herself by starting an organization for parents with child-abuse problems. It sounded interesting. Finally, in March of '75, I wrote a letter inquiring about Parents Anonymous. A few days later, Leonard Lieber called me and talked with me for a very long time. Before I even knew what I was saying, I heard myself telling him that I would try to start a group in my town.

"I can't recall just how I managed to get the group started. The group's first sponsor was a young pediatric nursing instructor at the local college. I found her by handing out our application forms at a child-abuse conference. She was enthusiastic about the group but fearful that her not being married, not being a mother, and not being over thirty would handicap her effectiveness. But I liked her and her practicality and her whole way of looking at life, so I encouraged her to give it a try. She did a beautiful job.

"I also had help from Jill, the regional coordinator for the area, who came in from Michigan to do some public speaking before our first meeting. She was tremendously effective on a radio phone-in show—the phones at the radio station weren't ringing, but the phone in my home was busy all day. We had about thirteen calls from parents during the first twenty-four hours of our group's existence. We were really gratified at the phone response—and then really disappointed when only one other parent actually made it to the first meeting. Two more parents came to the next meeting though, and even more came during the following week. Soon, our group included couples. Everyone felt pretty good at the response. By June of 1975, the group was pretty well under way.

"After two months of meetings, my sponsor took a vacation, and we met without her. I was acting as chairperson, and during one meeting I got very frustrated. For two months, it seemed, our group had done very little except tell stories— stories about what our parents had done to us as children, about what our children were doing to us, and about how we had retaliated. I was really sick of hearing the same old stuff week after week. Suddenly it occurred to me that we were locked into a pattern, and while it might not be destructive, it certainly wasn't productive.

"In the middle of one mother's story about how she had been put into a garbage can when she was a child, I blurted out, 'Listen, did it ever occur to you that maybe twenty years from now, your kid is going to be sitting in a P.A. meeting and telling everyone what a rotten bitch of a mother he happened to have, because you did mean things to him when he accidentally wet his bed?'

" 'Shut up!' she screamed at me, and started to cry.

" 'I won't shut up,' I said, 'What are you going to *do* about it? Are you just going to talk about it and cry about it?'

" 'NO!' she screamed at me.

" 'Well, are you just going to scream about it?'

" 'NO!' she screamed.

" 'Well, what are you going to *do* then?'

" 'I don't know,' she admitted.

"At that point, another group member suggested that she come up with a list of things she was going to do by the next time we met—and she did. We were on our way; we weren't playing any more. We were a real group, starting to do real work. When our sponsor returned two meetings later, she wasn't too surprised that we'd managed to move on without her guidance. We parents, however, were amazed that we'd accomplished even that step.

"It's hard to be a chairperson in a P.A. group, especially in a small community. The chairperson is the one who ends up filling most of the speaking requests, and it's hard to keep talking about your own life in public. Pretty soon, the audiences' reactions begin to get to you. I vividly remember wanting to throttle a young social-work student who said to me, 'You can't be very typical of a child abuser. I mean, you've been to college, and you talk as if you really love your kid.'

"Perhaps the most difficult problem we had with our P.A. group was financing it. No local funds were available for child-abuse treatment or prevention; so we raised the money for our basics at a charity bazaar bake sale. The $60 or so we made in one day covered our phone service and minimal office supplies.

"Some crises that occurred in other neighboring P.A. groups proved to be growing experiences for everyone. The most dramatic crisis occurred in the summer of 1976. The husband of one chairperson died from a lingering illness, and then, only a month later, the male cochairperson of another group fell dead of a heart attack. For once, everyone pulled together. Parents rallied around the families, and everyone stopped griping about how terrible their own circumstances were. Spouses who had been described as terrible suddenly became valuable; children whom parents had once wished dead were gratefully seen as being vitally alive.

"Another crisis that brought growth and reevaluation to our group occurred when a parent member had to be reported to the child protective services unit. The parent had joined the group when she was pregnant with her second child because, she said, she 'thought she'd have some problems.' She had given her first child up for adoption, and even while she was pregnant she feared she'd abuse this new baby. After she had the baby, she developed a neglect problem of unmanageable proportions. Nothing the group suggested, nothing the group said or did, could relieve it. When another member who happened to be a practical nurse confronted her about her situation, the only response was the baleful wail, 'I don't know how to take care of a house, let alone a baby!' We used the phone in the meeting room to call protective services then and there. An appointment was made for a social worker to go to the mother's house the next morning. The group member who's a nurse went with me to the mother's home the next morning and waited with her for the protective services worker to come. We took care of the baby while they talked. Other group members helped in the following weeks by demonstrating basic hygiene and nutrition to his mom. This crisis had another encouraging result: the protective services worker viewed our group as an asset and a resource to this mom. How incredibly, deliciously nice it was to be seen in a positive way by an authority figure!

"P.A. parents seem to have one universal blind spot—the protective-services worker. Most of the parents I know see the worker as either an authoritarian threat or a blundering ignoramus. We have great difficulty seeing the workers as just plain human beings, and we further compound the problem by demanding that they see us not as child abusers but as just plain human beings. In other words, we stereotype them while insisting that they view us as unique. Many abusive parents have had to deal with some sort of social worker or another throughout their lives—one who put them in a foster home, one who put them in an institution, one who put them through the court system, one who saw them through an out-of-wedlock pregnancy, one who placed a child for adoption, one who did some marriage counseling. And when a hospital treatment worker or someone from protective services steps in, it seems like the cycle is starting up all over again. It isn't too surprising, then, that many parents take a dim view of social workers. This is another problem we've had to deal with.

"And, finally, I personally have had to confront the problem that many other chairpersons have faced: 'I know how I got into P.A.; now tell me how to get out of it!' I reached a point where I simply had to quit. So I passed the group on to another chairperson and returned to the working world. My successor held a few meetings, decided that she couldn't continue, and the group died. People still call my home asking about P.A., and I talk them through their immediate crisis. Then I tell them that they have to drive fifteen miles to get to the nearest meeting. It makes me feel awful. It makes me feel guilty. I often think, 'Someday, I'm going to start the damn thing up again.' I just wish I knew when."

September 1976

During the spring of 1976, Leonard was in Chicago to attend the semiannual board meeting of the National Committee for the Prevention of Child Abuse and Neglect—a national advisory council on child abuse begun by Donna Stone. These meetings were held twice a year to provide an opportunity for people in the field to work more closely together, with the primary purpose of better educating the public about effective means of identifying, preventing, and treating child abuse. This particular meeting had a special twist to it, however.

Leonard was riding in a cab down Michigan Avenue with Brian Fraser, the Committee's Executive Director, when Brian turned to him and casually said, "By the way, the First International Congress on Child Abuse and Neglect is going to be held in Geneva, Switzerland, in September. A conference planning committee has mentioned that P.A. ought to be included. You can expect an invitation to present a paper there."

An invitation to Geneva! Further proof that P.A. was on its way.

Leonard spent the next few months working on a paper with Jean Baker, a Ph.D. psychologist from a firm called Behavior Associates, located in

Tucson, Arizona. Behavior Associates had conducted an evaluation of P.A. earlier in 1976. The paper would combine a history of P.A. and the evaluation's results, which offered conclusive evidence that P.A. worked.

Leonard went alone to Geneva—Jean couldn't go, and money was tight, so Jolly couldn't afford the trip either. He remembers:

"The butterflies had already hit me by the time I arrived to register for the conference at a hotel in downtown Geneva. Some of my colleagues from other U. S. cities recall how distant and aloof I seemed. It must have been my nerves—if I goofed here, I'd be letting everyone in P.A. down."

The conference began on the 13th; Leonard was scheduled to speak on the 15th. He learned early on that he would be giving his presentation in front of the entire group of 300 persons from over twenty countries who were attending the conference—and he came down with a respiratory infection in addition to a severe case of stage fright. The fact that each speaker was allowed only fifteen minutes didn't help either.

"Dr. Christine Cooper, a pediatrician from Newcastle-Upon-Tyne, was chairing the presentations that morning, and she made it a point to show us the warning and stop lights that she would employ to keep us from running over fifteen minutes. During the first two days, presenters had become very flustered over this—some literally giving up on their presentations because of the time constraints.

"Chris finally introduced me; I was numb, yet eager. As I spoke, I began to feel good about what I was saying, and I made it through—in fourteen minutes and fifty-five seconds. Chris had been ready to cut me off. There was silence from the group, then applause. Following a couple of questions and comments from the audience and many requests for materials, I took names and addresses of interested people from France, England, Sweden, and Norway, promising to send them information about P.A. once I returned to California."

A woman introduced herself as a reporter from the *London Times* and asked for a copy of Leonard's presentation to publish in their Sunday edition.

Not long after the conference ended, we heard from Chris Cooper. The next International Congress in London would devote more time to P.A., she promised. And would we send her some printed materials? She wanted to start a P.A. group in Newcastle.

November 1976

Our three-year demonstration grant would be ending in April of 1977, and we were worried about refunding. The P.A. national office would have to close if nothing came through. To the general population of potential P.A. members, this meant that fewer new chapters would begin and that some existing ones would die from lack of coordinated support.

Once again, we were rescued by the media. Toward the end of 1976, Leonard received a call from Norman Gorin, a producer for CBS's *60 Minutes*. Gorin wanted to do a feature on child abuse, focusing on Parents Anonymous, because he'd heard some pretty good things about the program. Several months before, he and Mike

Wallace had received a letter from a loyal viewer saying that she had been able to stop abusing her children after joining a local P.A. chapter. Before that letter arrived, Gorin and Wallace had known about child abuse, but they hadn't known about P.A.

Gorin asked to be put in touch with some P.A. parents in the Los Angeles area. Mike Wallace would interview two representative P.A. families, Jolly K., and medical and police personnel. The *60 Minutes* crew also wanted to film a P.A. meeting.

Leonard was nervous. How would P.A. look to the *60 Minutes* people? They had forty million viewers a week and tremendous credibility in the eyes of the American public. What if P.A. ended up looking weak or inconclusive? But we needed a shot in the arm from somewhere, and this just might be it.

April 1977

The show was filmed in January and February and aired in April. *TV Guide* happened to be doing a cover story on *60 Minutes* around that time, so P.A. was featured in that magazine as well.

During an interview Mike Wallace had conducted with one of the parents of a two-year-old girl, the mother had said, "When she—when she sees me get angry she looks up at me, and just has the most pathetic—most pathetic sad-looking face on a kid—you know—'Why Momma? Why me? Why are you doing this to me?'— you know—'What have I done to—to hurt you?' " That seemed to sum up everything that had ever been

said or written about child abuse, so the *60 Minutes*
program segment was called, "Mommy, Why Me?"

* * *

Wallace gave us his seal of approval and questioned why P.A. was being phased out due to lack
of funding. He also interviewed Gary, the ten-year-
old son of a P.A. family, and his mother. Gary
talked candidly about what his parents had been
like before and after joining P.A.

In early April, the Department of Health,
Education, and Welfare had granted us just enough
money to stay alive through the end of June.
Gary's words may very well have been what kept
the P.A. program alive after that.

The following is an excerpt from that *60
Minutes* segment:

Mike Wallace (to audience):...Ten-year-old
Gary...is the oldest of three youngsters in his
family. But his mother singled him out for physical
abuse because she saw in him the traits she hated
in herself—traits that her parents had despised in
her...

Gary (Gary was almost matter-of-fact about his
mother's anger.): I'd get her mad, real super-mad.
She'd just come over and whomp me one.

Wallace: What would she do?

Gary: She'd come out with her fists and, you know,
whomp me on the head or something like that....

Gary's Mother: ...I'd constantly beat that poor
child until it was unbelievable. And the school
didn't say anything, the nurse didn't say anything,
the neighbors didn't say anything. And I wanted

help, but I didn't know where to turn. And this was my way of saying help, and nobody heard me.

Wallace: Tell me something, Gary. What would you tell the kids at school, or the teachers or the neighbors, when they saw bruises on you?

Gary: I'd say that I did that while I was playing.

Wallace: You'd never tell on your mother?

Gary: Uh-uh.

Wallace: Why?

Gary: Because I was afraid she'd get put in jail....

Wallace (to audience): The police will finally get involved when the abuse gets so bad that the neighbors feel that they just have to report it.... Here's what we're talking about—a child malnourished by a parent, a child stabbed by a parent, a child burned by a parent—actual cases, investigated by the Abused Child Unit of the Los Angeles Police Department, one of a few such units in the United States. New York City does not have one. Chicago does not have one. Here, twelve full-time investigators follow up on two hundred, two hundred and fifty serious child-abuse cases every month. And they come from every part of the community—rich, poor, white, black. What the police are finding is that many youngsters who now commit violent crime had been victims of child abuse. The trouble is these investigators see just the tip of the iceberg. Only one of five serious cases of abuse and neglect gets reported. In 1975, there were about a million reports nationwide. That would mean there were five million serious episodes of child abuse in this country....

Wallace went on to interview P.A. parents and to explain how P.A. works. Then he discussed how it had been funded for the last three years and emphasized that the demonstration grant would expire at the end of that month.

Wallace:...That (grant money) has paid for the national office, the printing and distribution of P.A. information. But the most crucial function of the national office is the nationwide toll-free hot line that operates twenty four hours a day...(turning to Gary's mother) You get angry at Gary, still, today?...What do you do?

Gary's Mother: Well, we either make him sit down, or find out what he's doing, why he's doing it, instead of saying "Whap!" and that's it. We ask "Why?"

Wallace (to audience): And has P.A. made a difference to Gary? (to Gary): Do you mind your parents being strict?

Gary: Not really, because it makes me feel better...But, sometimes, when they're really super-strict, when they weren't in P.A., it made me feel kind of bad.

Wallace: What's the difference between being strict, and before they joined P.A.?

Gary: Well, before, they really beat me. But now it's changed. They'll talk to me and tell me what's right and wrong now.

Wallace: And before that, they would just hit, was that it?

Gary: Yup. That's right.

Wallace (to audience): The Department of Health, Education and Welfare earlier this month came up with enough money to keep the National Office of Parents Anonymous going through June 30th. After that, who knows?

July 1977

Not long after the *60 Minutes* segment on P.A. was aired, Joseph Califano, Secretary of Health, Education and Welfare, received a letter signed by thirteen members of the U.S. Senate asking that funding for P.A. be continued. This came in the wake of other letters from P.A. parents, professionals, and persons nationwide.

When the program was first run in April, the national office had been on the verge of closing. The WATS line serving parents in crisis had already been shut down since there was no more money left to keep it going. The *60 Minutes* show was rerun in mid-summer of 1977. By that time, extended funding had been set up for Parents Anonymous.

Natalie's story

We needed the media for the exposure they gave us, but we didn't need them to tell us that P.A. was doing a good job. We already knew that. The P.A. parents who kept us informed as to how their lives were changing gave us all the positive reinforcement we needed.

Natalie lives in a large city in eastern Kansas. She was thirty years old and a single parent with two children, ages six and four, when she joined P.A. in 1977.

"My father was an alcoholic. He would go out on binges and leave no money in the house. My mother was left with five children and no way to work and take care of us. When she went to an agency for help, three of us wound up in an orphanage, and my two younger brothers went to a foster home. I was three and a half when I went into the orphanage, and I stayed there until I was thirteen. There were between 500 to 800 kids in it, so nobody got any special attention. If I had a problem, I always felt like I had to take care of it myself; it never occurred to me to ask for help. I learned to be very independent. I saw my mother on some weekends. I never saw my father—by that time, he was a skid-row wino. I passed him in the street once, and he didn't even recognize me. My mother was always looking for the man to marry who would bring her kids home.

"I went to a foster home when I was thirteen and from there to a girls' school till I was nineteen. I always wanted kids. Somebody asked me once if I wanted a kid so I'd have somebody to love me, but that wasn't exactly it. I wanted kids so I could love somebody, so I could give them what I needed so much. I don't remember ever being hugged, except once when I was in the first grade. And growing up in an institution, I used to think that when I had kids, I would sing to them and hold them. I didn't know anything about what they'd really be like.

"I made the choice to be a single parent mostly because nobody asked me to get married. I didn't expect anybody to. I was twenty-four when I had my boy and twenty-six when I had the girl.

"My problems started when my son was two weeks old. He had a birth defect, and he cried all the time. I had moved in with my mother when her last husband died, and she was very demanding. I said nothing; I just complied. When my son wouldn't stop crying in the middle of the night, I was upset because I knew he'd wake my mother. And I thought *I* was a bad mother when I couldn't get him to stop crying. I swore at him and called him names. I never physically abused him—just verbally. At that time, I thought the whole problem was that I was living with my mother and I hated her. So I did a lot of reading on how to discipline. I realized I had a bad temper and thought that if I could just learn to control it everything would be okay.

"I struggled along, and when my daughter was born, I began to see a lot of her in me; and I didn't like her when she acted like me. By then, the verbal abuse was getting very bad. I would scream and yell at her, 'I hate your guts; I wish you were dead'—the worst things that came into my mind. And I called my son stupid. Even when I didn't say it—I implied it. My attitude came across as rejection. It got so they cringed every time I opened my mouth. I rarely spanked them, and when I did, it was just with my hand. But I was getting more and more scared of my feelings. I was scared that one of these times I would work myself into a fit and hurt them."

Finally, Natalie realized that she'd better get some help. When she called the Mental Health Association, they referred her to Parents Anonymous.

"I had heard a little about P.A., and I went into that first meeting hoping I would get some

242

help in controlling my temper. But inside I felt as if I were sick and different, as if I really needed a shrink. When I got in there, I found people who were willing to be so honest that I didn't feel alone with my problem any more. I was such a baby emotionally when I first got into the group; I wanted a mother figure, so I latched onto the cosponsor. I was jealous of other members who seemed to be getting her attention. I was confronted by several members about this, and the sponsor was very supportive. When I got that straightened out, I could work on my parenting problem. Just feeling that support around me, I began to notice changes. The most important single thing I learned in P.A. was be realistic about my anger. I saw that anger is neither good nor bad; it's what you do with it. It's *okay* to say to my kids, 'I'm angry with you.' I talked to my kids then about the changes I was trying to make, and I still do.

"I feel good about my relationship with my kids now. I've gotten to a point where I really like my daughter. And now that I'm able to deal with my mother, to speak up to her, I can like her, too. For the first time this past summer I was able to say 'I like you' to her and mean it. My problem hasn't completely disappeared; it's something that must always be faced and dealt with. What I particularly have to be aware of is how my unspoken attitude comes through to my kids. My body language may be implying, 'You're stupid,' even if I'm not saying it; and that's the same as saying it because that's the message they're getting.

"I never had any friends before I got into P.A., and now I have friends in the group and on the outside. I know I can call them and get

243

support. I'll probably always be involved with P.A., at least until my kids are grown and out of the house."

By this time, we were hearing from more and more men who were discovering that Parents Anonymous had something to offer them, too.

Mark and Shelley's story (as told by Mark)

"My younger son Danny was born on March 27, 1973. Within a couple of hours of his birth, he managed to twist out of his receiving blanket. This prompted the nurse to ask Shelley what medication she had taken during the course of her pregnancy. Her answer was simple: other than prenatal vitamins, she had taken no medication at all.

"This was only the beginning. For the next two years, Danny averaged six hours of sleep a night with a twenty-minute nap during the day. The rest of the time he usually spent screaming as hard and as loud as he could. As he grew older, he also became destructive—to himself as well as to others. At no time would he accept or give any type of affection. Our repeated pleas for help to his pediatrician were answered with, 'It's only a stage; he'll grow out of it.'

"In the meantime, the situation at home was going from bad to worse. Shelley was almost always yelling and crying; we were almost always at odds with our foster daughter. She spent most of her time hiding in her room or running to one of her friends. Looking back at the situation, I can't say that I blame her—I probably would have done the same thing if I could have. It was becoming too much for us to handle, and we were in the midst of a severe emotional crisis. On more occasions than I care to remember, I came close to causing severe physical damage to our son.

"In early February of 1975, Shelley came across an advertisement in the *Pennysaver News* that read, 'Having trouble with a child? Call ——.' And she did. Shelley explained our problem over the telephone and was invited to attend the next Parents Anonymous meeting in our area. After going to a couple of meetings, she asked me to accompany her. My attendance at that next meeting was my first encounter with P.A. You have no idea how happy I am that it wasn't my last.

"What first struck me about the meeting was the hurt and the pain that surfaced there. This was definitely no coffee klatch; the raw emotion was handled with dignity and without guilt. These people really *cared*.

"In the ensuing weeks, I found in P.A. the help and support I needed to keep me from harming my son. Help between meetings was never farther than a phone call away. P.A. showed me how to direct my stress and pain away from my son. As a result, I was better able to communicate with my wife. This probably saved our marriage. Shelley and I were provided with the support we needed while we continued to look for a long-term solution to our problem."

Part of Mark and Shelley's long-term solution for their son included getting him on the Feingold diet. This diet is one of the first that has been specially developed for hyperkinetic children. Its author is Benjamin Feingold, M.D., of the Kaiser Medical Center in Oakland, California.

Mark and Shelley were P.A. members for three years in Deer Park, New York, a suburban community of central Long Island. From there they moved to Georgia, where Mark entered Atlanta University as a graduate student, and the couple continued their involvement with P.A.

"When we moved from New York, we brought along the contact number for P.A. of Georgia, and three days after we arrived there, we called them. That's the unique thing about P.A. You can go anywhere in the U. S. and not feel alone. We got into a chapter there that had been in existence for only three weeks. Eventually, when that one got too big, we started a second one. I cochair one group, and Shelley is acting as temporary sponsor of another.

"New problems keep coming up in our lives, and going to P. A. helps us to work them out in a constructive way instead of taking them out on each other and the children."

* * *

We also heard from some men who didn't know about P.A. until it was too late.

In late 1974, a man named Jim began a correspondence with us while he was an inmate at Deuel Vocational Institution in Tracy, California. He had heard of P.A. while undergoing group therapy in the California Medical Facility.

I am deeply and sincerely interested in becoming involved with your effort. I would like to learn what your service consists of. I have experienced the agony of being an abused child, as well as the agony of being an abusive parent.

Physical abuse is a form of communication just as

246

surely as verbal conversation. My parents began communicating several things to me very early in life that became a more or less permanent part of my personality and strongly influenced my role as a parent.

I learned at a very early age what types of behavior in children were good and what types were bad. I used to be beaten severely on the buttocks with a board for very minor occurrences—some of which I had no control over, such as wetting the bed, and some that any small child would have difficulty avoiding. When viewed in the bright light of repeated painful beatings, these minor occurrences tend to take on an awful importance, an importance that cannot be easily altered in later life, even when a mature intellect insists that the importance is unrealistic. So some trivial types of behavior became "bad" to me.

I also learned that harsh physical punishment was the acceptable way to correct a child for doing those "bad" things. You don't usually question something you've never been without, so I accepted abusive treatment as a natural part of life because I knew of no other kind of existence. My parents had few friends, affording me little opportunity to compare them with anyone else. There were the only adults I had regular contact with. So beatings seemed natural and acceptable in child rearing.

Probably the most important lesson my childhood taught me was that beating a child was a way to handle personal frustrations. Even a small child notices that the beatings are more frequent and more severe when the abusive parent is frustrated or angry about something.

With that background in family relationships, I married at nineteen and became a father. I naturally imposed my concept of good and bad and my doctrine of harsh punishment on my family. For the first few years, I was considered a too-stern father rather than an

*abusive one. Later, as my emotional stability deterio-
rated, and the pressures mounted, I progressed to more
severe abusive treatment. This abuse was directed toward
our fifth child, who died of injuries at ten weeks of age.
This death resulted in my conviction for second-degree
murder.*

*I had sought help through the —— Department of
Mental Health before my daughter's death, but I tried to
get it without letting the psychologist or the members of
that group (all of whom were mothers) know I was in
the habit of beating a helpless infant.*

*About five hours before her death, I did go to my
psychologist and tell him the whole story and asked to
be locked up, as I was afraid I might cause her serious
harm. But he didn't take me seriously. He sent me home,
assuring me everything would be all right.*

*Finally in the California Medical Facility, I was in
psychotherapy for several years in a group composed of
men convicted of armed robbery, child molesting, rape,
assault with a deadly weapon, and three of us who were
convicted of taking the lives of small children. At that
time, the stigma problem did not concern me, as I was
severely depressed and suicidal. It was here that I gained
some understanding of the kinds of emotional dynamics
that lead parents to become abusive toward their
children.*

*It really is important to overcome the prejudice.
That prejudice is what kept me from getting help before
it was too late. If there is any way that I might
contribute to your effort, please allow me the privilege of
doing so.*

Over the next few months, Jim studied P.A.
literature, wrote regularly to the National Office,
and contributed an article and $10 to *Frontiers*. He
had been in prison a total of six years when he

was paroled in 1975. He immediately joined a Parents Anonymous group in Modesto, California. Several months later he got word that his ex-wife, the mother of his other four children, was remarried to a man who was seriously abusing the children and her; this man had even ordered her to get rid of them and put them in foster homes. Jim drove back to Indiana and brought his four sons back home to live with him in California. By then they were twelve, thirteen, fourteen, and fifteen.

In 1977, Jim became the chairperson of the Modesto P.A. group and began doing volunteer speaking engagements throughout his community. He wrote us:

Our group in Modesto is growing, both in size and—more importantly—in productivity. A great deal of trust has developed between some members, allowing for a deeper level of sharing. Much of the superficial babbling has been replaced by serious, meaningful discussion of feelings. It's really neat to watch the personal growth of these people who have become my friends and also experience some growth of my own in the process.

Jim and his four teenage boys now manage a poultry ranch in Ripon, California. At this writing, he has been asked to chair another group that is starting up in Manteca. A police officer is volunteering to sponsor it.

Another man, William J., braved the stigma of his crime and openly sought all the information he could on child abuse, even though there was no P.A. group in the maximum-security prison where he was incarcerated. He had served nine years of his sentence when he wrote the first of several letters to me in November of 1976:

Dear Patte,

I am an inmate at Patuxent Institution, a maximum-security prison for "Defective Delinquents" in Maryland. I received a ten-year sentence for manslaughter in 1968 in the child-abuse death of my three-month-old infant son. Earlier this year, I found out about P.A. in a newspaper article and promptly got in touch with Lee, the Maryland State Coordinator for P.A. I'd like a subscription to Frontiers. *I have a copy of the P.A. Chairperson Sponsor Manual, where I got your name. I have about twenty books now on child abuse/neglect, and I intend to start a new P.A. group, with Lee's help, when I get out. I'm making P.A. my life's work, and I want all the information and involvement I can get.*

In his second letter, William J. enclosed $2 to help keep *Frontiers* going. In December, he sent me a twenty-eight-page typed treatise entitled, "Parents Anonymous: An Alternative to Incarceration for Abusive Parents." When William J. got out of prison shortly thereafter, he began leading an active P.A. group in Maryland.

For a long while, the Parents Anonymous chapter at C.I.W. was the only prison chapter in the United States. However, in the years following the H.E.W. grant in 1974, Parents Anonymous prison chapters began functioning in Colorado, Delaware, Kansas, Indiana, Iowa, Maryland, and Washington. With a few exceptions, these are mainly in women's prisons because the lives of men in prisons are still in danger if they admit to other inmates that they are in for child abuse.

Two of these exceptions are the Washington State Correctional Institution in Shelton and the

Federal prison on McNeil Island in Washington State. The P.A. programs there are being formed to run as a whole-family therapeutic and preventive tool for the inmates and their visiting spouses, whether or not they are in on child-abuse-related charges. These couples will be able to learn better parenting and better interpersonal communication while their kids are waiting for them to come home.

November 1977

Parents Anonymous had long ago passed the point of being a "kitchen table" operation. We had gone official—with government funding, a national WATS line, a bonafide project officer, and a genuine paid staff. Our emergence as a national organization meant that we could no longer simply supervise and evaluate ourselves.

Between May of 1975 and April of 1976, an outside evaluation was conducted by Behavior Associates, a research firm located in Tucson, Arizona.[2] In reading their report, we had been happy to find that these "outsiders" were as confident of P.A.'s effectiveness as we "insiders" were. In our own working relationships with P.A. parents and in our travels throughout the country, we were convinced that P.A. was a success; Behavior Associates thought so, too.

During late 1977, Berkeley Planning Associates completed a forty-month evaluation of eleven federally funded three-year child-abuse and neglect service projects. The Parents Anonymous treatment modality, which was used by a number of the service projects, wasn't singled out as a focus of this research, but several results of the study showed some significant findings with regard to the P.A. model.

In their section on "treating abusive and neglectful parents," for example, the researchers noted that service recipients who used Parents Anonymous and similar forms of lay therapy were more likely to improve by the end of treatment than those who received other forms of service. In addition, the services that proved to be the most effective tended to be those that were the least expensive. The Parents Anonymous program was found to be the most cost-effective treatment available.

One particularly important conclusion stated that child-abuse and neglect services are maximized if "the program uses more highly trained, experienced workers as case managers but stresses the use of lay services and self-help services (such as Parents Anonymous) as part of its treatment offerings, as well as twenty-four-hour availability."

Once again, the "gut feeling" Leonard had had while talking to Jolly back in 1970—almost eight years earlier—had been reinforced.

December 1977

Between April of 1975 and May of 1976, Jolly helped launch and support P.A. chapters in Georgia, Connecticut, Florida, Pennsylvania, Wisconsin, Minnesota, North Dakota, Tennessee, Illinois, and Alaska. Having spent many years in the public eye, she gradually wound down her whirlwind tours and left more of the presentations to a growing number of able P.A. parents across the nation who were equally capable of representing the program. For them, Jolly had cut a path; it was no longer a phenomenon for a parent to present his or her personal story of the fear, anger, and shame of child abuse. By 1977, P.A. had become a respectable name to many people, and it was an honor instead of a burden to carry its banner.

In the fall of 1977, Jolly began a well-deserved respite from her role of "professional ex-child abuser" and took on the job of public-education consultant. In that capacity, she now travels to wherever her presence is requested by P.A. people, professionals, media representatives, and legislative hearing committees. She also travels to those areas that need a "shot in the arm"—new public awareness work through media and meetings—which she is so good at delivering.

* * *

Jolly's long-ago meeting with Leonard had had results that nobody could have foreseen. By the end of 1975, the number of P.A. chapters in this country and Canada had jumped to 250. At the end of 1976, there were 450 chapters—and the number of reported child-abuse cases per year had climbed to one million.

By the mid-seventies, every state had a mandatory child-abuse reporting law. These statutes require many professionals—such as doctors, teachers, nurses—to report suspected cases of abuse and neglect. The existence of such statutes, combined with stepped-up media attention to the problems of abuse, has served to increase general public awareness. In all states, persons who report abuse cases in good faith are protected from civil and criminal actions based on these reports. (By 1977, forty states had enacted penalties for the failure to make *required* reports, and all but three states have passed some form of legislation that authorizes courts to terminate the parent-child relationships under certain circumstances.)

For families afflicted with abuse problems, reporting laws have had a positive effect for several reasons; most important, reports are now made far earlier than before, and help is often made available before it's too late. In addition, the need for increased services has made the foster-home alternative less attractive simply because adequate foster families haven't been recruited fast enough. This has given rise to a new emphasis on providing services to abused families *in their own homes.* Instead of separating families at the first sign of a problem, there's a growing tendency to want to keep them together whenever possible.

P.A. is on the forefront of this movement. Largely because of its volunteers—who contribute approximately 500,000 hours of their time each year—more families are able to stay intact and work together on their problems. And both parents and children are benefiting. Parents are being allowed to keep their children, and children are getting what they really want—their own beds in familiar surroundings and more effective parents.

Carol Wollin's story

Carol Wollin is the divorced mother of two teenage children, a teacher at Long Beach City College, a licensed marriage and family counselor, and a county consultant on child abuse and parenting in the San Fernando Valley. She has been a P.A. sponsor since 1975.

"In 1972 I had gone back to school to get my Master's degree and was enrolled in a community psychology program at the college. I was interested in doing therapy with families in the community. I wanted to get away from the strict model of one-to-one, middle-class verbal kinds of therapy. At that time I had no connection with child abuse at all and knew nothing about it; I was simply working with families that had problem kids.

"I worked for two years at the Regional Center with developmentally disabled kids. I was hired as a Behavioral Interventionist, which meant that I would go into the homes and see the kids and talk with the parents. In many cases, I became like one of the family—a visiting psychologist in a very relaxed setting. It was unorthodox, and I enjoyed it. One day my supervising professor said, 'There's a family I want you to get into right away.' When I asked why, he answered, 'This lady says she's going to kill her kid.' 'Well,' I said, 'what do you do about that?' He said, 'I really don't know, but I think you'd better get in there very quickly.' I said, 'I'm really afraid. I don't know what to do about it.' 'Neither do I,' he said, 'but get in there and just do what you always do—find out what's going on.'

"I was really horrified. For reasons stemming from my own background, I had a need to try always to be a 'super mother,' involved in every aspect of bringing up my kids. I had been a Lamaze teacher; I had breast-fed my kids; I had been a director of the nursery school. I was always involved in what I saw as healthy parenting, so I had no idea what this family would look like or

255

what was going to happen. So I drove up in this residential section of Oxnard, and my anxiety was allayed a little bit because I figured, 'Well, this looks like a regular house, a regular block—it must be all right.' When I knocked on the door, I really expected to see somebody with horns. I expected that kind of stereotype. Then the door opened, and there was this perfectly charming twenty-three-year-old mother. The house was kind of chaotic, and she was walking over things; she had one little boy with Down's syndrome and another very precocious little three year old who was driving her crazy, and this was the one she thought she wanted to kill.

"During that next year, I had a unique opportunity to see their interactions because I was in the home every week. It wasn't like somebody coming to a clinic and saying, 'I have this problem.' I was right there, and I could see exactly what her little three year old was doing to make her angry. I found that a lot of the techniques I had been taught about how to control tantrums and other forms of behavior were helping her a lot. There were other elements there, like unreasonably high expectations of children's behavior, poor anger control, and a marriage in which she was extremely passive and her husband was very rigid and authoritarian. As I continued to do family therapy and marriage counseling with them, I noticed that my caring for her and kind of mothering her was washing over her and was also starting to wash over her child. She became much more tolerant and much more loving to her child because she was getting a lot from me.

"When it was time for me to do my Master's thesis, I started to look at some of the literature on child abuse. Much of it was anecdotal, nonexperimental, after-the-fact case histories. Very few people had had a chance to be involved with people who had this kind of problem. As I was starting home from Oxnard one day, I thought, 'Gee, the reason Mrs. S. is involved in this kind of thing is because she really doesn't know very much about parenting.' From this simplistic statement, I devised a Master's thesis around the fact that people with a child-abuse problem don't really know how to be parents in a mature way. Then I thought, 'I need a population. I need people to work with.' I called every contact I could find, but they all said, 'No, absolutely not. We will not have these people used as guinea pigs. They are very secret and private. We just won't allow you to do this.' I was getting more and more upset because I had a deadline and I couldn't get close to the people—that was during the summer of 1974. Finally, a friend of mine, a social worker, said, 'You know, my office mate at Olive View Hospital is thinking of starting a child-abuse program. Why don't you get in touch with her?' So I called her, and we went out for lunch. That afternoon, I was given the mandate to start a therapy program for child abuse at the hospital. I had worked with only one case, but this lady was saying, 'Well, gee, you did very well with that one case. Why not start a whole therapy program here? We'll call it a home intervention program for child abuse.'

"Around that time, a lot of people were getting interested in the whole area of child abuse. We went to conventions together and we learned together. We got several people from the college involved, along with several doctors from the hospital, and we formed a team. We set up a group-therapy program and then a home intervention program where you work closely with the family on the home base.

"Not long after we began the program, Tom and Vicki were referred to me. They had been physically abusing their two children. My approach toward them was, 'The reason this is going on is that you never learned alternatives to physical punishment. You've never learned how to control your anger. So let me teach you some things that I think really help.' I acted as a sort of a coach, training them in certain methods that I had been trained in. Finally, Tom said to me, 'What we need is a place for parents to go where we can *learn how to be parents.*' He wanted to start a parents' school. I contacted some people, and we made up a brochure, but it never got off the ground. Meanwhile, Tom had been going to a Parents Anonymous group in Hollywood, and it had folded. So he said, 'What we need is to start P.A. in San Fernando Valley. Since you've been such a help to us, would you be my sponsor?' I had never been involved with P.A., but by then I had heard of it, and I was interested in people helping themselves. So I decided it was something that I would like to do, even though I didn't know too much about it.

"In early 1977, an opportunity for me to begin parenting classes opened up in Long Beach at Cedar House—a big, old, renovated house used to provide on-site help of various kinds for families in stress. The director, Clara Lowry, was looking for somebody who was a parent, who knew about parent education, and who was sensitive to abuse problems. So I stumbled in and said, 'Hey, I can do this.' Working with Clara and with

258

Marilyn Johnson, the crisis counselor there, we got the classes underway in May of 1977. The classes were designed to meet the needs of a variety of parents—those who were experiencing a high level of stress and ran a high risk of abusing their children, those who had already engaged in abusive behavior, some court-referred parents, and some who simply wanted to acquire better parenting skills. This mixture worked out very well as long as the class leader was sensitive to the special needs of high-stress parents.

"I was, of course, playing it by ear, because it was a whole new thing. I began by conducting it like a regular class, but the feedback I got from the parents was that this was not what they wanted. They needed for me to start out where they were; they needed to be heard. The class model became an outgrowth of the P.A. format, then, beginning with an exchange of members' phone numbers and the encouragement of group supportiveness.

"The parents who come into this kind of parenting class are usually overwhelmed with the responsibility of parenting. They have a lot of personal frustrations, and they really need some answers quickly, so I start out from where they are and from what they tell me. They perceive the problem as 'The kid is doing something to me, and I can't handle what the kid is doing; and I can handle my feelings and reactions to the kid.' My feeling is that if I can give them something to do immediately, it might help the child feel that the parent is more in control, and the parent will feel that he or she can handle things better if there are techniques to use right away. So what I try to do in the first three or four sessions of the class is to *simplify* parenting, although I know it's not simple

259

at all. I try to impart to them that it's something they can be *trained* to do, that they can *learn* to do, and that things can change. I also make a guarantee that in five or six weeks, they'll see definite changes in terms of things that have been bothering them at home.

"The first couple of weeks, we talk about techniques other than punishment that can be used to decelerate tantrums—for example, you can send the child to his or her room, you can remove privileges, you can use rewards for reinforcement. Typically, what we find is that many of these parents don't know how to be positive or to praise or to reward the child in any way. So I teach them how to do that. When kids are reinforced and rewarded, they're more apt to act positively, instead of using negative, attention-getting behavior.

"Then we work on child-development information—At what age do you toilet train the child? What about sleeping behavior or eating patterns at certain ages? Is it reasonable to ask a child to clean his or her room and do chores at the age of two? Many of the parents have very high, unreasonable, unrealistic expectations of what their children should be doing, so we teach them what they can expect their kids to be doing at certain ages. We stress that parents can live through their children's stages because they don't last forever.

"When I was first developing this class, I didn't quite know where to go with it. I had started out by giving the parents child-development information, but I didn't know at what point I should introduce communication skills and empathetic listening and active listening.

Ultimately, my goal was to create nurturing relationships and respect between the children and their parents. I didn't want to *stop* at giving the parents control techniques, but I thought that would be a good place to start. As far as I knew, I was pretty much pioneering with this parenting format, which was adapted to the needs of parents with abuse problems; so I was always open to learning different kinds of techniques or approaches. It was at this point that Margot Fritz, P.A.'s training director, held the first training lab where she used sensitivity exercises and investigation into people's past parenting to break down barriers between professionals and parents. About twenty parents and fifteen professionals were thrown together, and in one exercise, we had to talk about how we had felt when we were children. We had to pick a certain age and talk about it. My mother died when I was ten, so I talked about how it had felt to be a child who had just lost her mother. I got in touch with pain that I wasn't even aware I felt.

"It was there, at the lab, that I realized how important the issue of mothering has always been to me. Having lost my own mother, I have always wanted desperately to be a good mother, to make up for my own lack of mothering. I'm sure that the reason I stayed in the area of child abuse was because it was addressing questions like 'What happens when mothering goes wrong?' and 'What are the actual aspects of being a mother?' When I went back to my parenting class, there was a TV movie called *Mary Jane Harper Cried Last Night* that was scheduled to be shown, and I asked my class to watch it. One thing I remember about that movie was that little girl just looking up at her mommy with all that pain and confusion in her eyes. But when the parents reported back, they hadn't seen that little girl at all; they had seen only the parent, *her* problems, and how hard life was for *her*. Nobody brought up the issue of the little girl and the pain that *she* was feeling. So I realized, 'I'm trying to teach communication skills and empathy skills to people who aren't there yet. They can't experience that empathy. I can teach it, but I don't know if they'll really understand it.' That's when I decided to incorporate the sensitivity exercise I had learned at Margot's lab into my class. I had each parent pick a time when he or she had been young and talk about how it had felt to live in that particular family and how it had felt to be abused. Once they were able to get in touch with the helpless child in them, they experienced the same feeling we did in the training lab: 'We don't want this for our kids; we were terribly hurt, and we're going to do everything we can to help to change it.' This was a real breakthrough. After that, I started Thomas Gordon's Parent Effectiveness Training (P.E.T.), which is aimed at developing empathy, communication skills, active listening, respect for the child's feelings, and recognition of your own needs as opposed to the child's. Whenever I use this, we really get into role playing. We experience how it feels to be a child being yelled at for wetting his or her pants, for example. We have the parent be the child—and boy, that's effective. The parent starts to sweat and really feel how it is to be a child again, being emotionally abused and yelled at and powerless.

"Following the P.E.T., we usually spend a whole session on anger control. We talk about things you can do before a situation reaches an explosive level—such as hitting a pillow or walking out or calling a friend. Parents have a lot of trouble accepting children's anger; most of them can't tolerate it. I tell them that they have a right to their own feelings of anger and that their children do, too. We also talk about sex education because many parents who were sexually abused as children are confused about sexual guidelines. I use the book *Your Child's Self-Esteem*,[3] which talks about how to build up self-esteem in a child and how to raise your own self-esteem. It also talks about what love is and how it's defined. For example, you may feel you love your child, but if you're not communicating your love or spending time with your child, the child isn't feeling that love.

"As it's taught today, the class is twelve weeks long and meets once a week, for three hours. Parents come with their children, and the children are part of a child-care program. We hear the children's side, too. At the end of the twelve weeks, the feedback I usually get from the parents is that the class really has fit their needs. Many of them were afraid to go to regular parenting classes because they felt that these classes were geared at an intellectual level and they wouldn't be dealing with feelings; they felt that they wouldn't be able to express themselves. There's also a lot of fear of classes in general. Many of the parents have a lot of anxieties about going to classes, doing homework, and getting a grade. I start out by telling them that *nobody can fail*. I stress that it's really an interchange and a sharing. I let them know that parents have a tremendous amount to offer *each other*. Even if they feel they've botched up their own situation, there's a great deal they can give to somebody else.

"Because they've seen positive changes and the class has proved nonthreatening, and because they've experienced success, most parents become very excited about the class and want to continue it. At this point, we don't offer advanced classes, so many of them go on to other parent education classes or to therapy groups, or they get in touch with other community resources that they might not have approached if they hadn't experienced a safe class. Many of them who never had therapy at all come in and learn about the group process. They become more open to getting some therapy if that's needed.

"I found out something else that's been kind of a bonus. In doing the role-playing exercises where parents delve into their own childhoods, I always have a couple of people around who had really happy childhoods. These people are able to share with the class how it felt to be really taken care of, to be appreciated, to be understood, and to be really cherished. Most of the parents in the program have no idea what a truly nurturing family can be like. Marilyn is one parent I like to have tell her story. She was the last of nine children, and her family lived on a farm in Minnesota. From the time she was born, she always knew that she was adored, that she was wanted, that she was wonderful and special. She remembers being held and touched and cherished constantly by ten or eleven different people. She would walk into a room, and everybody would turn around and say, 'Now there she is. Isn't she sweet? Isn't she wonderful?' And she would be picked up and held by everybody in the family.

Whenever she had something to tell, somebody would sit there and listen and talk to her. She was always being hugged, and she remembers how good it felt, how wonderful. She remembers sitting on her father's lap in front of the fireplace, nuzzling into this gentle man's shoulder, feeling totally safe and protected while he talked to her; she can still smell his cologne and his pipe. She can't recall anything unpleasant or discordant about her childhood. And to this day, whenever she goes home to her family, it's the same thing. They say, 'There she is,' and they all hug her and hold her and listen to her and think she's wonderful. Marilyn is the crisis counselor at Cedar House, and she has so much to give other people. When parents come into the House, she takes care of them and nurtures them. The fountain of giving and nurturing that was developed in her when she was young is still with her.

"Harriet, my teaching assistant in the Valley, also came from a large, cherishing family. Whenever the children wanted something, there was a doting grandmother or aunt or uncle who would spend time with them. Both women say that their families made them very strong and that they did realize how special their childhoods were. It's nice for other parents—and for me, too—to hear that there *can* be families where this happens."

* * *

The success of the parenting classes held at Cedar House generated countywide interest, and eventually an interagency committee was formed to develop a preventative team approach. Today, this committee consists of about thirty people—parent educators, mental-health workers, health workers, hospital workers, and Department of Social Services workers, among others. It also functions as a referral source and has generated tremendous interest in training other people to teach these classes.

A parenting class similar to the one held in Cedar House has been set up in the San Fernando Valley, and Harriet Kleinman has begun a new class that brings parents in right after they've had their first baby. This latter class has several aims: to instill confidence in parents about their own abilities to parent; to give them practical information on baby care; and to establish mother-infant bonding.

Carol Wollin is now a county consultant on child abuse and parenting; many of the parents from the Valley P.A. group are in her parenting class. As of this writing, there are other parent-education groups that have developed out of P.A. groups and several more that are beginning throughout the country.

March 1978

Our travels on behalf of Parents Anonymous have been a combination of hard work and sheer enjoyment. Some of our best times have involved long meetings with P.A. members, sponsors, and community-support people in their home cities and towns. Many of these have evolved from casual acquaintances into close friends.

The P.A. program in Atlanta was slow in getting off the ground for a number of reasons, but its potential was kept alive by the encouragement of a state child-abuse service specialist, a reporter from an Atlanta daily, and a few other concerned individuals.

Don Clapp, the director of a children's services planning agency in that city, decided to use his resources to establish P.A. once and for all. He had a busy enough schedule already—he also serves as the priest of a small Episcopal church in Calhoun, sixty miles north—but that didn't seem to bother him. In the spring of 1978, when Leonard was in Atlanta on other business, Don asked him to deliver a sermon, and Leonard was happy to accept the invitation.

Following the service, Don and Leonard went "down the street" to conduct a "secular" informational program on P.A. in the First Baptist Church of Calhoun. Eighty persons from a five-town area attended, including Judy Carter, the President's daughter-in-law and a resident of Calhoun.

April 1978

Perhaps the hardest thing to deal with in all of our P.A. travels was the knowledge that we would probably never again have the opportunity to see many of the new friends we made. Leonard has especially fond memories of some P.A. parents he met with and parted from too soon:

"I remember being dropped at the airport in Chicago sometime during 1976 by a woman who was involved in one of our chapters in a nearby suburb. On the way, she told me about her struggle to raise a severely handicapped son by herself. I haven't seen her in two years.

"In 1974, I attended a planning meeting of a

P.A. state organization in the Midwest. A parent at the meeting invited me to supper, and I accepted. We shared a modest spaghetti dinner—she, her three-year-old daughter, and I. While we were putting dinner together, her ex-husband's parents came over. They apologized for the fact that their son had virtually abandoned their grandchild and her, and they clumsily pushed a twenty-dollar bill into her hand.

"Early in 1978, a young P.A. father was responsible for picking me up at the local airport and taking me to my evening's lodging. A state P.A. organizational meeting was planned. I asked him to spend a block of free time at the hotel with me while other P.A. people from out-of-town were arriving.

"As we got to talking, I learned how important this forklift driver from Milwaukee had become in reaching out to other needy parents and educating the community about child abuse and P.A. When he returned the next day to take me back to the airport, his wife and kids were with him in the van, along with another P.A. member and child. He dropped them off and then made a point of proudly showing me the house they had recently bought in a modest neighborhood. This formerly abused military 'brat,' a guy who had been in the habit of messing over his own kids a short while back, holds down a decent job, pays his taxes, and is loved by his family. He uses his spare time to talk others into caring, and he chairs a P.A. group. He and others like him are what P.A. is all about."

June 1978

In late May, Jolly was scheduled to give several presentations in New Mexico. She knew that Sean, the boy she'd given up for adoption seventeen years before, was living in a town near where she would be speaking. Jolly hadn't seen Sean since he was ten months old. She decided to call the adoptive mother and ask for permission to see him. His adoptive mother agreed to the meeting. Jolly recalls the reunion:

"It was a very warm, positive, very friendly meeting. I hadn't wanted to have any contact with him until he was older. I didn't want to interfere or confuse him. But his parents are wonderful. They've told him about me, and he even saw me on *60 Minutes*. He asked me a million questions. He wanted to know what Faith and Roz were like. We talked and talked. He's turned out so well. They all went to hear me give my presentation. They've done such a beautiful job of raising him, just as I knew they would. I think we'll be able to see each other from time to time now as friends."

August 1978

By this time, Parents Anonymous had firmly established itself in the United States, Canada, and overseas. We had spent a good deal of time since 1975 traveling to various cities and towns within the continental U.S., giving presentations to P.A. groups and media people, congratulating the strong groups, and encouraging the ones who were having problems or just beginning. The Second International Congress on Child Abuse and

Neglect, which was scheduled for September 12-15, 1978, at the Imperial College of Science and Technology in South Kensington, London, provided us with a good excuse to see how our friends in England were doing.

The largest concentration of P.A. activity outside the U.S. is in Great Britain, where over fifty groups have begun to develop services to families in stress along the lines of our program. We wanted to meet with some of them to get a better idea of how we could help in their efforts to duplicate P.A. within the framework of their culture. We were also interested in learning, from a broader perspective, what was going on throughout Great Britain in the area of child-abuse services. We sensed that there were operative programs that we should know about. We were also curious to see how communities responded, if at all, to the issue of children and parents in stress.

The Second International Congress was being held under the auspices of the International Center for the Prevention of Child Abuse and Neglect, of which Henry Kempe was the moving spirit. Dr. Alfred White Franklin would act as chairman. He and Dr. Christine Cooper (whom Leonard had met in Geneva) are two pediatricians who are highly regarded as leading pioneering authorities on the subject of child abuse in England. Chris Cooper had, by this time, become an active P.A. supporter in Newcastle-upon-Tyne. Princess Margaret would be the conference's patron.

Leonard would deliver a paper on "Self-Help and Government, A Common-Sense Partnership in Child-Abuse Services." He would also present Margot Fritz and Jean Baker's paper on "The P.A. Service Provider/Service Recipient," since Margot was scheduled for surgery and would be unable to accompany us to London.

We planned on spending a few days prior to the conference doing some sightseeing. From there, we would be going to Lichfield, where Leonard would once again present both papers during a one-day workshop on violence. We would stay with Chris and Hazel Baker, who had organized the conference. Dr. Gary Faber, a P.A. board member, had introduced the Bakers to Leonard when they were passing through Los Angeles the year before.

After that, we would visit Maria Dobrowska, a P.A. coordinator in Nottingham. Maria, along with another professional who was also a troubled parent, had gotten P.A. under way there. We would spend an evening with P.A. people there, then drive to Edinburgh for a few days' stay, and then fly home again.

Michael, Leonard, and I would be gone for several weeks, and we knew that no small part of our task would involve trying to keep from abusing each other when the strain of constantly traveling together became unbearable.

London

Friday, September 8

September is considered off-season as far as tourism goes, but the crowds pouring through the Tower of London gave no indication of that. The longest line of all waited to see the Crown Jewels, guarded and displayed in the Wakefield Tower—a glittering fairytale splendor of crowns, orbs, sceptres, and swords.

We purchased several postcards of the Crown Jewels; one of the "bloody" tower, *sans* blood; and one picture of a very clean-looking block and axe, which was last used for the execution of Simon, Lord Lovat, in 1747.

Following a five-minute taxi ride over Tower Bridge across the Thames, we arrived at the London Dungeon on Tooley Street. We paid our admission and passed through tall black doors into the dank, stinking, cavernous interior to find that we were the only ones there. At my feet lay the wax body of a woman, bleeding at the mouth. A very real bug crawled around her nostrils and disappeared into her hairline. We moved from one shadowy alcove to the next; each contained horrifyingly realistic figures depicting Britain's barbaric past—the tortures, the ordeals, the punishments, the bloody battles. The recreated scenes were illuminated with a greenish light; the plaques explaining them were dimly lit by medieval torches on damp walls.

Legend has it that St. George, Patron Saint of England, rescued the King's daughter from the dragon that was trying to eat her and slew the dragon in the marketplace for all to see. The original legend tells of St. George as a Christian in a pagan country being tortured for his beliefs. These tortures included being tied to a cross and having his skin scraped with iron combs, in addition to being chained and nailed to a table, poisoned, immersed in a caldron of molten lead, and sawn in half. Finally, after being dragged through the city, he was beheaded.

In the London Dungeon, the execution of Simon, Lord Lovat, was not dismissed with a pristine picture of a chopping block and axe.

Instead, the body and bloodied neck were on the block, blood dripped down the block, and the severed head reposed in a basket on the straw-covered floor. A rotten skeleton hung high in a gibbet iron over a man who was being pressed to death with stones in the courtyard of Newgate Prison.

In 1282, David, Prince of Wales, was drawn and quartered for attacking Hawarden Castle. This punishment consisted of the victim being dragged by a horse through the streets on a sledge, after which he was hanged, cut down ten minutes later, and then disembowelled. His heart and bowels were burned before his face, and then his body was cut into four quarters and his head was spiked on the City wall. The quarters were sent north, south, east, and west of the city and buried in unconsecrated ground. This was known as "godly butchery."

The tortures that had gone on in the Tower were depicted and described. Among these were: the twenty-foot-deep pit; the cage called "Little Ease," which was so small the occupant could not stand, lie down, or straighten his back or legs; the rack; the iron gauntlet; and manacles. There was a hideous depiction of a family with the plague and even some live, large black rats scurrying around behind glass.

Way off in a corner where one could easily miss it was a small plaque headed *CHILDREN IN THE 13th CENTURY*, which read:

Children of the nobility were treated with a fair degree of harshness, and at an early age were sent away to other households to learn manners.

I for my part, believe that they do it because they

*like to enjoy all their comforts themselves, and that they
are better served by strangers than they would be by
their own children.*

*Besides which the English being great epicures and
very avaricious by nature, indulge in the most delicate
fare themselves and give their households the coarsest
bread and beer, and cold meat baked on Sunday for the
week, which however they allow them in great abun-
dance that if they had their own children at home, they
would be obliged to give them the same food as they
made use of themselves.*

ANDREA TREVISANO, 1497

There was another plaque, this one entitled *Infant
Mortality:*

*An estimate number of children surviving, after
being Christened between 1730 and 1749, was that
74.5% were buried before reaching the age of five years
old. They did not all die naturally . . . . "No expedient
has yet been found out for preventing murders of poor
miserable infants at their birth, or for suppressing the
inhuman custom of exposing infants to perish (in) the
streets."*

There was no depiction and no further mention of
the infanticide, mutilations, abandonment, and
severe forms of child punishment and ritual whip-
pings that had been condoned and supported by
law throughout history in every country. In fact,
there was no further mention of children at all,
except in the introduction to the booklet I bought
as I was leaving: "Welcome to the London Dungeon. We hope you enjoy your visit, but if you
don't, we won't be surprised, for contained in this
incredible premises are the realities and horrors of
our ancestors' lives. . . . My young children thought

it would be fun to put on an exhibition of the 'blood and thunder' of Britain's past—and here it is!"

I'm not easily sickened, but the feeling of nausea that I had when we left was still with me an hour later. Michael, on the other hand, was both enthusiastic and seemingly untouched by the gore.

"It was really *gross*," he said happily as we trudged along toward the underground. I looked at him sitting there as the tube doors slammed shut and the three of us were hurtled through the black underground tunnel. I thought of the old Calvinistic view that children were imps of darkness who had to have the evil beaten out of them regularly. "Perhaps what he needs is a good beating," I said jokingly to Leonard. Michael looked astonished. Who, *him*?

Monday, September 11

The day we arrived in London, Leonard received a four-page letter from Anne, the chairperson of Parents Anonymous of Croydon and Tandridge, a district south of central London that stretched through a depressed urban area, some affluent "middle class" territory, and some rural land. She had started the group a year before, after going on the usual round of professionals, including the doctor who was too busy to listen and the health visitor who didn't want to hear what she was saying about her feelings. She finally became so worried that she rang the NSPCC (National Society for the Prevention of Cruelty to Children), and though they acted promptly and sympathetically, she had to give them a great many personal

275

details, which they in turn put on file. She felt that the help they gave could easily have been given by another parent in a situation that would have been far less threatening and "bureaucratised." Thus she had set out to find like-minded people.

Their P.A. chapter now ran a twenty-four-hour telephone system with thirty-five trained volunteers and had had over 150 calls since beginning in January of 1978. More and more social services referrals were coming in every week.

"I didn't know about P.A. in America until I'd been working on the idea of a group for three months," she later told us. "We chose to use the name because it encapsulated the ideas of confidentiality and self-help we were especially concerned with."

We planned to meet Anne and two other P.A. parents on a particular street corner and then go to a Chinese restaurant that somebody had recommended.

Anne's letter had sounded quite proper, and I fantasized some upper-class tweedy stereotype; but the three young women who suddenly appeared around the street corner in the gathering dark looked like casually dressed American suburbanites. As we were walking the several blocks to the restaurant, Jay spoke of the universal problem of tending young children when you're bone tired and can't get any sleep because of a screaming baby. They had been discussing taking another member's child overnight so that the overwrought parent could get some relief, and Jay asked us if this sort of thing was done in our groups. We assured her that anything was done that worked. Then Dorothy said that their group's biggest problem was their English reserve—they often lapsed into social chatter because nobody wanted to talk about what was really bothering them.

"We're also very defensive about shrinks and professionals and health-care people who lord it over us with their expertise," she added.

Anne went on to discuss the fact that people simply didn't seem to care about one another. "Neighbors can be killing each other next door and nobody will lift a finger," she said. "People on the street will watch you struggling to get through a door with a stroller and two babies, and nobody will help. I don't know—maybe it's all part of the apathy and depression. The country's been so poor for so long." Although we had been in London for only five days, I had picked up that feeling of indifference in the shops and on the street.

When we reached the restaurant and got ourselves settled, Michael, who had been surrounded by discussions of child abuse and P.A. since he was three years old, sat calmly consuming his food while the usual talk of problems, crises, and tragedies swirled around him.

I heard Anne at the other end of the table saying something to Leonard about the torn perfection of a relationship between parent and child: "The parent sees the relationship with the child at first as a perfect tapestry and tends to feel that this perfection is irrevocably ripped apart or wrecked once the first bout of violence has been unleashed. And since it is wrecked anyway, it becomes easier to do violence again."

I looked over at Anne and felt a sudden rush of kinship. She was putting into words what I had felt years before, when I was in my twenties. I thought that the same might be said about our relationships with ourselves. Each of us comes into the world in a state of grace—you might call it perfection—and then the negative messages we receive about ourselves divide us into "bad me's" and "good me's." I started to say something to that effect, but apparently we had all said too much as far as Michael was concerned. It was late, and he was tired. He signaled the waiter and asked him quietly but firmly to please bring the check.

When we went to take the women back to their car, they couldn't remember where it was parked. At that point, any remaining cultural differences dropped away.

Tuesday, September 12

Imperial College, the site of the conference, was a disappointingly modern building. As we registered, people we hadn't seen since some previous conference in the U.S. bobbed out of the milling crowd, greeted us, and then disappeared again.

Two simultaneous formal receptions were scheduled for 6:30 that evening—one provided by Her Majesty's government at Lancaster House and the other provided by the Greater London Council at County Hall. The invitation we received was to Lancaster House. At around 6:00 P.M., several huge buses gathered us up from the conference site and delivered us there. The program had stated succinctly that special facilities for children would not be provided, and Leonard was concerned that they might not let us in because we had Michael with us; but there seemed to be no problem. The doors opened, and we were led from the austere exterior into dazzling Louis XV decor.

278

The 150-year-old Lancaster House had a reputation for welcoming those who were working for social reforms. It was there, we were informed, that Lord Shaftesbury had advocated the reforms that led to the Factory Act, and Charles Sumner and William Lloyd Garrison had pleaded for the abolition of slavery.

We checked our wraps, and after an interval standing in the marble-columned splendor of the central hall, we were led up the double staircase with its gilded balustrade to a huge stateroom where we were formally announced and received. Michael was not only cordially received, he even had his picture taken while shaking hands with a Cabinet member.

At a little past eight, the big buses deposited us back at the Conference site, and from there we took one of London's big red doubledecker buses back to Kensington. There was an old man sitting beside Leonard and another old man in the seat ahead of me. When the old man ahead of me discovered that we were Americans, he turned around to face me and began mumbling something about the war. I leaned closer to try to catch what he was saying and realized that he was very drunk. He went on and on. I couldn't understand any of it, but Leonard caught the name of General Mark Clark and answered him with a mention of June 6, 1944.

The man sitting next to Leonard said, "Don't pay any attention to him." But Leonard continued to listen and answer where it was appropriate. The old man was turned toward us, but he seemed mostly to be talking to himself, reliving his part in the war. I wanted desperately for him to stop blowing his sour breath in my face, and I was

relieved when the bus came to our stop. But I was
also glad that Leonard had talked to him.

"He was one of the walking wounded,"
Leonard said. "When that man next to me said,
'Don't pay any attention to him,' it occurred to me
that this is the way people often speak to the
powerless—young *and* old. He once had power,
though, and fought to give the other guy the right
to say 'Don't pay any attention to him.'"

We strolled to Boccaccio's on Kensington
Church Street to finish off the evening with some
Italian ice cream. When we came out, the church
bells at St. Mary Abbot's were ringing loud and
wild. We wandered down to the end of the street
to see what was happening, but the huge old
church was dark and deserted.

The war memorial rose in the dim light, a
stone woman with a wreath in her left hand and
an inscription in her right hand: "Wake Remem-
brance of the Gallant Dead." A Lockwood's Spark-
ing Lemonade can rested on the top step of the
monument, next to the inscription on the base: "In
Memory of the Men of Kensington and Those Men
Serving in Kensington Battalions Who Gave Their
Lives for King and Country in The Great War.
1914-1918, 1939-1945." I wondered if there was a
memorial somewhere for the ones who came back
in such shape that they have to get drunk to
forget.

Wednesday, September 13

I attended a morning workshop on "Children in
Institutions." One of the participants was a woman
named Noele Arden who, like Jolly K., had spent
her childhood being placed by her mother in

280

various institutions. She went from children's homes to a workhouse, to a remand home, to an approved school, to an adult mental hospital, and then to her final destination—Rampton, the special hospital designed for antisocial patients suffering from mental subnormality. Very few patients who are committed to this kind of hospital are intelligent or articulate enough to record their experiences. Thus, the savage punishments—ranging from public canings and severe beatings to long periods of solitary confinement—are kept from the general public's knowledge.

When she was twenty-four-years old, Noele Arden somehow managed to obtain her release from Rampton and went on to write her harrowing biography of mistreatment, brutality, and neglect: *Child of the System*. The book was dedicated to "those who cannot speak for themselves."

I came away from that workshop with one presenter's vehement pronouncement still ringing in my ears: "In most cases, the only criterion for judging a foster home is whether or not it has good plumbing."

Before we went to lunch, Leonard introduced me to Jill Korbin, a young cultural anthropologist who had spent several years making cross-cultural comparisons of child rearing practices in both large and small societies throughout the world. In the area of preventing child abuse, she has called for the establishment of special child-care centers where children can be cared for full- and part-time to ease the burden of parents under stress. In addition, she has advocated providing preadolescent children with child-care experiences in healthy, positive settings where they can begin to learn about the needs of infants and very small children and to explore their own feelings about parental responsibility.

Outside, a tall man greeted Leonard, and I was introduced to Bob ten Bensel,[4] a pediatrician on the P.A. Advisory Board who travels around, according to Leonard, with a fascinating "slide show of horrors." He's regarded as one of the leading pediatricians in the U.S. concerned with the study of child abuse and neglect. Among medical lecturers on the subject, Dr. ten Bensel has one of the most thought-provoking formats. Using materials from the field of art history, he has compiled a collection of historical data on the family throughout the past centuries, which he has developed into a slide-show presentation, focusing on the abuse of children in our history. His pictorial review accompanies a discussion of infanticide, abandonment, use of discipline, the evolution of parent-child relations, institutional abuse, and cross-cultural child-rearing practices.

His aim is to create an awareness that child abuse and neglect is not a new phenomena, and that current problems are deeply rooted in many past cultural practices. Once armed with that awareness, it is hoped that we can become agents of change, more in touch with our feelings about our own childhood, and thus able to deal more effectively with troubled families.

We saw part of the presentation later that day. Leonard had said that it never failed to evoke a heavy emotional response from the audience, and that afternoon was no exception.

That evening, Leonard and I took a taxi to the Saint Vedast Church in the east central part of London, where P.A. of London was hosting an informal get-together for conferees who were involved in or interested in Parents Anonymous. A smiling red-haired woman was waiting outside the church as we arrived.

"I'm Jean," she said. She gave us directions and remained there on the curb to help more people find their way inside. (I later learned that she was Jean Renvoize, who had authored three novels and the book *Children In Danger: The Causes and Prevention of Baby Battering* which had first been published in May of 1974 when there were no other British books on child abuse. She, too, had found that the only texts available on the subject at that time were those by Kempe and Helfer.)

We walked through the courtyard and into a room with about twenty-seven other people. We were seated around a huge antique table covered with a gold plastic tablecloth and a generous spread of red and white wines, crackers, cheese, and something vaguely resembling potato chips, which looked and tasted like salted styrofoam. We sat to the left of Sally, Dawn, and Pat, the parent who had started the London branch of P.A. When Pat stood up and introduced herself, we were both stunned by her physical resemblance to Jolly K. She was large and overwhelming, with the same blunt manner of speaking.

Dawn was the current chairperson. She had that pensive, pinched-rose beauty that one glimpses now and again in paintings of English children of long ago.

Sally—vibrant, with a thick cloud of dark hair that moved with her every gesture—was a London social worker who ran the training sessions for the P.A. phone volunteers, approximately thirty parents who were backed up by volunteer professional social workers, doctors, and health visitors.

We met Alan, a volunteer from London; Jean, a volunteer from Birmingham; Tony, another volunteer; Jane and Colin, a couple with two kids and another on the way. Colin was involved with Government Children's Services. He and Jane had been phone volunteers since last year. Ethel, a volunteer with the Greater London Council, ran a recreation group for mothers with young children. She was Irish and a former abused child. There were several Parisians, professionals, a woman doctor, and a man from the Ministry of Health. Tak Oka, a Japanese who was the London Correspondent for the *Christian Science Monitor*, was covering the conference for that paper; he was also translating for the French people. Ann, a social worker from Liverpool—one of the areas of highest unemployment—had first seen mention of Parents Anonymous in a newspaper article eight months before. She was encouraging a grass-roots movement in her area and was involved in putting together foster parents' meetings to make them more supportive of natural parents.

Helen, from Athens, Greece, was a social worker in an Athens hospital. There were three women from P.A. of Australia—Rosemary, Liz, and Diana; all had had abuse problems. Liz worked with a halfway house; Diana was a psychologist; Rosemary was a P.A. chairperson.

The questions that American parents and professionals had been asking and answering for each other and themselves over the past five years were pouring forth once again here. From Australia: "How can we get more men to participate?" From Greece: "What can we do about the problem of paternal tyranny and the lack of guilt about child abuse?" From France: "What do you say over the phone?" And there were other questions as well: "How do we go about overcoming authoritarianism?" "What about ensconced cultural traditions?" "What can we do about women who feel uncomfortable with men counselors on the phone, and vice versa?"

"Underneath, nobody really *wants* to harm their child," someone said.

"We all have a dream of the perfect, happy family we'll have," Jean commented.

And, from Dawn, "You start to break down these barriers with caring and loving—across the table or on the phone."

Jane was once a parent with a problem; she has since become a phone volunteer with the London group. She remembers, "The first time I called P.A., the member who answered said, 'How are you?' not, 'What have you done to your child?'"

Another person entered the conversation with "What you say on the phone isn't as important as conveying an attitude of warmth and listening and acceptance." And we all agreed with the person who concluded, "Training is needed to help develop phone skills. The art of listening doesn't come any more 'naturally' than the art of parenting."

Sally briefly explained, "Our phone-training course consists of once-a-week meetings for five consecutive weeks. During these intensive two-hour sessions, volunteers explore their feelings about anger, children, and themselves; some would-be volunteers self-select out. Growth is always slow and painful, though, and shouldn't be rushed. The most exciting thing about P.A. is watching the growth of a parent who calls in 100 percent needy and ultimately winds up helping other parents."

We all wanted to know what kinds of calls the phone volunteers from all over the world were receiving. Dawn said that one small bit of publicity in her local newspaper had brought forth persons from every walk of life with every parenting problem. Ethel described the terror of a young doctor's wife who, after being reassured for a full five minutes that her anonymity would be protected, spoke for an hour and fifteen minutes about her feelings; it was the first time she'd been able to talk to anybody about her problem.

The conversation turned to professionalism. Diana from Australia said, "P.A. helps parents rid themselves of guilt; this can't be done in a professional-recipient relationship." And Rosemary from Australia asked Leonard, "How do you deal with professional burn-out?"

"For one thing," he answered, "I'm nourished by sessions such as this."

Leonard and many of the others would be making their formal presentations the next day, but the real "people" meeting was taking place that night. Hands across the international table had little to do with world-wide conferences or speeches. Our understanding of one another came, as it had since P.A.'s inception, when people were able to unashamedly bare their problems and concerns to each other, warmed by hospitable surroundings and mutual acceptance.

When the church bell struck nine, we were told that we would have to vacate the room fairly quickly for some unknown reason. There were people there that I hadn't had a chance to talk to or even identify, and it was with a sense of frustration that I watched them leave, knowing that I would probably never see them again.

Ethel insisted on driving us back to Kensington, saying, "You couldn't easily get a cab this time of night in this part of town." She took us on a somewhat roundabout route so that we could see London at night—*she* loves London at night, when the Parliament buildings are bathed in a soft pink light and the traffic has thinned, and the harsh daylight doesn't expose the meanness alongside the beauty. Ethel was originally from Dublin. She had come from a violent home and had become interested in P.A. because she realized how much it would have helped her parents.

Thursday, September 14

In the morning, Leonard participated in a panel with Parents Anonymous Australia and Parents Anonymous London. There were about seventy people in the room.

P.A. Australia had established a successful telephone system and home-visiting service, but their groups had been successful for only short periods and in only a few cases. The interaction between professionals, volunteers, and members was improving. At first, professionals hadn't worked out as sponsors or on the phone because they were felt to be distant, uncaring, and indifferent; but these barriers of hostility and suspicion were gradually being broken down.

Sally pointed out that P.A. London had been successful in using backup professionals for telephone volunteers. If a volunteer took a particularly difficult call in the evening, for example, there was usually a professional available. They were doing what they could with virtually no money. There were, we learned, twenty-four branches of differing P.A. telephone services throughout England, which operated on shoestrings or less.

During lunch, Michael went off with Debbie Ezell, our P.A. national administrative assistant, who had flown over for the conference. Leonard and I walked a few blocks just to get out in the air. We saw four London bobbies in full dress on horseback; we also saw a woman wheeling a pram with a very proper-looking baby in it, neatly and perfectly asleep under a hand-knit shawl and embroidered sheet folded out just so.

"That's the kind of baby that creates false advertising for the joys of motherhood," I couldn't help commenting.

We did not see Princess Margaret, patron of the conference, make her entrance into the college cafeteria to have tea and officially greet whoever was up there. (We had heard a rumor that she was in the Fijis and wouldn't be showing up.) When we returned to the main entrance of the Sherfield Building, we saw the maroon Jaguar limousine and the small crowd of people gathered near it awaiting her exit.

She came down the stairs then and everyone applauded. She wore a white-and-pink figured silk shirtwaist dress and off-white sandals; and she had a gracious, determined smile that didn't make it to her eyes. Her eyes were quite sad. She waved in acknowledgement of the applause, and then the attendant held the car door open and shut her up deep inside the Jaguar and drove off.

During the Wednesday night meeting at St. Vedast Church, Ethel had told us that Princess Margaret personally stumps for Parents Anonymous.

Lichfield

Friday, September 15

Leonard managed to drive the rented car out of London, with Michael navigating and me hanging out the window on the left side to tell him when he was brushing too close. By mid-afternoon we had arrived at BBC Birmingham, where we met Chris Baker, a law instructor and magistrate who was also Chairman of the Lichfield and District Mental Welfare Committee. Chris and Leonard did a five-minute radio news-interview with the BBC, and then we followed Chris back to the Bakers' house. There were no numbers in the address—it was simply "Rockville, Oakhurst, Lichfield, Staffordshire, England."

The house was on a lane surrounded by rose gardens and countryside. Lavish rose gardens were a common sight in England, but I hadn't yet gotten used to them. Chris led us through a huge wooden door into an entryway that ran nearly the width of the old place. The house had been derelict when the Bakers bought it in the early fifties and had been partially put together after the war with parts from other buildings that had been damaged or destroyed. The front door was salvaged from a church, and the oak staircase leading to the five bedrooms upstairs was 250 years old.

The Bakers' home was filled with antiques, most of them from Hazel's family. Hazel, Chris's wife, was a child psychiatrist; she had apparently been delayed with a patient that evening and would be there soon.

We went into the living room where Chris offered us drinks. A little ratty-looking black dog that had greeted us with ecstatic leaps over the furniture finally settled down. "That's Aphrodite," Chris said. "We called her that because she was the only pup to be saved in a whole litter that was being drowned. One of the children in the neighborhood managed to pull this one out of the water, and he brought her to us."

The room was chilly in spite of the heater going in the fireplace alcove, and the late-afternoon autumn light coming through the leaded windows didn't quite illuminate the corners. I had to look closely to see the faces in the photographs of all the Bakers' grown-up children—graduations, weddings, grandchildren.

Michael and I had settled on the floor near the heater with a huge illustrated English travel book when Hazel Baker came in. I got to my feet and greeted the tiny woman who stood there in a plain cotton dress, a shapeless sweater, and sandals. I remained standing for a few moments; I had the vague sensation of once again being in the presence of royalty, the kind that can't be conferred by anything but strength of character and a workaday dedication to doing the right thing. But then she smiled and dispelled any remaining chill in the room.

The aroma of warming stew was drifting through the door-way behind her. She said she would have some sherry with us before seeing to the vegetables.

Feeling completely at home, we followed her to the huge kitchen and fed our dirty laundry into the old front-loading machine while she chopped vegetables on an ancient, scarred white table surrounded by four fat black-and-white cats. When the laundry was done, I looked around for the dryer, but there was none. I asked if she had a dryer in the basement. "No," she smiled, "the dryer is over your heads." She pointed up at a gigantic wooden apparatus that went the width of the kitchen. It was a 200-year-old drying rack. She lowered it to eye level with pulleys, laid the wet laundry over it, then raised it back up to ceiling height.

We were just sitting down to dinner when the phone rang. Hazel sighed with exasperation as she went into the hall to answer it; but in a few seconds I heard her greet whoever was on the line with fondness and delight in her voice. Then laughter. When she returned to the table, she explained that it was one of her patients.

"You must have a very warm relationship with them," I said.

"Oh, well, *yes*," she replied. Her tone implied a mild shock that it should be any other way. It was obvious that Hazel Baker was a complete stranger to the fifty-minute hour.

Before we went up to bed that night, Hazel asked if I wanted a hot-water bottle. We had been standing talking while she rummaged around in the large pantry searching out some canned orange juice for the next morning. She suddenly produced a cozy, pink, fur-encased hot-water bottle.

"No, thanks," I said. "I don't think I'll be needing one."

"I always take one up with me," she answered. It was a small, homely gesture that

291

seemed, when I reviewed it later, to be the crowning achievement in hospitality.

Lichfield,
The Friary-Grange School

Saturday, September 16

The autumn day was sunny and crisp, and there was almost a party air of excitement as we entered the school to register for the one-day conference "ANSWERS TO VIOLENCE." The members of the Lichfield Mental Welfare Committee were briskly going about their tasks of directing cars in the parking lot, handing out programs, and serving coffee, tea, and cookies.

At a few minutes before nine, we were all directed upstairs and into a beautiful, modern amphitheater. There were 280 people attending that conference, ninety-five percent of them pro-fessionals—teachers, psychiatrists, nurse trainees, social workers, and probation officers. The cost was £2.50 (about $5.00) per person, including tea, coffee, and a full lunch.

Three other people were on the program besides Leonard. The first was F.H. McClintock, Professor of Criminology at the University of Edinburgh, who discussed and analyzed different types of violence and violent crime, different levels of criminal justice intervention, and alternative strategies.

As Professor McClintock was talking, I noticed a lovely, solemn young girl sitting next to me drawing doodles on her note pad. They looked very much like the doodles I create when I'm talking on the phone. Judging from the sober attention she was paying to the speaker, I would have expected her to be taking neat and accurate notes, but her pad was blank, except for the doodles. Just as I was wondering who she was, Chris introduced her as the next speaker.

Gwynedd Lloyd is the Coordinator of Intermediate Treatment at Panmure House in Edinburgh. In a soft Scottish burr, Gwynedd described Panmure House—a nonresidential neighborhood center where kids from twelve to seventeen who are having trouble in their relationships with family, school, peers, and themselves can go.[5]

Following her presentation, Gwynedd Lloyd showed us a movie about Panmure House. We saw teens and preteens interacting with each other and with counselors in a give-and-take setting, helping each other toward growth, increased self-esteem, and more assertive behavior. We watched kids coming out of their shells, taking charge of their lives, and talking about what Panmure House meant to them.

Leonard was scheduled to give his paper, "Self-Help and Government: A Common-Sense Partnership in Child-Abuse Services," plus some comments about Margot Fritz's training project, after lunch. Leslie Brannon, an elegant English gentleman, took the stage that afternoon, and in melodious Shakespearean tones that would have put John Carradine in the shade at his peak, gave Leonard the most lavish introduction of his life. It took us all a few moments to recover.

Leonard's presentation touched on several major issues, including the following: (1) P.A. has become a network of "extended families" providing treatment for persons who have never had a healthy family experience. (2) There seems to be a case for government to strengthen self-help groups which are supportive of their members' emotional well-being. (3) Many top-ranking government officials and public office holders have become involved, in most of the United States, in making the P.A. program part of the social-service delivery system. (4) The P.A. national program is decentralizing to allow for more local control by its members and other supporters. (5) We all must be more concerned about the needs of all families, not just those who already show signs of serious stress. (6) In preparing any human service or training program, we must be aware of the emotional distances between professionals and service recipients. Any such activity must be developed to give us all a sense of working together on commonly shared problems.[6]

When Leonard was through answering questions, the people in the audience descended on the stage like locusts and took every scrap of P.A. literature we had put out.

After tea, the Reverend David Collyer, organizer of the Double Zero Club for "Rockers" and "Hell's Angels" in Birmingham, told his harrowing but funny experiences in personally facing down youths in gangs, until they came to trust him. In looking for ways to discover and provide nonviolent opportunities for the "disprivileged," Collyer had progressed from "comforting the afflicted to afflicting the comfortable." He was, in short, a maverick preacher who brought the smell of the streets into middle-class living rooms so that those people might become as sensitive to the causes of violence as they were to the incidents of violence —and all with sharp good humor.

The conference ended with thunderous applause and a general feeling of a job well done.

We all went back to the Bakers' house to prepare for that evening's party. Committee members and friends were coming over later that night, each of them bringing food. A light wind was blowing, and I felt the need to take a long walk before the guests began to arrive for the party; when I asked Hazel for suggestions, she pointed out the wooden sign down the road that read "Footpath." I took the footpath through a field and up a hill to an old dilapidated gazebo, which seemed to contain at least fifty years of pigeon droppings. Seen from there, the community of Lichfield was a postcard from long ago.

When I got back to Rockville House, Leonard and the Bakers were in the living room, talking about the war. Hazel and Chris had met in the hospital during the war. He had been wounded, and she was a doctor. The conversation moved to families. Hazel's father had invented the gun sight that was used in the Spitfires that helped to defeat the Luftwaffe in the Battle of Britain.

The guests began arriving with dishes of food, and the table was soon laden with quiche, trifle, cold meats, salads, and puddings. The group radiated a sense of wanting to be there to see us and one another. There were, I learned, twenty-five persons on the committee, and it had taken nine months of planning to put on the conference. These were all interesting facts, but I couldn't help wondering out loud, "What's the secret of this smooth organization? What makes it work?"

"Well," one woman said, "we don't all love each other every minute, but when we have differences, we talk them out immediately, before they have a chance to fester. And everybody on the committee has a job to do, and they know how to do it. They follow up on every detail of that job until all of the foreseeable snags are eliminated."

"And we're so exhausted," another put in, "that whenever we do something like this and it's all over, we swear we'll never do it again; and three weeks later we're back at it planning another one."

"But the inspiration that gets things moving in the first place is Hazel. Hazel is the moving force."

We looked across the room at the tiny woman who was out of earshot. My first suspicion had been correct—*she was* the queen.

Sunday, September 17

On Sunday morning, a page-long story on Parents Anonymous, the conference, and child abuse appeared in the *Birmingham Sunday Mercury*. It stated that there was already a P.A. group in Birmingham and that one would be started in Lichfield the next day.

The idea comes from America, where there are already 700 groups....A volunteer has agreed to spend two hours each Monday night for the next twelve months, just waiting for Lichfield 51213 to ring. The Lichfield volunteer ... is a former probation officer and now lectures on social work.

He will coordinate the group until a leader can be found among the parents themselves. Then the social worker will take on the role of a sponsor, a professional adviser to help with "particular hang-ups."

The coordinator says: "These groups are starting up in a higgledy-piggledy way all over the country. Here we have a traditional facility for picking up issues through the Lichfield and District Mental Welfare Committee. Those local people involved knew that there were people in the area who were potential child abusers . . ."

Later that morning Chris took us on a walking tour of Lichfield. We strolled past ancient buildings with wavy roofs and gables, Samuel Johnson's birthplace, and a marker noting the place where somebody had been hanged or beheaded. We arrived at the Lichfield Cathedral. Hundreds of years old, it was the only one in England with three spires. Chris rattled off facts and dates like a professional tour guide. Finally we just stood there, staring up at it in silence.

We walked back through town to St. John's Hospital, now a home for elderly men. In the archway leading to the quadrangle was an anonymous plaque that read:

> *It is admirable to consider, how many millions of people come into and go out of the world, ignorant of themselves and of the world they have lived in.*

At Rockville House again, we shared a meal of roast lamb and fresh vegetables before leaving. Once again, the warmth of shared experiences had turned strangers into friends.

Nottingham

We knew, from Maria's correspondence, that P.A. of Nottingham was one of the oldest and strongest of the new groups in England, having begun in early 1978.

Maria Dabrowska had attended both the conference in London and the one in Lichfield, but she had somehow disappeared each time before I'd had a chance to meet her. Now we were an hour late arriving at her office.

Maria is personal services manager at something called "Family First Trust," which, we soon learned, is a community-based charity that combines many enterprises, the main one being to provide housing for single-parent families or anyone else in desperate need of a home. It also offers a contemporary settlement house program with a philosophy that stresses the need to prevent family problems from reaching an irrevocable stage. Family First Trust was founded and directed for ten years by Ruth Johns, a journalist from a wealthy, prominent family. It is headquartered in Ruth's original home, so, of course, Maria's office looked nothing like an office. And the young woman who rushed headlong out the door to meet us bore no resemblance to the middle-aged, smiling peasant in a babushka I'd been expecting.

She took us to her home, where we were introduced to her four younger sisters and her brother. We met Vanda, Regina, Christina, Heinrich, and Theresa, who was working a jigsaw puzzle on the coffee table and didn't respond to the introduction. When she did look up, she stared at us out of eyes that weren't quite expressionless but instead seemed to be looking inward at something she couldn't quite comprehend. Theresa, I realized, had Down's syndrome.

Maria regarded her lovingly and asked if she wanted supper. Theresa shook her head and continued working her puzzle—not a baby puzzle, but one of the sprawling, complex ones with hundreds of pieces. She was halfway through.

Before sitting down to supper, we found that

the girls had given up their rooms so that we would be comfortable during our stay. Then Vanda served us delicious meatballs, beet salad, potatoes, carrots, and fruitcake.

Maria hurried around putting things together so we could make it back to the office in time for the 7:30 meeting of P.A. parents and professionals. In her sweater and skirt, she looked like a schoolgirl trying to cope with an overloaded schedule by making up time on the road. We were already out the door when she suddenly gasped, "Oh, I forgot to go to the loo!" As she sped back down the stairs, a young parent from Leicester who was trying to start a P.A. group there showed up to accompany us to the meeting.

On the way, I asked Maria how she had gotten involved with P.A.

"In August of 1975," she answered, "I started visiting single-parent families when I was working for the Family Services Unit in London. I realized that children were being damaged, but I wasn't sure what to do about it or how to draw the parents out. I worried when I left them, and I felt that I had just two alternatives: I could report the family or leave the situation as it was.

"Then I got to know Sandra,[7] who was a parent and professional. When I started talking to her about *her* feelings about abuse, I knew that there were families whose feelings weren't being articulated. We became very close, and I finally put another troubled parent in touch with her. I realized later that I was trying to start a sort of Parents Anonymous, but that was before I knew there was such an organization.

"Very soon after that I read an article about a Middlesex woman who was running P.A. there out of her home. I corresponded with her, and Sandra and I spent from February to September of 1976 discussing the idea with professionals all over. We began training volunteer parents to help people over the telephone, and we started our phone service on November 1. Even though Sandra and I were timid about going after publicity, we went on the radio to talk about P.A. Then I traveled to Toronto to learn more about P.A.; I had been under the impression that it had begun there. The woman who was coordinator for that region told us about Leonard Lieber and said that we should contact him in California. When we found out about a TV program called *Grapevine* that publicizes self-help groups, we wrote to them, and in August of 1977 they offered to do a feature on P.A. on BBC Nottingham. They also produced a fact sheet on how we set up our group and circulated it to anyone who requested it. The group began regular meetings in September.

"Our phone service went slowly and sporadically. We had virtually *no* referrals from professionals; many of them were very suspicious of us. I wrote to all of the directors of professional services and got only one response."

Before Maria had finished telling her story, we had arrived at the meeting. The rest of the story was told there. We walked into the large living room at Family First Trust to find more food and drink laid out buffet style on a huge table. Again, nearly everyone attending had contributed a dish of some kind.

The group was made up of both parents and interested professionals—the area director of Social Services; a child psychiatrist; an inspector from the National Society for the Prevention of Cruelty to

Children; a senior nursing officer; a consulting pediatrician at a children's hospital; a woman from Norway; a teacher; the chairperson of the local P.A. group; a principal group social worker in a mental hospital, who had been the local P.A. sponsor for a year and a half; a probation officer employed by St. Mary's House, a drop-in center for ex-offenders; and Angus Walker, the current director of Family First Trust, who had taken over from Ruth Johns in 1976.

Following Leonard's talk about P.A. in America, we held a question-and-answer period. When one English woman remarked that it's difficult for the English to break through their reserve and bare their feelings, another one wryly commented that the English were just beginning to admit that they *have* feelings.

The sponsor spoke of building trusting relationships within the group and discussed the difficulty of open and honest communication. Maria mentioned how much skill it takes to say the right thing in order to *allow* someone to be open. It had taken her three years of fumbling, she said, to gain just a little more of that skill.

When we left the meeting, Angus Walker gave me a packet of information about Family First Trust. The envelope holding the material was a child's watercolor of what looked like a lot of blue sky and sunshine on thick paper, folded and stapled.

As we talked a while longer with Angus and Maria, we realized that Family First Trust was offering a fine program for distressed families, and that because of the efforts of Maria and Sandra, P.A. had become an integral part of that treatment service.

"Were you born here?" Leonard asked Maria on the way back to her house.

"In Wales," she answered.

"Your family must have been refugees, then."

"Yes, they were. My father was a watchmaker. He could do anything mechanical. He came from a small village in Poland near Warsaw. When Hitler invaded Poland, my father took to the hills and actively resisted; he was ultimately arrested and tortured, but he never gave them any information. He was shipped to Siberia then and sentenced to ten years as a political war prisoner.

"He was released after several years, when the Russians made the alliance with the allies. He was sent with other Polish soldiers to fight in Monte Casino, Italy, in 1943 or 1944—I'm not sure exactly when. They fought alongside the Americans and the British there; they were also sent to Egypt."

"Your father was a war hero in an army that never officially existed," Leonard commented.

"I guess he was," she said. "Hardly anybody realizes that there was anything left of the Polish army after 1939."

*   *   *

The next morning, following an interview Maria and Leonard did on BBC Nottingham, we gathered in Maria's dining room to look through an old, scuffed photograph album. There was a picture of her father and his army buddies bathing in a water hole, laughing; a wedding picture; a large group of people standing outside of what looked like barracks; her father's good-natured, slightly worried expression; her mother's round and girlish face.

302

Maria's story

"After the war, my father wound up in Camp
Mona, a displaced persons' camp in Wales. That's
where he met my mother. They married just before
the camp was disbanded; they would have been
separated at that point if they hadn't. That was in
1948. My mother had been in various camps from
1939 on, and she spent most of the war in an
African jungle. Finally, her group was shipped off
by the Red Cross to any country that would have
them, and she wound up at Camp Mona.

"I was three years old when my sister Theresa
was born in 1953. At the hospital, they kept Therea
away from my mother for two days. Mother was
sick with anxiety, feeling that something was
wrong and not knowing what. My father had a
heart attack. The people at the hospital tried to talk
Mother and Father into giving Theresa away, but
my parents were shocked at the idea. They had
both come from small, close villages where such a
thing was unheard of; they wouldn't have thought
of shutting her away anywhere.

"My parents were very poor at that time. We
were living in Caernarvon, Wales. My father first
worked as a typewriter repairman; then he began
taking in watches to repair and turned part of our
house into a workshop. When Theresa was still a
baby, they made plans to move to Brooklyn. We
already had our passports and everything, but we
weren't accepted into America because Theresa was
mentally handicapped. It was obvious from her
passport picture that she had Down's syndrome,
but nothing at all was said until we were ready to
go. Mother and Daddy had sold everything, and
they had to start all over again. I remember the

empty house, the piles of boxes and crates. They were allowed to buy a derelict house. It was in terrible, slum condition; my father fixed up the house himself, and it took him months.

"My parents learned English on their own. I remember them wandering around with dictionaries in their hands and using all their spare moments to study. We were the only Polish family in Caernarvon, and we kids were known as 'the children of the Polish watchmaker.' My father disciplined us, but he always seemed fair. I seldom felt the punishment was unjustified. We had a good relationship, but he was hurt when I challenged him verbally. He had been brought up very strictly, with regular beatings. Though he almost never talked about his childhood, he had the traditional patriarchal view of 'respect your elders.'

"My father's shop was always open to the public; he never refused anybody anything. He lent people money, and people just kind of hung out there—we had tea and supper with whoever was hanging around when it was served. I remember my father sitting in a cramped position for hours, repairing watches, then getting up and pacing back and forth to ease his muscles.

"When I was nine, my father returned to Poland for the first time in twenty-one years. He had waited until he became a naturalized citizen of Great Britain. He felt the Polish government might hold his involvement in the resistance against him. I was the only one who traveled with him when he went back. We went on the train and stayed two weeks on the old farm where his brother was still farming. It was 1960, but the conditions were very primitive; the food was terrible. My father cried when he saw an old close friend his own age who had no teeth.

"We stayed on in Caernarvon until my father became very ill. He was nearing retirement, but the people never let him alone; they would even bring him their watches to be repaired when he was sick in bed. We moved to Nottingham when he was sixty-one because our nearest relatives were here, but he was never happy being retired. He died in January of 1975.

"Theresa comforted my mother when Daddy died. She patted her and said, 'Daddy's asleep.' She's so loving. I always felt closest to Theresa. I was introverted; I read a lot, and I thought of Theresa as my special friend. I took her around the neighborhood with me and got into scrapes because people made fun of her. I was always aware of her as a human being. I was very sensitive to being different because we were the only Polish family in a Welsh community; so I could appreciate Theresa's being totally different. It was Theresa who taught me that every human being has dignity. I was very young when I started wondering why people couldn't learn to accept retarded children at home. I knew that Theresa was better off at home. She learned more from being around the family and she was toilet trained early because of all the loving attention she received.

"Theresa was in public school only a few weeks when she started coming home and going into strange rages, making terrible, angry faces. It was frightening, and we couldn't figure out what was wrong. Finally we learned that the teacher was apparently a very harsh disciplinarian, and we realized that Theresa was copying the anger she saw around her. The family took her out of school, and the authorities threatened prosecution if my father and mother didn't put her back; but they refused, so the school authorities provided a tutor in our home.

"When I decided that I really wanted to be a doctor, I went to Leeds University for two years before deciding against the profession. Partly I was afraid of the responsibility involved in being a doctor. I didn't want to kill anybody.

"I applied as a trainee social worker and was rejected; I never knew why. I was told to go work as a volunteer for a year. I got a job in a children's home for that period, then applied again and was again rejected. I went home and 'licked my wounds' for a while. Then I went to work for North London Social Services as a volunteer for four months, and they offered me a paying job for a month at a day center. I was twenty-two then. I never applied for a professional course that would certify me as a qualified social worker because I lacked confidence. Instead, I applied for a diploma in social studies, which would allow me to make placements under supervision. I got a two-year study grant and worked two days a week as a probation officer, but I found that the job required me to be a narrowly-confined agent of the court rather than a friend to the deviant. I was bursting to give, and nobody seemed to want what I had to offer. I went to work for the Family Services Unit in London, but I still felt that I was allowed to get involved with the people only on the surface. They were labeled as 'problems,' and there was never enough emphasis on helping them to help themselves.

"So I dragged on to get my diploma in social

studies. My father died while I was in my second year. I carried on for him, for his memory. It's what he would have wanted. When I asked for a placement in Nottingham at St. Mary's House, I was rejected because I wasn't on a 'professional course.'

"Finally, I picked Family First Trust out of a hat. I didn't even get dressed up for the interview. I was so discouraged by that time that I didn't care; I figured they could just take me as I was. I expected to be rejected again.

"I knew I liked Family First because of the feeling of honesty I got from them—they didn't hide behind a professional facade. I felt a great rapport with the place and people, and I was overwhelmed when Ruth Johns said that she wanted me. She expressed faith in my ability and gave me the confidence I needed to do the job as I saw it. The autonomy has been wonderful. Angus took over in 1976, and he carried on her vision, developing community answers to community problems.

"I love my work; I see it as an integral part of my life, and being in a warm, loving family recharges my batteries."

It was time for us to leave. Vanda offered us more cake, and she and Maria teased each other about who was head of the household while their mother was in Canada attending the birth of a grandchild.

As we passed by the living room, Leonard looked over at Theresa, who was quietly, patiently putting the pieces of her puzzle together.

"Good-bye, Theresa," he said.

I heard "Good-bye, Theresa," with an echo of "Good-bye, Ellen Jo." The girls came out to the car

to wave us off. Theresa came out and stood
between them, smiling a very special smile at us.

* * *

Maria and Angus and Family First Trust would
continue to be strongly committed to developing
P.A. in Nottingham and to participating in its
development throughout Great Britain. Maria,
along with Anne and many others, would become
part of a national planning committee for P.A. of
England.

Maria Dabrowska hadn't become a doctor, but
I think her father would have been proud. He was
a hero in an army that never officially existed. His
daughter is a hero in an unofficial army that is
rallying its troops all over the world.

October 1978

Leonard wanted us to see Edinburgh because, he
said, it was the most beautiful city he'd ever seen.

And it was. Edinburgh Castle floated high
above the city, visible from any direction.

Inside the castle, inside the Scottish National
War Memorial, in the Hall of Honour, is written
this inscription by Thucydides:

*The Whole Earth is the tomb of heroic men, and their
story is not graven only on stone over their day, but
abides everywhere without visible symbol, woven into the
stuff of other men's lives.*

* * *

On October 5, we turned in our rented car at
Heathrow Airport in London and flew home to

Redondo Beach. Two hours after our return, Leonard was back taking calls on the WATS line. There was a woman, fighting back tears, scared of her feelings, convinced that she was the only person in the world who wanted to hurt her kids. A man, bewildered and angry because his wife had left him and his kids were rebelling against him. Another woman, isolated in a rural area with two little kids and a husband who traveled a lot; she was from an area of West Texas where there were no P.A. chapters, and she wanted to tell us that she might be able to start one herself.

January 1979

On January 11, 1979, the Public Broadcast System aired a special on child abuse, *Raised in Anger*, hosted by Edward Asner. The show focused on the P.A. program in Pittsburgh, highlighting the positive impact P.A. has had on families there and elsewhere. The response to the program was overwhelming, with P.A. membership gaining nearly 1,000 members nationwide. And of course, there were more phone calls.

With all of that, it was still business as usual, until the phone call from Betty on March 4.

4
Hope for the Future

It has been nearly ten years since that day back in 1970 when I read about Betty Lansdown in the newspaper and concluded that her life probably wasn't worth living.

My life has changed a great deal since then, largely because of the work I've done with Parents Anonymous and the friends I've made along the way.

Betty's life has continued to change, too—again, largely because of her involvement with P.A. There are two more chapters of her story that need to be included here. One was written in 1975. The other was written just this month.

In early 1975, Betty gave me a little one-page, handwritten piece for *Frontiers*. "I don't know if you think it's good enough for *Frontiers*," she said, "but it helped me a lot just to put it down on paper."

I ran the piece in the spring issue. It was called "Pictures."

Today I brought my children's pictures to work with me and sat them on my desk. Each of these pictures is at least three to five years old (depending on which one of my six children you are looking at). I would love to have recent pictures of my children but I can't because I do not know where they are.

I've always kept the pictures out of sight from other people because I couldn't handle the questions of where the children are or any other conversation regarding my children with those who didn't know my situation with my children. It hurt too much and I felt too guilty about why they are not living with me.

It hurts not knowing where or how they are; but

now I can put their pictures on my desk for anyone to look at and ask questions about if they choose to.

Thanks to P.A. I now can handle not having my children with me and the realization that I will never have them. (At this point I am not even sure that I will ever have any other pictures of my children.)

I thank P.A. for helping me with my feelings and to a point within to stop hating myself for everything that happened which led to having my children taken away. I also thank P.A. for giving me a second chance at life (a good one this time) with or without my children. I realize for the first time that I am worth something good without my children.

Betty has now been happily married to Jim Kojaku for well over a year. Jim is completely aware of her background and supports her in every way.

On March 4, Leonard received a call from Betty Lansdown Kojaku. She had been reunited with two of her children the day before—children she had not been allowed to see or have contact with for ten years. On the night of March 3, the children's father had phoned her from Ontario, California, to say that the three kids had been asking him if they could see her; on that day, the youngest daughter, Trenia, had run away. She didn't have Betty's address or phone number, but she'd said that she was going to find her mother somehow.

At that point, nobody knew where Trenia was. Betty got permission to go down and see the other two children the next day. The boy and two girls had been seven, five, and three years old when their mother had disappeared from their lives.

Betty didn't get any sleep that night. The next day, Jim drove her down to Ontario. There was no number on the house, but Betty saw a teenage girl standing at the top of the steps holding a dog in her arms. The little girl who had been left clinging to a freeway fence was now fifteen. Betty recalled:

"I knew it was Jannie; it just had to be. I said, 'I'm Betty.' She looked at me for a minute. Finally she said, 'I'm Jannie.' We held each other for a few minutes. I didn't realize until later that the dog was biting me on the arm. We all sat down in different parts of the room and talked about where Trenia might be, where we could look for her. Finally I came unglued and asked Jannie if she would mind sitting next to me. So she came over and held me, and I held her, and we just cried together.

"Tim came in then with his grandparents. He had blonde hair and blue eyes. I knew it had to be Timmy. He was going on seventeen, and he looked like a grown young man. We hugged each other, and he sat down with me. When the relatives left and we had a chance to talk a little bit, he told me, 'I've always said I didn't hold grudges against anybody or anything, but it was a lie. I did hold a grudge against you. But I realize now that all of this hasn't been your fault. I realize I can't erase everything that's happened in the past, and we can't change that, but maybe we can go on from here.' I said, 'Yes, that's the only way it can be.' "

They spent the afternoon looking for Trenia. They didn't find her.

As Betty and Jim were leaving, Jannie gave Betty one of her school pictures. On the back she had written, "To Mom, from your daughter Jannie. I love you. Hope to see you again, soon." She told her mother that while she wanted to see her again, she didn't want to go to Betty's house to visit. She needed time to get used to her.

"It hurt," Betty said, "but I wanted her to know that I respected her feelings. I had hurt for them for years, knowing what they had to go through. I had kept myself busy doing what I had to do so that one day I'd be together enough to be of value to them if I ever had a chance to be with them. All those years I had thought about how it would be if I ever got together with them again—whether it would fall into place or fall apart. But I did know that whatever any one of the kids needed, I was willing to try to provide it for them—whatever they needed from me."

On Monday, March 6, Betty got a call from a social worker who asked if she was Trenia Lansdown's mother. Trenia had spent the weekend with a friend whose father counseled juvenile runaways. On Monday, she had gone to her school counselor and said that she wasn't going back to her father's house but wanted to find her mother instead. The counselor took her to the social worker, the social worker told the family where she was, and then she got in touch with Betty.

On March 8, Betty was reunited with Trenia at a temporary foster-care shelter in Ontario. Betty took a motel room, and the social worker offered to let Trenia stay with her. Trenia later described the experience.

"Mom and I talked all night. We tried to catch up on thirteen years in eight hours. I knew the stuff they'd said about her couldn't all be true because no person could be that rotten. And my sister and brother had told me things that were totally different from what the family had told me—things that they remembered. So I wanted to hear Mom's side of the story before I made a judgment. I just had to find out the truth.

"My Aunt Sherie was the one who first started encouraging us to see her. She used to like my mom, and she said, 'You guys should get to know her before it's too late. I've met her, and I know she's a good woman.' But I never even knew what she looked like; I never even saw a picture of her. Dad had us calling different ladies 'Mom,' and even after I'd been talking all night with my real mom, I wasn't really sure if she *was* my real mom; I still wondered if maybe it was just somebody who was willing to take me in because I was a runaway. So I said to her, 'Before we go up there to see that social worker, how do I know you're my real mom?' "

"We talked some more," Betty added. "One of the things she finally asked me was how her brother died. She needed to know, and I could understand that. I told her. It was hard, but I told her."

They went back on Tuesday morning to see the social worker, and Trenia said, "I want to go home with my mom." The social worker turned to Betty and asked, "What do you want?"

"I want her," Betty answered. Then Betty phoned Jim to tell him they were coming home.

Over the phone, Jim said to Trenia, "We know it's going to be hard. There are going to be rules that you'll have to follow; there are going to be some things that are going to be hard for you to swallow. But we're willing to try to work with you to give you the best of what's good for you. And any time we tell you something that doesn't seem right to you, we'll explain why we feel that way,

317

and you're free to express your feelings. You have some say in the matter."

Trenia was moved by this phone conversation.

"Here was this man I'd never met, never seen, never even heard of before, who was willing to care for me, to take me in, to listen to me. I never had that before. I had felt all my life that nobody ever listened or cared about me."

Trenia had been with Betty and Jim for about two weeks when she became depressed one night and finally, in tears, confided to Betty that she missed having Jannie and Tim around.

"I wasn't surprised," Betty admitted. "I knew that for all those years, they felt that all they really had to hang on to was each other."

On March 25, Tim called and asked if he could come to live with them. That permission was joyfully granted. A few days later, Jannie left Ontario and joined her brother and sister in their new home. The three children, who had felt themselves to be alone for most of their lives, were together again, but this time they were in a place where they wouldn't have to depend solely on each other for emotional support.

"I had never given up the belief that one day, if I didn't find the kids, they would somehow find me," Betty said. "Now that it's happening, I'm not afraid of it. Because of what I've learned, what I've dealt with in P.A., if I need help coping with whatever situation might come up, I'm going to ask for it, really quickly; and I know I'll get it. I have all the supports around me that I need."

In March, P.A. had received a service grant, part of which was to be directed toward expanding services to U.S. military families in Europe. We knew through the stories of P.A. parents like Wayne that child abuse was a real problem in military families—largely because it was often ignored.

Leonard has been particularly interested in finding out more about child abuse in military families.

"Recently, on a trip to Charleston, South Carolina, to work with our state organization there, I heard comments from civilians (professionals in counseling agencies) that gave me further insight into the unique status of military families.

"An hour's drive away from Charleston is a U.S. submarine base. Within the community are hundreds of Navy families. For months at a time, naval personnel, many of whom are fathers of young children, are away at sea in cramped living quarters. When they return for shore leave, they are eager to resume their roles as husbands and fathers; but all too often, their children and spouses are unable to adjust to their pattern of absence and return.

"The little ones have recognized their mother as the family leader and setter of rules and limits. When their father returns home, he is a 'visitor' to some children, a 'stranger' to others, and a 'friend' to still others. He needs to reassume the leadership role at home, but the entire family finds this difficult to adjust to, simply because they have trouble dealing with the constant disruption that combat training causes.

"The professionals near Charleston spoke of

the pure agony that many of the couples and their children continually face.

"Throughout the early part of the 1970s, it seemed as though any negative parenting behavior in the military that didn't require law-enforcement intervention was 'invisible.' In other words, if a G.I. didn't kill or nearly kill his child, he didn't have to worry—at least not about reprisals from his superiors. If he did overly brutalize, he was a good candidate for a quick discharge or transfer. No one thought much about helping these fathers and their families.

"During the past few years, the U.S. Army and Air Force have attempted to correct this situation. Both branches of the service have established child-abuse education and intervention strategies through 'offices of child advocacy' or base hospitals. The Navy has been slower to move in this direction, though a few enlightened staff members at a couple of bases have taken some positive steps.

"But not much seems to be happening in the way of preventing the alienation of military family members from each other. Our colleagues in Charleston believe that the military must provide *preventative* services in the form of family-life education. It isn't enough to acknowledge the sacrifices that our service people are making; we must also back up their efforts in a way that will begin to safeguard their families.

"My personal observations have led me to believe that child abuse within officers' families is still kept in the closet. This undoubtedly is in part because of the aspirations of career officers to move up in rank. A charge—or even a loud whisper—of child abuse could do serious harm to an otherwise honorable service history.

"I believe we have to acknowledge that military families not only provide an especially important service to our country but are also very susceptible to family problems. We owe it to them—and to ourselves—to do something extra special for them. In the long run, we'll be doing something extra special for ourselves."

U.S. military families who are located overseas often face even greater problems than those who are based in the States—problems such as language barriers, increased isolation, difficulties in adjusting to an unfamiliar culture. More and more wives are finding it harder to get jobs, and since soldiers' pay is frequently low, this is adding to their financial burden. We hope that P.A.'s expansion into Europe will help some of these families to feel less alone, less desperate, and more able to cope with themselves and their children.

May 1979

Today, Parents Anonymous numbers about 1,000 groups, not only in the United States but in Canada, England, Australia, and U.S. military bases in Germany. The days of struggling with grant applications in somebody's kitchen are long gone—now money worries take place in an office. P.A. is now a recognized and respected self-help organization that continues to thrive and grow.

Leonard has been a constant moving force within P.A. When he isn't traveling, making speeches, or otherwise promoting the organization, he's taking crisis calls on the WATS line. Occasionally, he'll sit back and reflect on where P.A. has been. More often, he likes to contemplate where P.A. is going and what it can become:

"Where Parents Anonymous as a movement and treatment modality will go from here really depends on the wishes of its constituents and government representatives. It's only one attempt to deal with child abuse. It isn't always successful, it isn't for everyone, and it must be considered an *adjunct* service to others, which must also be supported. It's also an acknowledged member of the self-help community of services and as such must be considered from now on whenever one examines alternatives in dealing with most human problems.

"Inasmuch as P.A. chapters will survive only if they have community support, my hope is that every community in the United States that is concerned about child abuse and neglect will somehow embrace the idea that self-help is an important part of protecting families against the ravages of child abuse and neglect. By the end of the 1980s, I wouldn't be surprised if nearly every county in the United States had a Parents Anonymous chapter that served as an adjunct service to local public welfare, mental health, law enforcement, and judicial agencies.

"I really don't see the P.A. national office growing any larger because that would take away from the sense of accomplishment and responsibility that each P.A. chapter must have if it's going to survive. It would also place too much authority and control in the hands of too few people. P.A. parents' self-esteem must be increased by their *own* efforts, not through messages from 'on high.' The

P.A. national office should continue to provide the impetus for growth and public understanding through contact with the media and other national organizations. It should be a clearinghouse for communication between state P.A. chapters and should be able to disseminate a large volume of literature to P.A. groups and other community persons everywhere.

"It's important to keep our strong P.A. state offices functioning; we've been helped to do this by our supporters at the National Center in Washington. In September of 1977, the National Center began providing financial support to enable the P.A. national program to decentralize by placing a great deal of responsibility in state offices. By May of 1979, thirty-five such state offices had been funded and were operational in the United States. They coordinate services between local P.A. chapters, community agencies, and the general public. It is our hope that within a very short time every state in this country will have an active Parents Anonymous coordinating office to carry on this work.

"We're continuing to expand overseas, too. During this month, the national P.A. organization in Britain convened its first annual planning meeting in Lichfield to more effectively plan P.A.'s development in that country. And, by the end of this year, there will be a P.A. coordinating unit in Europe primarily responsible for coordinating needs of U.S. military families there; the function of this unit will be very similar to that of a Parents Anonymous state office.

"Judging from the results of the evaluation that was done by Behavior Associates in 1976 and from later research performed by the Berkeley

Planning Associates, P.A. is a system that has arrived and will stay. We should now direct our attention to determining how P.A. will continue to provide even greater services.

"It may be time for P.A. people to look beyond their local chapters and consider advocating adequate parental education in schools, community respite–care centers, closer examination of what increases the possibility of child abuse in a given community, and so on. These decisions will have to be made on a regional and local basis; national and state P.A. representatives can lend support and leadership.

"We're getting more and more requests from P.A. people to look into the possibility of establishing some services for their kids. As time goes on, I believe that we're going to see many effective no-cost or low-cost therapeutic children's groups running simultaneously with P.A. chapter meetings. We're already seeing the growth of such programs in places like Cleveland, Pittsburgh, and South Bend.

"Jolly has some special wishes of her own about P.A.'s future. For example, she would like to see P.A. imported to non-English-speaking countries around the world; she believes that P.A. holds a universal set of answers for a universal problem. This expansion would, of course, include translating P.A.'s printed materials into several languages. She would also like to see P.A. establish 'homes' where entire families could live for a period of time, surrounded by skilled, caring people who would help them to learn to deal with their feelings and relationships in a healthier manner. Costs could be borne in various ways, both publicly and privately. She feels that treating child abuse in a live-in way would be far more effective than the one-or-two-hours-per-week form of therapy usually available to families.

"I think that we need to look at domestic violence as an umbrella-type of problem area in which child abuse is only one part. Self-help groups for spouse abusers—both men and women—and for children who attack their parents are other programs that the P.A. national organization could effectively initiate. It would be nice to see mental health, protective services, spouse abuse, special child-abuse programs, and the like working hand in hand, possibly under the same roof. This would be one way that representatives and treatment specialists in the whole field could be closer together in a sort of 'treatment family' and provide a highly visible, coordinated approach to families in stress.

"Whatever direction local P.A. organizations may choose to take, family advocacy and the delivery of quality, low-cost service to the community should and will be the ultimate result. In a time when resources are shrinking all around us, we have to become more creative and economical in the way we use what's available to enhance the quality of life around us. In its ten years, P.A. has shown that it can do just that."

June 1979

People who are involved with and interested in P.A.—whether as parents, sponsors, professionals, media representatives, or coordinators—often cross paths. One story of intersecting lives involves two people who have never met. They live thousands of miles apart, yet they have much in common.

Hazel Baker, our friend and colleague in Lichfield, England, was recently involved with her husband, Chris, in helping to put together the first national planning meeting of P.A. in England. It was held in Lichfield on May 12, 1979.

Terry Payne lives in Charleston, South Carolina, where he is employed as a worker in the Youth Bureau—a service organization for "children in trouble." Now married and the father of a small child, Terry became interested several years ago in Parents Anonymous. He thought that it offered a potentially effective approach to families in the Charleston area who had child-abuse problems. In 1975, he sponsored the first P.A. chapter in that area, and with the support of cosponsors and other caring community people, he has continued to work with his P.A. chapter. Recently, Terry was one of several persons who were instrumental in establishing P.A. of South Carolina, the coordinating unit for P.A. throughout that state. It is housed in the office where he works.

Hazel and Terry may never meet, yet their lives are intertwined.

In World War II, Hazel's father invented the machine-gun sight that helped the British to win the air war during the Battle of Britain. Only two out of 150 pilots in one R.A.F. unit survived the bitter battles—aided by a precision gun sight. Following the war, one of them, Dennis Payne, became a consular officer in the English Foreign Service. He was assigned to the office in Atlanta, Georgia, where he is now Vice-Consul. He and his wife had several children—one of them named Terry.

Both Hazel Baker and Terry Payne have made commitments to P.A. They live across an ocean from each other, but they are not strangers in any sense. Instead, they reflect that part of the human spirit which is constantly working to make some sense of the lives we hold in common.

5

A P.A. Reader

Forms of Abuse

Parents Anonymous recognizes six forms of abuse. We do not excuse any form of child abuse and believe that any one form of abuse can be, and often is, equally as destructive as any other form.

Parents Anonymous does agree that some parents have this problem to a lesser degree than others. We hope that, through our program, we will achieve an equally effective rehabilitation for those parents who have this problem to either a lesser or a progressed degree.

P.A. knows that, due to human imperfection, most parents at some time or another are subject to episodic abusive behavior. However, we feel that if the abuse becomes an ongoing pattern, then it is a behavioral problem and is, in fact, child abuse.

The six forms of abuse recognized by P.A. are—
- physical abuse
- physical neglect
- sexual abuse
- verbal abuse
- emotional abuse
- emotional neglect

Parents Anonymous's Interpretation of the Forms of Abuse

- *Physical abuse*: Physical abuse has been officially described as "any injury to a child other than injury sustained accidentally; that is, willful cruelty and applied trauma."[1] P.A. goes along with this definition, but we take it further; we also include the *attitude* of the abuser. P.A. believes that when a parent physically handles a child in such a way that the handling is used only as a means of venting the parent's anger, with no intent to discipline, then it is physical abuse. A single slap, then, can be as abusive as a broken arm if the attitude of the parent is abusive. The difference in the degree of trauma the child experiences may depend on the degree of abusive attitude on the part of the adult, which in some cases may be only a degree of control or of strength.

• *Physical neglect*: The lack of a proper amount of food, clothing, medical care, and attention to hygiene are some forms of physical neglect. We also include the lack of parental guidance, supervision, and general care in our interpretation of physical neglect.

• *Sexual abuse*: We recognize two forms of sexual abuse—active and passive. The active sexual abuser engages in sexual acts with a child, while the passive sexual abuser takes no action to prevent such abuse when he or she is aware of it, thereby allowing it to continue.

• *Verbal abuse*: Included in the general definition of abuse is "the use of insulting, coarse, or bad language about or . . . to scold harshly, revile." We all know that we can be easily destroyed by words, especially when we're young. P.A. defines verbal abuse as words that are aimed at tearing down or destroying a child's image of himself or herself. If a child is called a stupid idiot every day of his life, for example, he'll most likely grow up believing that he *is* a stupid idiot.

• *Emotional abuse*: All forms of abuse are emotionally abusive. Emotional abuse is present whenever a parent provides a negative emotional atmosphere for a child. This can be done in a number of subtle ways. Maybe a child isn't hit or called any names, but instead is made to feel like two cents because he didn't bring home all A's on his report card. Or maybe a child's toys are given away because she didn't clean her room. Or maybe a child is continually asked why he can't be good like his older sister. This is also called *psychological abuse*, and there are as many varieties of it as there are parents. It can be even more damaging in the long run than physical abuse.

• *Emotional neglect*: Emotional neglect may be described as *passive emotional abuse*. The parent provides neither a negative nor a positive environment for the child; the child is shown no feelings at all. He or she is shown neither anger nor warmth; he or she is neither spanked nor held closely, neither hated nor loved. It's as if the child doesn't exist. The only message he or she ever gets from the parent is "Don't bother me with your life." This form of abuse may not be as prevalent as others, but it's every bit as damaging. The child who is treated like a nothing grows to regard himself or herself as a nothing, a zero.

Once we recognize and understand what abuse is and the harm we do when we're abusive, we feel guilty. But nothing is accomplished by wallowing in guilt. We don't want our guilt about our destructive behavior to make us feel like losers. That will keep us from trying to change. What we *do* want to do is to learn what it is that we're

doing to ourselves and our children. Then we want
to learn how to stop.

The Parents Anonymous
Guidelines for Achievement

1. I will recognize and admit to myself and to
other P.A. members the child-abuse problem in my
home as it exists today and set about on an
immediate course of constructive actions to stop
any further abusive actions in my home.
2. I want and accept help for myself and will
follow any constructive guidance to get the
strength, the courage, and the control that I must
have in order that my child(ren) will grow up in a
loving, healthy home.
3. I will take one step, one day at a time, to
achieve my goals.
4. I may remain anonymous if I desire, but I may
identify myself and at any time call upon other
P.A. members or seek constructive help before,
during, or after my problem of child abuse occurs.
5. I must understand that a problem as involved as
this cannot be cured immediately and takes constant working within the P.A. program or other
constructive guidance.
6. I admit that my child(ren) is (are) defenseless
and that the problem is within me as a parent.
7. I believe that my child(ren) is (are) not to be
blamed or subjected to my abusive actions regard-
less of what the cause is.
8. I promise to myself and my family that I will
use, to the fullest extent, the P.A. program.
9. I admit that I am alienating myself from my
child(ren) and my family, and through the P.A.

program, I will make myself the center of reuniting my family as a loving, healthy family unit.

10. I admit I must learn to control myself in order to achieve harmony in my home and to earn the love and respect of myself, my family, and society.

The Parents Anonymous Guidelines of Allegiance

1. I, as a member of Parents Anonymous, will always respect the anonymity of fellow Parents Anonymous members.

2. I, as a member of Parents Anonymous, will always promote a true and honest understanding of Parents Anonymous and the problem of child abuse, and will help fellow members and society to better understand the Parents Anonymous program.

3. I, as a member of Parents Anonymous, will never suggest that we have the total responsibility or the total answer for the rehabilitation of the person with an abuse problem.

4. I, as a member of Parents Anonymous, will never suggest that any form of abuse is more harmful than another form or that any member is more abusive than another.

5. I, as a member of Parents Anonymous, will never judge, condemn, or make light of another person's problem of child abuse.

6. I, as a member of Parents Anonymous, will always remain supportive to other members and persons with child–abuse problems in their struggle to overcome their problems.

7. I, as a member of Parents Anonymous, will always extend a helping hand to any persons who express a desire for our help with parenting difficulties.

8. I, as a member of Parents Anonymous, will never deny help because of race, color, creed, national origin, religion, economic status, or form or severity of abuse problem.

9. I, as a member of Parents Anonymous, will never attempt to coerce, threaten, or harass another person into involvement with the Parents Anonymous program and instead will use the methods of invitation, attraction, and encouragement to reach out to troubled parents.

10. I, as a member of Parents Anonymous, will always uphold the Parents Anonymous concept, the Guidelines of Achievement, and the Guidelines of Allegiance.

Background of a Parents Anonymous Parent

Parents with abuse problems may have many different personalities, but they also have certain common threads running through their lives.

Almost universally our parents were abused themselves as children. However, a person need not have been physically abused in order to become a physical abuser as a parent. Emotional abuse and deprivation can be, and is, as damaging to the human psyche as physical abuse.

The abuse our parents sustained as children has in effect taught them that they are unloved and unlovable, and this results in a very low sense of self-esteem and self-confidence. This sense of themselves as unworthy of love is usually coupled with a sense of helplessness and powerlessness. They feel helpless to change themselves and powerless to change their environment and their lives for the better. Our parents react to real or imagined interpersonal threat with a feeling of panic; their typical response is to withdraw from persons and situations which frighten them. Their panic is either released in anger toward an inappropriate target—their children—or suppressed and added to their storehouse of unexpressed fears. This creates a cycle of threat-then-fear reaction which our parents internalize and carry with them into adult life. As adults, they tend to become reactors rather than actors, responding to life situations and significant relationships out of a fear of punishment and the loss of love.

For our parents the abuse they sustained as children has created a basic insecurity and anxiety in them. The irrationality of their parents' anger has conveyed to them a sense that their parents were unreliable and untrustworthy because their responses to their children did not make sense to the children. At a time when the children's own personalities were forming through interaction with their parents, they were learning, (a) that they were "bad persons" and (b) that people can't be trusted. As children, our parents also learned that they were small, weak, dependent, powerless figures who had no control over their environment. Typically children will respond to such an emotional climate in one of two ways—they will become passive and manipulative, or aggressive and manipulative. In either case, their basic lack of self-esteem and their inability to trust others will program them to behave in ways as adults which, to emotionally healthy individuals, will seem either anti-social or hostile. As adults, these parents often become emotional isolates and carry with them a load of anger that is historical in origin but crippling to them in the here and now.

Abused children usually grow up to become adults conditioned to being and feeling abused and to creating an emotional climate for themselves which fulfills their expectations. If parents can be helped in the interactive process of the chapter meeting to see the ways in which they set themselves up to be rejected by others, they can begin to recognize the ways in which they do it "on the outside." Part of the therapeutic experience of P.A. is for our members to discover that in spite of their rejecting behavior they are accepted and liked for themselves. The acceptance that parents find in chapter meetings makes it possible for them to begin the process of relearning ways of relating to others that will not result in their rejection. As parents begin to relate to others more positively and as others respond to them more positively, their self-esteem rises and some of the old anguish and distrust is dissipated. If parents can be helped to get in touch with some of the historical material which is the source of their underlying anger, they can begin to leave the past behind them so as to free themselves to respond to the here and now.

With the forms of abuse which result in death or critical injury to the very young child, there is usually involved an extreme element of self-punishment. The more nearly new a human life is, the more it seems to be an extension of ourselves, and the more closely we identify with it. For the parent with intense feelings of self-hate, the expression of those feelings toward a being who, in a sense, appears to be an extension of self, becomes an extreme form of self-punishment—"I am punishing that which is unacceptable in myself."

Sometimes the parent projects onto the child characteristics or qualities of the other parent, and these projections can be the key factor in abuse. Mothers are often heard to make remarks like, "He's just like his father." This is followed by a lengthy discussion on just how "bad" the father was or is, and it is obvious that the mother is abusing the father she perceives in the child. In addition, the anger she feels toward the father for failing her in their relationship is scapegoated onto the child.

Such parents need help in discovering the ways in which they project the "bad" characteristics of the other parent onto their child. If they can be helped to experience their child as separate and distinct, as an individual in his or her own right with a unique personality and qualities, they may free themselves from these projections which result in abuse.

Another dimension of abuse is the fact that when parents abuse they almost invariably follow the abuse episode with an intense effort to make up to the child for their abusive behavior. In effect, this conditions the child to the expectation that abuse will be followed by an outpouring of love and concern on the part of the parent. This outpouring may be the most intense closeness the child experiences in his or her relationship with the parent. This may account for the distressing fact that children whose parents are making a concerted effort to stop abusive behavior will goad the parent into abusing. The child may well believe that when the abuse stops, the love and closeness will stop as well. The emotionally needy child whose parent(s) are attempting to stop abusive behavior will need a great deal of reassurance from the parent that the cessation of abuse does not mean the end of loving closeness.

When this is carried to its logical conclusion, it also means that abused children will grow up to be adults who need abuse in their lives to reassure themselves that they are loved. Parents who permit their spouse to verbally or physically abuse them will often describe how loving the spouse is after such an episode. These parents will need help to see the ways in which they set themselves up to be abused by their spouse in order to get the love and attention they crave. They will also need help in the area of tuning in to their own needs, verbalizing these needs, and getting them met in adult ways.

An assumption that is often made is that child abuse is usually a problem that involves one parent and one, singled-out child. Parents Anonymous does not go along with this. We take the position that child abuse is a family problem, affecting the lives and functions of every member of the family. In our experience, when two parents are in the home and abuse is a chronic problem, both parents are contributing to the abuse. As a rule one parent will be the "active" abuser, while the other is the "passive" abuser. Both parents are, in fact, engaged in contributing to the abuse. It is a rare case indeed when one parent can honestly claim total ignorance of the other parent's abuse problem. For this reason we urge both parents to attend chapter meetings so that both can be helped to see the ways in which they contribute to the pattern of abuse.

In sum, then, we are saying that abusive parents, because of their childhood conditioning, will provide themselves with an abusive relationship; and they need help in understanding this dynamic and in finding more rewarding, less punitive ways of meeting their needs, preferably as a family unit.

Excerpt from Parents Anonymous
Chairperson-Sponsor Manual, 1975
Margot E. Fritz, Director of Training

Questions Most Often Asked by Parents and Other Lay Persons About Parents Anonymous

Q: *Is the first child in the family the one most likely to be abused?*

A: Not necessarily. It seems as though the child who becomes the "target child" is that youngster who is a reminder to the parent of a particularly negative quality which the abusing parent focuses on. For instance, if a parent has a very negative self-identity—which is usually the case—that child who most resembles the parent in characteristics, appearance, behavior, and so on, may be singled out because of the negative reminders that child provides the parent.

Or, a youngster may be conceived or born during a particularly stressful time for the family. Perhaps someone loses a job; perhaps there are financial troubles or similar domestic difficulties—these tend to give the child some form of negative identity.

Q: *Are handicapped children more likely to be abused?*

A: Interestingly, we're learning from persons who work with various types of handicaps—such as mental retardation, cerebral palsy, and so on—that a number of children develop these afflictions *because* they were physically abused about the head when they were very, very young. Thus, a handicap may not lead to abuse; instead, abuse may lead to a handicap.

It is true, however, that a child with a handicap poses extra stress for a parent. If that parent is unable to deal with the feelings that are aroused, the child may become more of an at-risk youngster than other children in the family (if there are other children). It's important for the parent of a handicapped child to identify and admit to the feelings of shame, doubt, guilt, and so on associated with having a handicapped child and reach out for help so as not to take out these negative feelings on the child.

Q: *Is it worse to physically abuse a child than it is to yell or to call him or her names?*

A: From our experience in working with members of our program throughout the country and in speaking with other persons in the field of child abuse and neglect, it's our opinion that the scars from physical abuse tend to heal fairly quickly. However, the "scars" caused by emotional and verbal insults to a child's personality, whether or not they're accompanied by physical abuse, tend to go away quite slowly if at all. Many people who were emotionally and verbally abused as children often say that they would have preferred a very non-emotional spanking.

P.A. members have generally found that it's much easier to stop physical abuse than it is to stop emotional abuse. The latter is much easier to inflict upon a child simply because name calling involves no physical work.

Q: *If a child is seriously abused, does this mean that he or she will grow up to be an abusing parent?*

A: Not necessarily. We know many persons, who, for whatever reason, have been able to separate themselves from their childhood experiences and become better parents. Quite often, the difference between these folks and those who do end up abusing their children is the presence of a very special, significant person in their lives. An aunt or an uncle or a teacher may be able to nourish some very special positive feelings in the child that may make up for a lot of the negative things that the youngster is experiencing in his or her own immediate family.

We do find that many young people today are deciding not to have children or are putting off having children indefinitely because they themselves were abused as kids and are afraid of their own potential for child abuse. We suggest that they reach out for help from various resources—including Parents Anonymous groups—so that they can learn how to deal with these feelings and stop worrying about hidden fears.

Q: *Is it child abuse for one parent to intervene and beat on a large teenage son who is becoming physically assaultive toward another, smaller parent?*

A: What we're talking about here is self-defense or coming to the aid of someone else. Even though the teenager may be acting in response to earlier abusive behavior he experienced within the family, he must still begin to assume responsibility for his own actions. The only thing we can do at this point is to help him to understand that while he may have reason to be angry at a parent, that doesn't give him the right to abuse them in turn.

In this kind of situation, the entire family should seek some kind of therapeutic treatment. If the teenager isn't willing to get involved in any kind of program, then the parents need to find some counseling on their own that will help them to work through their feelings and remove some of the guilt that they're undoubtedly experiencing over their child's behavior.

Q: *Who is most likely to abuse a child—a father or a mother?*

A: Most authorities tend to believe that the person most likely to abuse the child is the person who spends the most time around the child. Thus, if a mother spends most of her time at home with the children and if there are certain stresses that she's not able to deal with, she may more likely be the abusive parent. However, if a father is put out of work and the woman switches roles with him and becomes a member of the labor force, the father may be uncomfortable with being the parent "in residence." Given minor stresses and particular difficulties in dealing with a dependent infant child, the father may become abusive.

There are disagreements about who is more likely to abuse if both parents are around a child an equal amount of time. The best thing to do in this circumstance is to look closely at each parent's background to determine if either one of them was seriously abused as a child; this can help to identify potential risk situations.

Q: *Is there help for a parent who feels the potential for abusing his or her child but hasn't actually abused yet?*

A: In most communities today, the parent who is willing to look for help can usually find it. More and more communities are establishing reach-out type services or are responding to requests from parents through mental health or social service agencies. The Parents Anonymous program lends itself fairly well to this type of parent who voluntarily requests reassurance, guidance, and whatever other kinds of assistance he or she may require.

The greatest danger for a parent is not to admit the feelings of potential abuse that may be growing within and to let these feelings remain unexamined until it's too late. Then, of course, the parent may not voluntarily seek help; instead, he or she may receive mandatory services from the community, which are certainly less desirable than preventive measures.

Q: *What if one parent wants help and the other doesn't?*

A: This is a difficult situation, one in which one parent wants to begin a growth phase in his or her life and the other isn't ready for change. We suggest that the one parent who is motivated acknowledge his or her need to reach out for services and to use them. If the other parent is unwilling to make any change or keeps insisting, "I don't have a problem," then there is a likelihood that the relationship between the two will diminish in quality. The growth rate of the one will leave the other person behind, and it's very possible that the relationship will dissolve.

Of course, the best situation is one in which both parents attempt to make a positive change for themselves; this must be encouraged whenever possible.

Q: *Do single parents abuse more often than married parents?*

A: The tendency is to believe that child abuse is more prevalent among single parents, whether divorced, separated, never married, or whatever. This isn't necessarily true. However, the stress of being a single parent is extremely great, and if someone is unable to deal with stress adequately, the burden of being a single parent may simply be too much. It's therefore very important that single parents who are feeling a lot of stress reach out for help. In addition, those persons who are aware of single-parent families which may be in some danger should also be willing to offer whatever services they can as friends, neighbors, or relatives. If necessary, they should also ask local authorities to provide special kinds of services to keep the family from falling apart.

Q: *What kinds of help are available for abused children?*

A: Many communities are starting to develop low-cost therapeutic child care, special therapeutic nurseries, and so on. However, most communities are *not* offering special programs for abused children because we've been led to believe that such kinds of treatment programs are generally very costly. The fact is, we don't have the resources needed to fund all the services to abused children that we would like to provide.

Parents Anonymous is attempting to provide services to youngsters while continuing to help their parents. However, we believe that every community should try to develop a *preventive* type of service for families at risk. And abused kids should have access to voluntarily-based treatment settings.

Q: *Isn't it better to remove an abused child from his or her home than to allow the child to stay there?*

A: If certain kinds of service have been provided to the family to "defuse" the volatile situation which exists there, then in most cases the children can safely be left at home. In other words, supportive services should be provided to the parents, and if their case is referred to an agency, then sufficient supervisory service should be made available through protective services or some similar agency.

We've spoken with many adults who were removed from their own homes as children, and most of them would rather have seen help provided to their parents so that their families could have stayed together.

In some cases, of course, it's necessary to remove children from their homes, particularly in cases involving physical abuse of very small children. We believe that such children should not be placed back in their own homes until their parents have received several months of some form of therapeutic intervention. Following this, an evaluation should be made to determine whether the children should be returned to their families. And in a very small number of cases, we believe that some parents should not have the responsibility for raising small children. Arrangements should be made for long-term out-of-home placements for such children to enable them to live in stable home situations as soon as possible.

Q: *Can all child abusers be helped?*

A: No. There are some persons with extreme child–abuse problems for whom rehabilitative methods of treatment have not yet been devised. The percentage of persons in this category is small, yet these are people who probably should not be with their own children or others. In some special circumstances persons with extremely serious child–abuse problems should be considered for possible removal from the community.

However, every instance of child abuse and neglect should be looked at as an individual situation. Only as a last resort should separation between parent and children be considered, as we are learning more and more effective ways of keeping families together safely.

Questions Most Often Asked by Professionals About Parents Anonymous

Q: *Does Parents Anonymous observe the child-abuse reporting laws in all fifty states?*

A: Most reporting laws in this country are similar. The P.A. organization believes in their intent which is to provide service while protecting the health and safety of children and their families.

When a parent comes to a P.A. chapter, they learn from the other P.A. members that reduction of child abuse is every member's personal responsibility.

In most instances, P.A. members have shown marked improvement in their parenting skills as a result of P.A. participation. However, if signs (well-known to a P.A. group) indicate that a member is losing his or her grip on a situation which could be corrected by assistance from an outside source, a report to a public agency is made. This step can be taken because most members choose to give up much of their anonymity to other group members in their honest wish for help and involvement with others who care. When a P.A. parent needs help, the other members will do what must be done to protect the children and to meet the needs of their parents. This preserves the image of responsibility which the P.A. organization has worked so hard to achieve.

New members are not automatically reported just because they have come to P.A. with past or potential problems. The main task is to begin the treatment process. If it doesn't work, then the use of anonymity cannot be used to shield or condone child-abuse problems.

Q: *How does P.A. work with other community agencies?*

A: P.A. prides itself on helping its members to develop a better set of attitudes toward the helping services. Abusing parents usually grew up seeing authority figures as potential abusers; the relationship between a P.A. sponsor and the members of a P.A. group is meant not only to allay the parents' concerns about persons in authority but also to help P.A. members realize that not all professionals need be mistrusted and feared.

349

Thus, P.A. members tend to learn more about their community agencies than usual—they want to know which services can best assist their families. Our P.A. sponsors become "windows to the service world" for members who may need to consider individual therapy, family therapy, marital counseling, possible out-of-home placement on a temporary basis for a child, and so on.

In many cases, P.A. groups not only refer their members to existing community agencies when needed or advisable, but these agencies also refer their clients to P.A. groups.

Q: *Do courts ever refer parents to Parents Anonymous?*

A: More and more members of the bench in both family courts and in other court settings involving criminal child-abuse charges are referring persons to P.A. In several communities, the P.A. program is seen as an adjunct service to courts, law enforcement and social service agencies, and so on. Quite often, a P.A. group may be the only child-abuse treatment service available within a certain area.

Incidentally, what goes on in P.A. groups with court-referred members is not reported back to the court or its designated representative on a verbatim basis. Rather, a court-referred person's attendance at P.A. is reported as regular, irregular, and so on.

Often, a P.A. group will assist the court in later determining the advisability of returning a child to a court-referred P.A. parent's home.

Q: *Parents who are court-referred, then, will often attend P.A. because they have to. Isn't it true that a* *parent has to want to use a program like P.A. before he or she can be helped?*

A: Not necessarily. In the past, it was often assumed that child abusers couldn't ever change their behavior, especially if they weren't highly motivated to do so. Parents Anonymous groups across the country have found that court-referred persons have benefited just as much from participation in P.A. as those who attend on a voluntary basis. True, a court-referred parent may spend his or her first six months in P.A. griping about the unfair legal system. After this initial period of adjustment, however, other P.A. members will very firmly help that person to deal with his or her reasons for being in P.A. Thus, we usually assume that it will take approximately six months for the "average" court-referred person to really begin to grow and change because of what P.A. has to offer.

Q: *Is it usually just one parent in a couple who abuses a child?*

A: P.A. believes that whenever there are two parents or child-care givers in a home, both are responsible for whatever occurs. Even though one person may be the "active abuser" and actually inflict the verbal or physical abuse, the other allows the situation to go on or, in some cases, becomes a "passive abuser" by setting up situations that prompt the active abuser to strike out.

Q: *What type of parent stands to benefit most from P.A.?*

A: Parents Anonymous seems to work best for those persons who are more "explosive" with their negative behavior or those who have physical and verbal-emotional *abuse* problems. Those with *neglect* problems are at the other end of the spectrum;

they tend to require more individualized help and attention than a P.A. group can normally give. Usually, however, anyone who can use the spoken language, possesses at least average intelligence, and can function within some form of group process will do well in P.A.

We also serve many thousands of persons who don't attend P.A. meetings but who use the one-to-one counseling relationship with local P.A. members over the telephone.

Q: *Can an abusing parent who is mentally ill effectively utilize a P.A. group?*

A: Our experience has been that persons who are actively mentally ill or psychotic with hallucinations may have difficulty using the usual P.A. setting. Persons like these are normally in need of greater service and supervision than a P.A. group is able to provide. In addition, their illness may disrupt the P.A. group process.

P.A. groups do include persons who have been hospitalized at one time or another for some form of mental illness, but their participation in P.A. is based upon their being relatively free of acute symptoms at that time.

Q: *Can a protective-services worker be a P.A. sponsor without experiencing a conflict of interest in his or her regular job?*

A: Many P.A. sponsors have been or currently are protective-services agency personnel. In most cases, their supervisors see their participation in P.A. as totally separate from their job responsibilities. All we ask of someone who is a protective-services worker and wants to be a P.A. sponsor is that he or she wear two hats. That is, he or she should assume responsibility for expertise as a protective-services worker but should also be ready to assume separate responsibilities as a P.A. sponsor. The skills learned as a protective-services worker can be quite effective in a P.A. setting, and just because a sponsor is also a social worker does not mean that he or she will necessarily report incidents of child abuse that are discussed within the group setting. On the other hand, a family in need of referral to protective services can benefit from a P.A. sponsor with this experience, since he or she will have access to and knowledge of the quickest and most desirable forms of intervention.

We should caution that various locales may have different philosophies regarding this matter. These philosophies should be made clear at the outset of any relationship between a protective-services worker and a P.A. group.

Q: *What is P.A.'s success rate?*

A: It's hard to talk about "success rates" in terms of numbers when discussing P.A.'s effectiveness. We can report that research done by Behavior Associates of Tucson, Arizona, in 1976 indicated that participation in a P.A. chapter often enabled persons to stop physically abusing their children within a number of weeks after joining P.A. The problems of emotional abuse and neglect were also dealt with effectively, but these usually took a matter of months rather than weeks.

P.A. isn't for everybody who has an abuse problem. In fact, the dropout rate for persons who join P.A. may be 20 percent or 30 percent during the first few weeks when it becomes clear that P.A. expects its members to do a lot of hard work and to change their behavior patterns. It's very difficult for many persons to deal with the idea of change, and for that reason a number of people choose not to remain involved with P.A.

The thousands of parents who have stuck with P.A. over a period of time have shown degrees of marked success in improving their parenting. This success is often directly related to the amount of time they've spent in P.A. For example, someone who stays in P.A. for a year or more will probably never go back to abusing his or her children, either in the manner or with the frequency that brought him or her to P.A. in the first place. They actually end up becoming better parents than the norm in a community. In addition, they tend to become paraprofessional experts on child abuse and are thus even more valuable to their communities.

An Evaluation of Parents Anonymous, May 1975-April 1976

Under the terms of our OCD (Office of Child Development) grant, an outside evaluation of P.A. was conducted by a research firm, Behavior Associates of Tucson, Arizona. Their staff carried out an extensive study to determine the impact Parents Anonymous was having on its members. The following material, prepared by Jean Baker of Behavior Associates, summarizes their findings.

*   *   *

EVALUATION PROCEDURES

In order to develop evaluation procedures and instruments which would be acceptable both in form and content to the target population, the Behavior Associates evaluation staff worked very closely and intensively with Parents Anonymous staff and board of directors; with small groups of representative members, chairpersons, and sponsors of Parents Anonymous chapters; and with representatives from the funding agency, the United States Office of Child Development. In this way the information needs of all of the significant information users were carefully considered throughout the development and implementation of the evaluation plan.

The particular aspect of the program evaluation which will be described here is the impact study which evaluated the overall effects of membership in Parents Anonymous and the satisfaction of the members with the program. These effects were assessed by means of in-depth interviews with thirty-nine P.A. members in five different cities in the United States and by a written questionnaire designed specifically for the purpose and entitled *Parents Anonymous—Your Personal Profile*. (Individual copies are available upon request from Behavior Associates.) The dimensions to be measured by the evaluation instrument were determined on the basis of the input from the program staff, the program "consumers" and the funding agency, as well as reviews of the literature relevant to child abuse and neglect. The following dimensions were among those selected:
• Self-esteem
• Feelings about parenthood and children
• Satisfaction derived from parenthood
• Knowledge of child development
• Social contacts and use of community resources
• Frequency and severity of abusive behavior

- Perceived benefits of membership in P.A.
- Opinions and feelings about child abuse
- Demographic and family characteristics

The *Parents Anonymous—Your Personal Profile* questionnaire was mailed to all (356) identified P.A. chapters at one specified point in time, April 25, 1976. Each chapter sponsor and/or chairperson was asked to cooperate in the program evaluation by requesting that all of their chapter members be requested to complete the questionnaires and return them anonymously to the evaluators. Questionnaires were returned from approximately 35 percent of the chapters to which they were sent. At the time the data were analyzed, 613 individual questionnaires had been received from P.A. members in thirty states.

A time-series evaluation design was utilized in the study in order to determine if significant program effects could be demonstrated to be a function of length of time in the Parents Anonymous program. For purposes of this design, the participants were divided into categories determined by the amount of time they had been in the program. The time categories were one month or less, two months, three months, four months, five to six months, seven to eight months, nine to ten months, eleven to twelve months, thirteen to eighteen months, and nineteen months or more. These particular time categories were selected in order to equalize as much as possible the number of persons in each group. Statistical measures were used to test the significance of differences in mean scores on the questionnaire among the different time groups, and additionally to test whether actual scores for individuals who had been in the program longer were significantly higher or more positive than scores for those who had been in the program a shorter length of time.

A pre-post evaluation design was not considered feasible for a program such as Parents Anonymous due to problems of anonymity, of frequently changing chapter membership, of varying time periods of group attendance (i.e., no specific program beginning and ending), and of the probable reluctance of members to submit to a pre-test immediately upon attending a Parents Anonymous chapter meeting. In addition, the appropriate control groups, essential in a pre-post program evaluation design, were not possible to obtain.

EVALUATION RESULTS

Characteristics of Individuals Participating in the Parents Anonymous Program

The return of 613 individual questionnaires from 35 percent of the P.A. chapters to which they were sent constitutes a large enough sample to be considered representative of the population as a whole. This statement is not meant to imply that this sample group is representative of the general population of abusive parents, but only of that group who have become members of Parents Anonymous chapters. A brief description of this population follows:

83 percent females and 17 percent males

93 percent voluntary members and 7 percent court-ordered members

Mean age—29.3 years

Income Level

Over $20,000—7 percent

$10-20,000—38 percent

Under $10,000—47 percent

Mean educational level—12 years of school
  with 25 percent reporting some college

Mean number of children—2.6

Mean age of children—5.9

21 percent have had a child or children
  removed from their custody by
  court orders

Ethnicity

Anglo—69 percent

Black—4 percent

American Indian—3 percent

Mexican-American—2 percent

Asian-American—1 percent

Other or no answer—20 percent

Marital Status

Married—64 percent

Divorced—18 percent

Separated—10 percent

Single—6 percent

Widowed—1 percent

<u>Abuse Pattern in Own Childhood</u>

75 percent experienced some form of abuse

17 percent experienced sexual abuse

Emotional abuse and emotional neglect were reported as the two most serious abuse problems.

<u>Abuse Patterns Toward Their Children</u>

77 percent reported verbal abuse

53 percent reported physical abuse

43 percent reported emotional abuse

28 percent reported emotional neglect

7 percent reported physical neglect

4 percent reported sexual abuse

Certain findings about the P.A. population were derived from the personal interviews alone and must, therefore, be considered as more tentative. These findings were:

<u>Children's problems</u>

58 percent reported that at least one of their children had some form of handicap or special problem.

33 percent reported that at least one of their children was hyperactive. (This was the most frequently reported special problem.)

92 percent reported that one of their children was the focus of their abuse

Parents Anonymous Members Evaluate the Program

In general the members expressed high levels of satisfaction with their membership in P.A. In answer to the question, "How much benefit has P.A. been to you?" the overall responses were as follows:

"A great deal."—69 percent

"Some."—28 percent

"Very little."—2 percent

"None."—1 percent

In order to determine whether perceived benefits increased with time in the program, a regression analysis (trend analysis) was performed to assess whether individuals who had been in the program a longer time tended to answer more positively than those who had been in the program a shorter period of time. This analysis demonstrated a statistically significant effect ($p < .01$) of time in the program, showing that a gradually increasing percentage of persons reported that they had benefited "A great deal" as length of time in the program increased. For example, among those persons who had been in the program one month or less, 42 percent reported "A great deal of benefit." Among those who had been in the program longer than one year, 87 to 90 percent reported, "A great deal of benefit."

In addition to the question about general benefits of P.A., the respondents were also asked the following question: "Taking into account all factors related to your child-abuse problem, not just the frequency, how much improvement do you feel you have made in your ability to handle the problem?"

Again there was a high level of perceived improvement—50 percent of the total sample answered "A great deal of improvement"; 34 percent answered "Some improvement"; 14 percent answered "A little improvement"; and 2 percent answered "No improvement yet."

Length of time in the program was again significantly related to a more positive response to this question as measured by the regression analysis ($p < .001$). For example, of those who had been in the program over eighteen months, 76 percent reported "A great deal of improvement" compared to 23 percent of those who had been in the program one month or less. After two months in the program the percentage reporting, "A great deal of improvement" rose to 40 percent, and this general trend continued throughout the various time categories.

Changes in the Abusive Behavior Patterns of P.A. Members

Obviously, the primary goal of the P.A. program is to change the abusive behavior of its participants. It was not possible to obtain actual behavior indices, therefore, we relied upon the reports of the participants to several questions about their abusive behavior. Among these questions were the following:

"How often are you physically abusive to your children now?"

"How often were you physically abusive to your children before joining P.A.?"

The mean scores of the respondents who had been in the program one month indicated that their current frequency of physically abusive behavior was between "Once a Month or Less" and "Almost Never." The mean score of the same group prior to joining P.A. represented a frequency close to "Several times a Month." The differences in scores between the two questions were compared by a t test for means from dependent (matched) samples and the differences were statistically significant ($p < .001$). Similar t tests were performed for each of the other time categories and all groups showed significantly less frequent physically abusive behavior after joining P.A. Then a regression (trend) analysis was used to determine whether there was a significant decrease in frequency of physical abuse as a function of time in the program. The time categories relative to length of time in the program were those described earlier. Although there was a trend in the hypothesized direction, it was not statistically significant.

The results of these two statistical analyses suggest that the decrease in reported frequency of physical abuse appears to be an almost *immediate* effect of entering the P.A. program, and that the decrease does not significantly change with time in the program. This latter finding is not surprising since the overall frequency of physical abuse of the respondents who had been in the program only one month was close to "Almost Never." In other words, there was little room for improvement over time on this particular variable.

**Frequency of Physical Abuse
As Reported by P.A. Members**

Frequency	Before Joining P.A.	After Joining P.A.
Almost Every Day	19 percent	1 percent
Several Times a Week	16 percent	7 percent
Several Times a Month	20 percent	13 percent
Once a Month	13 percent	18 percent
Almost Never	32 percent	61 percent

The findings with regard to verbal abuse patterns were somewhat different. The two questions used to measure this variable were:

"How often are you verbally abusive to your children now?"

"How often were you verbally abusive to your children before joining P.A.?"

Again, a t test for matched samples showed significant ($p<.001$) differences in the mean scores between the two questions for the respondents who had been in the program even one month or less. This analysis revealed that before joining the P.A. program the average frequency of verbal abuse had been close to *several times a week*. After being in P.A. a month or less this frequency changed to *several times a month*. Again this finding suggests an immediate program effect.

In contrast to the pattern for physical abuse, however, the decrease in verbal abuse continued over time in the program as indicated by the regression analysis ($p < .05$).

Frequency of Verbal Abuse
As Reported by P.A. Members

Frequency	Before Joining P.A.	After Joining P.A.
Almost Every Day	48 percent	12 percent
Several Times A Week	22 percent	24 percent
Several Times A Month	12 percent	27 percent
Once A Month	5 percent	15 percent
Almost Never	13 percent	22 percent

Changes in Self-Esteem of P.A. Members

Poor self-esteem and feelings of inadequacy or worthlessness have been frequently reported in the literature and by therapists who have worked with abusive parents (Steele, 1974; Steele and Pollock, 1974). In order to evaluate whether changes in feelings about self occurred as a function of membership in P.A., twenty-three positive and negative self-descriptive items were presented in the section of the evaluation questionnaire entitled, *My Feeling About Myself As A Person*. The respondents indicated the frequency with which they experienced each of the feelings, and a summary score was obtained reflecting the extent of positive self-description.

A regression (trend) analysis was performed to determine whether scores on the self-esteem measure were more positive as a function of length of time in the program. The results indicated a significant relationship ($r=.83$, $p<.01$) between the self-eseem score and months in the program, thus demonstrating a program effect indicating more positive self-reports for persons who had been in P.A. longer periods of time than for those who had been in shorter periods.

According to an item analysis, the major theme appearing in the changes in self-descriptions of P.A. members suggests that of a developing feeling of personal competence as well as increased ability to deal with stress, a most important finding in light of the generally accepted view of child-abusing parents as lacking in impulse control and problem-solving skills.

Changes in Social Interaction Patterns of P.A. Members

Among the psychological characteristics often reported for child-abusing individuals are those of social isolation and reluctance to seek help (Kempe and Helfer, 1972). A program for child abusers might, therefore, be expected to exert some influence upon these behaviors. Six items on the P.A. evaluation questionnaire were designed to assess these aspects of the P.A. participants' lives. These items were the first six questions on the section entitled *My Ways of Dealing With Stress* and they dealt with frequency of social contacts, with seeking help from others, and with use of community facilities for child care. Again, a regression analysis, for determining the relationship between time in the program and frequency of social contacts indicated a positive correlation between these two variables ($r=.65$; $p<.05$).

Changes in Feelings About Children and Parenthood

Negative attitudes toward children (Steele and Pollock, 1974) and toward parenthood have also been mentioned in the literature about child abusers. Two sections of the evaluation questionnaire contained items relative to these dimensions—the seven-item section entitled *My Feelings About Myself As a Parent* and the eight-item section entitled *My Feelings About My Children*. These two sections were combined because statistical analyses suggested that the two subtests were actually measuring the same variable.

No significant relationships were found between scores on this measure and length of time in the program. For example, mean scores for those who had been in the program for one month did not differ from those who had been in the program nineteen months or longer (47.4 vs. 47.5). Thus, no program effect was found relative to satisfaction with parenthood or feelings about children.

However, the mean score of 47 (out of a total possible of 60) which was the average score for the new members of P.A., represented fairly positive attitudes toward children and toward parenthood at the beginning of participation in the P.A. program.

Changes in Knowledge About Child Behavior and Development

Child-abusing parents have been frequently reported as having unrealistic expectations for their children's behavior relative to the children's actual developmental levels (U.S. Department of Health, Education and Welfare, 1975; Kempe and Helfer, 1972; Spinetta and Rigler, 1972; Steele and Pollock, 1974). An eleven-item scale on the evaluation questionnaire entitled *My Understanding of Children* was used to measure the dimension of knowledge of child development, based upon the hypothesis that increased knowledge of child development might result in a reduction of unrealistic demands upon one's children, thereby fostering a more harmonious parent-child relationship.

The regression analysis showed a significant positive correlation between length of time in the P.A. program and the score on this measure ($r=.75$, $p<.05$) thus indicating a positive effect of the P.A. program on the members' knowledge about children's behavior and development.

Parents Anonymous's State Organization Contacts (as of May 1, 1979)

ALASKA
Center for Children
and Parents
1343 "G" St.
Anchorage, AK 99501
907-277-1494

ALABAMA
P.A. of Alabama, Inc.
P.O. Box 6142
University, AL 35486
205-348-5000

ARIZONA
P.A. of Pima County
3833 E. 2nd St.,
Rm. 7
Tucson, AZ 85716
602-881-1794

ARKANSAS
P.A. of Arkansas
4313 W. Markham
Hendrix Hall Rm 131
Little Rock, AR 72201
501-371-2773

CALIFORNIA
Carol Wollin
11726 Blix St.
N. Hollywood, CA
91607
213-985-3170

COLORADO
Rocky Mountain P.A.
7380 Bradburn Blvd.
Westminister, CO
80030
303-427-1429

CONNECTICUT
P.A. of Connecticut
60 Lorraine St.
Hartford, CT 06150
203-236-5477

DELAWARE
P.A. of Delaware, Inc.
2005 Baynard Blvd.
Wilmington, DE 19802
302-658-5177

FLORIDA
P.A. of Florida, Inc.
Roberta Sussman
15935 Prestwick Place
Miami Lakes, FL 33014
305-885-9752

GEORGIA
P.A. of Georgia, Inc.
1260 Winchester Pkwy.
Ste. 202
Smyrna, GA 30080
404-432-0671

HAWAII
Linda Santos
P.A. Central Committee
c/o Catholic Social
  Service
250 S. Vineyard
Honolulu, HI 96813
808-537-6321

IDAHO
Jolene Hoole
1900 W. Quinn #184
Pocatello ID 83201
203-237-7782

ILLINOIS
P.A. of Illinois
1035 Outer Park Drive
Rm 404
Springfield, IL 62704
217-787-7679

INDIANA
Edythe Richardson
Bureau of Community
  Nursing
200 E. Washington St.
Rm. 1760
Indianapolis, IN 46204
317-633-3270

KANSAS
P.A. of Kansas, Inc.
539 E. Santa Fe
Olathe, KS 66061
913-782-2100

KENTUCKY
P.A. of Kentucky
447 Carlisle Ave.
Lexington, KY 40505

LOUISIANA
D.D. Beam
P.O. Box 6151
Bossier City, LA 71111
318-742-0421

MAINE
P.A. of Maine, Inc.
125 State St.
Augusta, ME 04330
207-622-5650

MARYLAND
P.A. of Maryland, Inc.
1123 N. Eutaw, Ste. 405
Baltimore, MD 21201
301-243-7337

MASSACHUSETTS
P.A. of Massachusetts
c/o Office for Children
120 Boylston St.
Boston, MA 02116
617-727-0067

MICHIGAN
P.A. of Michigan
2230 Witherell St.
Detroit, MI 48201
313-237-0943

MINNESOTA
Wilder Foundation
919 LaFond
St. Paul, MN 55104
612-645-6661

MISSISSIPPI
Council on Children
MVW Box 329
Columbus, MS 39701
601-327-4072

MISSOURI
Cindy Jones
Rt. 1 Box 108
Nixa, MO 65714
417-765-2105
417-839-6534

MONTANA
Sheila Rice
4-C's
1601 2nd Ave. N.
   Rm. 414
Great Falls, MT 59401
406-727-3083

NEBRASKA
Barbara Fox
1601 Euclid Ave.
Lincoln, NE 68502
402-435-3165

NEVADA
Regional Resource
   Center-Nevada
John Sarb
4220 Maryland Park-
   way S., Ste. 308
Las Vegas, NV 89109
702-384-0713

NEW HAMPSHIRE
Ellen Dorr
RFD #2 Box 243
Lancaster, NH 03584
603-788-4023

NEW JERSEY
Joyce Mohamoud
14 Maple Ave.
Plainsboro, NJ 08536
609-799-4023

NEW MEXICO
P.A. of New Mexico
2107 N. Kingsley
Hobbs, NM 88240
505-393-1776

NEW YORK
P.A. of Rochester
121 N. Fitzhugh St.
Rochester, NY 14614
716-454-5060

NORTH CAROLINA
Kathy Jonas
1115 East Park Drive
Gastonia, NC 28052
704-865-6017

NORTH DAKOTA
P.A. of North Dakota
P.O. Box 2093
Minot, ND 58701
701-852-1376

OHIO
P.A. of Ohio, Inc.
1001 Huron Road
Cleveland, OH 44115
216-781-2944

OKLAHOMA
Ann Hardy
Parents Assistance
  Center
2720 Classen Blvd.
Oklahoma City, OK
  73106
405-525-7339

OREGON
P.A. of Oregon
3214 SE Holgate
Rm. 311
Portland, OR 97202
503-238-8818

PENNSYLVANIA
P.A. of Pennsylvania
300 Sixth Ave. Bldg.
Rm. 210M
Pittsburgh, PA 15222
412-562-9440 or 9441

RHODE ISLAND
P.A. of Rhode Island
62 Jackson Walkway
c/o YWCA
Providence, RI 02908
401-861-2910

SOUTH CAROLINA
P.A. of South Carolina
4360 Headquarters
  Road
Charleston, SC 29405
803-744-3381

SOUTH DAKOTA
Barbara Audley
P.A. National Board
Extension Service
South Dakota State
  University
Brookings, SD 57006

TENNESSEE
Charlotte Bryson
5515 Shelby Oaks
  Drive
Memphis, TN 38134
901-382-3880

TEXAS
P.A. of Texas
5415 Maple 319
Dallas, TX 75235
214-688-0727

UTAH
Blythe Rodriquez
P.O. Box 9782
Ogden, UT 84409
801-399-3311

VERMONT
P.A. of Vermont, Inc.
P.O. Box 434
Barre, VT 05641
802-476-7328

VIRGINIA
P.A. of Virginia, Inc.
Frank & Marlene Jones
6516 Wailes Ave.
Norfolk, VA 23502
804-461-3690

WASHINGTON
Faye Benjamin
3402 N. 24th St.
Tacoma, WA 98406
206-759-3814

WEST VIRGINIA
P.A. of West Virginia
1212 Lewis St. #305
Charleston, WV 25304
304-343-4196

WISCONSIN
P.A. of Wisconsin, Inc.
P.O. Box 11415
Milwaukee, WI 53211
414-963-0566

WYOMING
P.A. of Wyoming
2712 Thomes Ave.
Cheyenne, WY 82001
307-632-6673

DISTRICT OF
COLUMBIA
FACT Hot line
Box C
1690 - 36th St. NW
Washington, DC
  20007
202-965-1900

Parents Anonymous Literature as of 1978

Chapter Development Manual (C.D.M.)

Chairperson-Sponsor Manual (C.S.M)

I Am A Parents Anonymous Parent (I.P.A.P.)

Frontiers (Subscription by donation)

Public Information Pamphlet (P.I.P.) (Child Abuse)

Parents Anonymous Pamphlet (P.A.P.) (Losing Your Kool With Your Kids?)

Child Abuse Is Scary (Facts and feelings for those who may need to report)

Now You've Done It (A Handbook for New Mothers)

The above are available by mail by writing to:

> Parents Anonymous National Office
> 22330 Hawthorne Blvd., Ste. 208
> Torrance, California 90505

Panmure House, Edinburgh, Scotland
(A Center for Teens in Trouble)

Panmure House is a nonresidential establishment catering to young people of secondary school age residing within the city of Edinburgh. It was opened by the Edinburgh Corporation Social Work Department in June, 1974, in an attempt to alleviate the increasing pressure on social workers and residential schools arising from the needs of young persons at risk in the community. The sphere of work within which the unit operates is that which is commonly referred to in social work terms as "Intermediate Treatment." The name of the unit is derived from the building which it occupies—an historic eighteenth-century building situated just off the Canongate in Edinburgh's Royal Mile.

The young people who come to Panmure House have, by definition, all come to the attention of "the authorities" and have given cause for concern. The vast majority of the young people who have passed through Panmure House have been in trouble for offending against the law or have had problems with school attendance, either through truancy or through being excluded from school. However, such prerequisites are not essential for attendance at Panmure House, nor do they represent the main criteria for determining whether or not a particular child is an appropriate referral for Panmure House.

All the young people who attend Panmure House have at least one thing in common—they have been referred to the centre by a social worker. From this it is clear that these youngsters have already demonstrated a need for some form of support. When a social worker does not believe that a young person's needs can be met in a normal supervision or case work relationship but that the case does not merit so drastic a measure as removal from home, Panmure House offers a middle alternative.

In general terms a distinction can possibly be made between two broad categories of young people at risk and in need of support. First there is the model of the subcultural delinquent who largely through the influence of a local delinquent peer group gets involved in a pattern of offences. There is no reason to believe that such a youngster need have personality or social inadequacies, and this problem would appear to us to be more appropriately tackled at the level of the group or community from which the young person comes. A second broad category of young people who come to the attention of social workers are those who are inhibited by difficulties in forming and sustaining relationships and communicating feelings and needs, be it with school, authority, parents, or more critically with their own contemporaries. Such young people come to the attention of different agencies through offending against the law or through difficulties at school, but such incidents are symptoms of the real problem; it is this more basic problem, that of relationship and communication difficulties, that we are best equipped to tackle at Panmure House.

Any young people may experience these difficulties without manifesting them in the above mentioned ways—but it is, unfortunately, far harder for young persons to receive help unless their problems cause inconvenience for other people. Consequently, the majority of young people referred to Panmure House have caused an inconvenience.

Typically, a young person who attends Panmure House may be either overly aggressive or excessively withdrawn. The majority of our young people lack any real support in their lives. This is one of the main criteria for offering them a place at Panmure House. Many of them come from broken homes, have experienced emotional deprivation throughout their childhood to an astonishing degree, and experience consistent rejection from those with whom they come into contact, be they schools, youth clubs, peers, and many other agencies and individuals. Many are sent to Panmure House as a last resort, either in an attempt to avert removal from home into residential establishments or because there is no other resource for them.

We have been asked to provide facilities for a wide range of young people exhibiting a wide range of difficulties both in variety and degree. The age group we serve falls broadly into that of secondary-school children. Within that range we now concentrate on the thirteen to seventeen age group. The reasons for this are to be found in our particular styles and methods of working, and in the facilities available in Panmure House.

Aims and Objectives: A primary aim is to develop meaningful relationships between the adults that work here and the young people who are referred to us. The young people are brought together in such a way that individuals within the Panmure House Community, both adults and young people, become significant people in each young person's total life experience.

Panmure House is not a total institution; during their period of attendance, these young people spend a limited amount of their time at Panmure House each week. Consequently their experience at Panmure House must be directly related to their life experience outside. Outside life is complicated by problems resulting from the attitudes and actions (or inaction) of other persons and agencies as much as by the young people themselves.

We also wish: (1) to provide opportunities and stimulate motivation for the young person to realise other people's perceptions of himself/herself and the reasons for these; (2) to explore the problems in the young person's life and the factors contributing to these problems.

Also we consider and explore possible courses of action to resolve these problems.

It is necessary to convince them that there are people who consider them to be individuals of worth, and to allow them to experience positive relationships, and enjoyable and successful achievements.

A second central aim is to seek solutions to the problems in the young person's life. These are usually characterised by a lack of motivation and opportunity for constructive or recreational activities in which to channel their energies and interests.

During their period at Panmure House, young people will often exhibit or develop interest in activities or in getting out and meeting other people in social and recreational contexts—interest which they often pursue once they leave Panmure House. It is a necessary part of our work at Panmure House to facilitate this development. In many cases we work with other agencies to produce other relevant and supportive environments for the young people. Another essential aspect of our work is with the families of our young people and with their schools.

Two further aims are providing opportunities for learning and developing powers of self-direction, and for learning the value and power of cooperation. It is a constant aim of the staff at Panmure House to minimise their intervention with regard to control and decision making in Panmure House and to place as much of this as possible in the hands of the young people both at an individual and community level.

"Self-Help and Government: A Common-Sense Partnership in Child-Abuse Services"
(Excerpts from Leonard's Paper
 Presented in London and Lichfield,
 September, 1978)

A colleague of ours from Great Britain recently traveled to the United States with a particular interest in studying the Parents Anonymous program so that she could better establish it in her community upon her return home.

She asked for the names and locations of several P.A. contact people with whom she could spend time chatting about their work and of her own concerns. We directed her to colleagues of ours in several communities on the eastern seaboard.

When our British colleague was about ready to leave the U.S.A., she called to reflect on her visits here. She commented on how the people she met presented a very similar "package" of feelings and ideas to her. She commented on their openness, warmth, high degree of expertise and willingness to share the issues surrounding the success of their respective Parents Anonymous organizations.

She said that she felt as though they were all part of the same family. And now that family called P.A., numbering thousands of troubled parents, skilled and caring professionals, and even more lay citizens, has grown to become a huge, loving, therapeutic family that is stretching beyond oceans, reflecting a much larger set of issues than how to treat and prevent child abuse.

In a nation fearing governmental control of family life, yet dazed by rapid change in the institution of the family, we have tapped the public treasury to establish another alternative to the family.

The intimacy of communication in P.A. groups, the growth of new permanent friendships and other special, long-term relationships between those associated with the program, suggests that we have tampered with a process. Or have we?

I offer that the American family is basically not in the throes of destruction now, nor has it been for generations. The *type* of family, yes. Preindustrial extended, agrarian families, twentieth-century nuclear families, and so on, have changed, for whatever reasons.

The nature of a family group reflects the state of organization (or disorganization) of a society and how it influences an individual.

In the case of an alienated twentieth-century, abusing parent, who experienced an unhealthy extended or nuclear family as a child, and who can find no solution to his own failure at nuclear family living, a normal behavior pattern might very well be membership in a loose-knit "extended family" not necessarily based upon blood ties, but upon basic human needs for identification, emotional support from others, skills in making positive social relationships, parenting, and so on. In essence, we see this evolution of group members very reflective of healthy behavior-seeking mechanisms on the part of P.A. members.

The Issue of Government Support

So where does government have a place in directly sponsoring, not controlling, but enabling, alternative family groups to flourish?

Sol Tax, an anthropologist at the University of Chicago, notes that the United States government has always professed as its mission "to promote the general welfare." He sees public policy clearly served by strengthening self-help groups that are supportive of persons. His view is that groups supportive of people protect their health—physical and emotional. And health strengthens the social and economic fabric of any culture.

By the above comments, I certainly do not mean to suggest that any government begin total support of a family—therapeutic or not. My experience as a public welfare worker in Los Angeles County during the 1960s and as a mental health worker in the 1970s taught me how angry a family group or individual adult can become when they realize that they are almost totally dependent upon others for sustenance.

My experience has also raised a number of issues over the long-term practicality of the classical psychotherapeutic relationship between "patient and therapist," which, in my opinion, has too often created as many chains as keys to the locks.

No, what is suggested here is a multi-national policy designed to provide minimal support toward those life alternatives that enhance living in these perilous times.

Child-Abuse Opinion Survey

In 1977, persons holding high public office or top-level jobs in family and child welfare and other human services throughout the United States responded to a study questionnaire produced by an evaluator of the Parents Anonymous project.

We may argue over whether P.A. should be subsidized as a quasi-family, but findings of the study seem to reflect the merit in some governmental assistance for a program that has a beneficial effect on the prevention and treatment of child abuse.

(1) Over 85 percent of the respondents believed that *nonphysical* forms of abuse and sexual abuse were major social problems, and they favored more programs in their states for the prevention and treatment of same. (In a 1976 study of the P.A. program, emotional abuse was found to have been significantly reduced through member participation. [Behavior Associates, 1976])

(2) Only 12 percent thought that more severe legal approaches were needed against child abuse, the general feeling being that punishment does not alter abusive behavior.

(3) Less than half regarded temporary foster home, residential treatment or permanent legal separation of child from parent as successful means to deal with child-abuse problems.

(4) Over 90 percent of the respondents were positively disposed toward the self-help approach of Parents Anonymous in dealing with abused families and a similar number called for continued expansion of this modality in their states.

Parents Anonymous State Office Project

A year after the many above-mentioned respondents made their views known, they found themselves actually demonstrating their support of such ideas and strategies.

With the assistance of the National Center on Child Abuse and Neglect in Washington, D.C., the national program of Parents Anonymous has begun to decentralize its functions.

In this manner, each of the fifty states has an opportunity to work closely with state-level P.A. offices in providing P.A.'s "alternative-family/child-abuse treatment program" in a fashion that best suits the needs of a state, but which is also formulated by P.A. parents, lay citizens, members of P.A. boards of directors, professionals, and government officials.

In this manner, the fear of distant centralized government control is minimized, while the voice of a concerned populace is given an opportunity to share a task with local government and, ultimately, is able to gain self-worth and respect plus credibility in creating a service "for the people by the people," a credo too seldom observed, though often held as a distant ideal.

Although a new age of enlightenment is upon all of us, it is one in which the family is threatened by more and more stresses.

The liberated woman is often a prisoner of those pressures placed upon her as a single parent. The same applies for single fathers, who strive to nurture their children in families that are beset by inflation, decreasing quality child-care services, less physical space on the planet in which to grow, and so on.

Contraception, in all of its forms, has not really stemmed the growth in numbers of pregnancies among teenagers in the United States. And, as we know, many teenage mothers are choosing to keep their babies with them instead of placing them for adoption, as had been past practice.

Unfortunately, teens are usually ill-equipped to handle active parenthood, yet too little is being done to provide parenting skills and mutual support mechanisms, which can be so invaluable for a child thrust into the role of parent.

And what about the "normal, intact family"? It, too, is constantly threatened by a horde of contemporary pressures. In so many places in the world, the cost of living requires that both parents work outside of the home, reducing even more the quality time available for parents and children to be together. These families need assurances that supports are available, though it becomes increasingly hard to find such backing.

Not to be neglected—and they are too often—are the poverty-level families of our society.... Under-employment and dependence on subsidy add stress, but not nearly as much as the surroundings that poverty provides.

We must all regard ourselves—as children and as parents—as being in jeopardy, needing mutual support and protection. This process will involve a partnership between government and its people—one in which mutual trust and support can elevate the political process for all concerned."

Notes

1. Beginnings

1. See Thomas Gordon, *P.E.T.*, *Parent Effectiveness Training: The Tested New Way to Raise Responsible Children* (New York: New American Library, 1975). P.E.T. parenting courses are taught nationwide.

2. Ray E. Helfer, M.D., and C. Henry Kempe, M.D., *The Battered Child* (Chicago: University of Chicago Press, 1968).

3. Eda LeShan, "When a Child Drives You Crazy," *Woman's Day* (New York: Fawcett Publications, Inc., 1975).

4. Dr. Apthorp joined the Parents Anonymous Advisory Council in May, 1973.

5. James Apthorp, M.D., from an article in Feb. 8, 1970 issue of *Family Weekly*.

6. See Section 5, A P.A. Reader, page 331, for further explanation.

7. See Section 5, A P.A. Reader, pages 334 and 335.

8. C. Henry Kempe, M.D., and Ray E. Helfer, M.D., eds., *Helping the Battered Child and His Family* (Philadelphia: J.B. Lippincott Company, 1972).

9. Since the organization has been known to members and to the public as Parents Anonymous since 1971, it will be referred to as Parents Anonymous, or P.A., throughout the remainder of this book.

2. P.A. Grows Up

1. "A Project to Rescue Children from Inflicted Injuries," published in *Social Work*, January, 1962. (Reprinted by Practicing Law Institute, New York City, in Volume 3 of "Effective Utilization of Psychiatric Evidence.")

2. Senator Alan Cranston of California took over the reins of the subcommittee in 1976; he and his staff have remained supportive of P.A. through the years.

3. The current extension of this law provides the federal funding that supports the P.A. national office.

4. Leigh——was the group sponsor and a P.A. board member.

5. Beth attends regular therapy sessions with her youngest son at Richstone Center. The center began as a small-scale therapeutic play experience for children of P.A. parents in one Los Angeles area group. It has since become a larger-scale parent-child therapy program funded by the state of California. The Richstone Center was first conceived by Allene Goldman, an early-childhood-education specialist and former P.A. sponsor who is now a community consultant and a professor at Eastview Junior College in Dallas, Texas. Beth first read about the Richstone Center in *Frontiers* in September, 1978.

6. Lt. Jean Land succeeded Nurses Best and Gray as sponsor of the P.A. group at C.I.W. In 1976, she lapsed into a coma following a motorcycle accident and has never recovered. Corrections program

supervisor Nina Klein took over sponsorship and is still sponsor at this writing.

3. On the Road

1. After serving as an R.C. for several years, Helen Magnuson is now cosponsor of a P.A. group and a resource person for the community.

2. See Section 5, A P.A. Reader, pages 354-367, for a summary of the Behavior Associates' findings.

3. Dorothy Corkille Briggs, *Your Child's Self-Esteem* (Garden City, N.Y.: Doubleday & Co., Inc., 1970).

4. Robert W. ten Bensel, M.D., M.P.H., Professor and Director of the Maternal and Child Health Program, School of Public Health, University of Minnesota

5. See Section 5, A P.A. Reader, page 373, for a further description of Panmure House, a center for teens in trouble.

6. See Section 5, A P.A. Reader, page 378, for excerpts from Leonard's speech.

7. Sandra was the "colleague from Great Britain," referred to in Leonard's paper (See Section 5, A P.A. Reader, page 378), who had traveled to the U.S. to study various P.A. groups on the East Coast.

5. A P.A. Reader

1. California Statute on Child Abuse and Neglect (Sec. 11161.5 of Calif. Pen. Code)

Suggested Reading List

Child Abuse

Chase, Naomi Feigelson. *A Child Is Being Beaten.* New York: Holt, Rinehart and Winston, 1975.

Coigney, Virginia. *Children Are People Too: How We Fail Our Children and How We Can Love Them.* New York: William Morrow, 1975.

Forward, Susan, and Buck, Craig. *Betrayal of Innocence: Incest and Its Devastation.* Los Angeles: J.P. Tarcher, Inc., 1978.

Helfer, Ray E., M.D., and Kempe, C. Henry, M.D., eds. *Battered Child.* 2nd ed. Chicago: University of Chicago Press, 1974.

Kempe, C. Henry, M.D., and Helfer, Ray E., M.D., eds. *Helping the Battered Child and His Family.* Philadelphia: J.B. Lippincott Company, 1972.

Kempe, Ruth S., and Kempe, C. Henry. *Child Abuse.* Cambridge, Mass.: Harvard University Press, 1978.

Wheat, Patte. *By Sanction of the Victim.* New York: Major Books, 1976. Reissued by Timely Books, P.O. Box 267, New Milford, Conn. 06776, 1978.

Parenting—Child Development

Leach, Penelope. *Babyhood.* New York: Alfred A. Knopf, Inc., 1976.

Leboyer, Frederick. *Birth Without Violence.* New York: Alfred A. Knopf, Inc., 1975.

Mack, Alison. *Toilet Learning: The Picture Book Technique for Children and Parents*. Boston: Little, Brown & Company, 1978.

Spock, Benjamin, M.D. *Baby and Child Care*. Rev. ed. New York: Pocket Books, 1976.

Parenting — Communication and Relationships

Briggs, Dorothy Corkille. *Your Child's Self-Esteem*. Garden City, N.Y.: Doubleday & Co., Inc., 1970.

Faber, Adele, and Mazlish, Elaine. *Liberated Parents, Liberated Children*. New York: Avon Books, 1974.

Gordon, Thomas, M.D. *P.E.T., Parent Effectiveness Training: The Tested New Way to Raise Responsible Children*. New York: New American Library, 1975.

Hale, Dale, and Wheat, Patte. *You're Getting Closer*. Los Angeles: Price/Stern/Sloan Publishers, Inc., 1978.

Young, Leontine. *Life Among the Giants*. New York: McGraw-Hill Paperbacks, 1971.

Stories, Dates, and Places
You've Encountered in the Book

Stories
Beth   page 118
Betty Lansdown   page 50
Betty Stratigos   page 139
Bobbye G.   page 86
Carol Wollin   page 254
Cathy M.   page 103
Don   page 221
Gwen   page 225
Jolly K.   page 25
Kay   page 212
Leonard   page 29
Linda   page 208
Linda W.   page 183
Marcie   page 194
Margot   page 109
Maria   page 302, 303
Mark and Shelley   page 244
Marlene   page 214
Mary Y.   page 81
Natalie   page 240
Patte   page 4
Rosemarie Biggins   page 89
Sara   page 150
Wayne   page 201

Dates
November 1969   page 12
January 1970   page 13
November 1970   page 14
December 1970   page 17
January 1971   page 36
February 1971   page 39
March 1971   page 48

June 1979   page 325

Places

"We are each of us the product of those who have loved us . . . or refused to love us."

—John Powell